FAITH FAMILY
MINUTE
A Daily Devotional for Busy Families

Dr. Dan Coflin

Faith Family Minute:
A Daily Devotion for Busy Families

Copyright © 2016, 2017 Dan Coflin
Published by Coflin Family Publishing

ISBN: 978-0-9970643-0-8

Scripture quotations from the following sources:

"Scripture quotations taken from the Amplified® Bible, Copyright © 1954, 1958, 1962, 1964, 1965, 1987 by The Lockman Foundation Used by permission." (www.Lockman.org)

Scripture taken from the Common English Bible®, CEB® Copyright © 2010, 2011 by Common English Bible.™ Used by permission. All rights reserved worldwide. The "CEB" and "Common English Bible" trademarks are registered in the United States Patent and Trademark Office by Common English Bible. Use of either trademark requires the permission of Common English Bible.

All scripture quotations in the publication are from the Contemporary English Version Copyright © 1991, 1992, 1995 by American Bible Society, Used by Permission.

The ESV® Bible (The Holy Bible, English Standard Version®) copyright 2001 by Crossway, a publishing ministry of Good News Publishers. ESV® Text Edition: 2011. The ESV® text has been reproduced in cooperation with and by permission Good News Publishers. Unauthorized reproduction of this publication is prohibited. All rights reserved.

Scripture taken from The Expanded Bible. Copyright © 2011 by Thomas Nelson, Inc. Used by permission. All rights reserved.

All scripture quotations in this publication are from the Good News Translation in Today's English Version- Second Edition Copyright © 1992 by American Bible Society. Used by Permission.

Scripture is taken from GOD'S Word®, © 1995 God's Word to the Nations. Used by permission of Baker Publishing Group.

Scripture quotations marked HCSB are taken from the Holman Christian Standard Bible® Copyright © 1999, 2000, 2002, 2003, 2009 by Holman Bible Publishers. Used by permission. Holman Christian Standard Bible®, Holman CSB®, and HCSB® are federally registered trademarks of Holman Bible Publishers. Unless otherwise noted, all Scripture quotations are taken from the Holman Christian Standard Bible ®, Holman CSB® are federally registered trademarks of Holman Bible Publishers.

"Scripture taken from The Message. Copyright © 1993, 1994, 1995, 1996, 2000, 2001, 2002. Used by permission of NavPress Publishing Group."

"Scripture quotations taken from the New American Standard Bible®, Copyright © 1960, 1962, 1963, 1968, 1971, 1972, 1973, 1975, 1977, 1995 by The Lockman Foundation Used by permission." (www.Lockman.org)

"Scripture taken from the New Century Version®. Copyright © 2005 by Thomas Nelson, Inc. Used by permission. All rights reserved."

NET Bible® copyright © 1996-2006 by Biblical Studies Press, L.L.C. http://netbible.com All rights reserved.

THE HOLY BIBLE, NEW INTERNATIONAL VERSION®, NIV® Copyright © 1973, 1978, 1984, 2011 by Biblica,Inc.® Used by permission. All rights reserved worldwide.

"Scripture taken from the New King James Version®. Copyright © 1982 by Thomas Nelson, Inc. Used by permission. All rights reserved."

Scripture quotations marked (NLT) are taken from the Holy Bible, New Living Translation, copyright © 1996, 2004, 2007, by Tyndale House Foundation. Used by permission of Tyndale House Publishers, Inc., Carol Stream, Illinois 60188. All rights reserved.

NLV New Living Version: Public Domain

Scripture quotations are from the New Revised Standard Version Bible, copyright © 1989 the Division of Christian Education of the National Council of the Churches of Christ in the United States of America. Used by permission. All rights reserved.

Scripture quotations are from the Revised Standard Version of the Bible, copyright © 1946, 1952, and 1971 the Division of Christian Education of the National Council of the Churches of Christ in the United States of America. Used by permission. All rights reserved.

J. B. Phllips, "The New Testament in Modern English", 1962 edition, published by HarperCollins.

Scripture quotations marked (TLB) are taken from the Living Bible copyright © 1971. Used by permission of Tyndale House Publishers, Inc., Carol Stream, Illinois 60188. All rights reserved.

The Voice Bible Copyright © 2012 Thomas Nelson, Inc.

WEB: World English Bible – Public Domain

Introduction

So what's different about this devotional?

It is designed to gather together a busy family
before each member hurries off to begin the day.

There are 7 segments to each day's devotional:

#1. Scripture:

Like most devotionals, it begins with a
scripture to be read by one family member.

#2. Promise or Command:

The scripture is followed by a question: Does this scripture contain a promise to receive or a command to obey? Let every family member look for something specific the scripture is saying to him or her.

#3. Prayer:

Join hands and pray the prayer aloud.
The prayer is based on the scripture
reading for that day.

#4. Proclamation:

Together declare aloud the proclamation.
You are declaring the promise of God's
Word over your lives by purposefully
speaking what God has said about you.

#5. Memory Verse:

At the beginning of each week, there is a memory verse to learn. Because there are a multitude of translations of scripture, I have chosen to give the King James Version for the memory verses most of the time; however, I purposefully eliminated the old English forms of pronouns such as "thou" and changed them to "you" and other simple modifications such as leaving off the "th" at the end of certain words as "speaketh" and make it "speak." This makes the memorization simple and more understandable without changing the meaning or message. Let each member of the family rehearse aloud the memory verse. (You might want to write out the verse on paper or record it in your phone or tablet so you can review it often throughout the day.) Make it your goal for every family member to quote the verse by the end of the week.

#6. Blessing:

Daily declare to one another, "I love you.
You are blessed, and you are a blessing."

#7. Hugs:

Don't let any member of your
family run off without a hug.

Introduction

How do I apply these principles?

Jesus said, "Man shall not live by bread alone but by every word that proceeds out of the mouth of God."

It is not enough to simply read the Bible and expect our lives and the lives of our family members to be radically changed. We must "apply" the Word of God to our lives. We must make the scriptures we read enter and fill our hearts. This is something we must do "on purpose." We must let the scripture speak to us personally. Reading scripture with a purpose of looking for a promise to receive or finding a commandment to obey will help us apply the living Word of God that will transform our lives.

Prayer is another necessary part of our daily fellowship with God, and prayer is also a part of this devotional. The importance of hearing members of our families pray and them hearing us pray reinforces the value of prayer and establishes a daily practice that lasts a lifetime.

A vital aspect of prayer is proclamation. We must discover what God's Word says, apply it to our lives personally and pray accordingly, but then we should proclaim the will of God over our lives and our families. Speaking what God says about us and declaring that word establishes the course for our day.

The psalmist wrote, "Your word I have hidden in my heart that I might not sin against you" (Ps. 119:11). The Word of God is to be written in our hearts, and one way that can be accomplished is by memorizing scripture. Make it your goal to memorize one verse of scripture every week.

One of the last components of this devotional is a spoken blessing each family member gives to another. The words "I love you" are powerful and necessary for each of us to hear every day. As we say to each other "I love you" and seal that word with a heartfelt hug we have set the stage for a wonderful day.

– *Dan Coflin*

January 1st

Scripture: Ephesians 4:21-24 (NLT)

"Since you have heard about Jesus and have learned the truth that comes from him, throw off your old sinful nature and your former way of life, which is corrupted by lust and deception. Instead, let the Spirit renew your thoughts and attitudes. Put on your new nature, created to be like God—truly righteous and holy."

In your prayer journal, identify in this portion of scripture a promise to receive or a command to obey.

Prayer:

Heavenly Father, I choose this day to put out of my life every action and attitude that I know is displeasing to you. I ask for your grace to empower me to always choose what is right. This is a new year and a new day. Your Word says that your mercies are new every day. I thank you for your forgiveness for every wrong choice I have made in the past. I put on, like a new garment, the new man that you have created me to be. I praise your wonderful and holy name, and it is in the name of my Lord Jesus Christ I pray, Amen.

Proclamation:

I am the righteousness of God in Christ Jesus. I am led by the Spirit of God today. I hear his voice and walk in his ways. The blessings of the Lord come upon me and overtake me. I am truly blessed of the Lord. He is my shield and fortress, my high tower and place of refuge. I am kept from every evil work, for if God is for me then who can be against me?

Memory Verse: 2 Corinthians 5:21

"For he has made him (Jesus) to be sin for us, who knew no sin; that we might be made the righteousness of God in him."

To every family member: *"I love you; you are blessed, and you are a blessing."*
Don't forget the hugs.

January 2nd

Scripture: Philippians 1:2-6 (NIV)

"Grace and peace to you from God our Father and the Lord Jesus Christ. I thank my God every time I remember you. In all my prayers for all of you, I always pray with joy because of your partnership in the gospel from the first day until now, being confident of this, that he who began a good work in you will carry it on to completion until the day of Christ Jesus."

In your prayer journal, identify in this portion of scripture a promise to receive or a command to obey.

Prayer:

Father, thank you today for your grace and peace you freely give me. I want to be a person of prayer who will stand in agreement with you and my family and my church, as we are all partners together in the work of the ministry. As covenant partners we all share alike in different gifts and abilities you have given us. I pray the deposits you have made in us, of spiritual things, will not be wasted. I pray those gifts and that anointing will grow and develop and become useful to you. Father, help us become more and more fruitful in every good work you have called us to perform. Be glorified in our lives this day; I pray in Jesus' name, Amen.

Proclamation:

The scriptures declare that I am in partnership with God and other members of his church in order to do and accomplish God's good purpose. I am anointed with the Holy Spirit and equipped with spiritual gifts God has given me. I am yielded to God and submitted to those he has put in my life to teach me and instruct me in spiritual things. I will function in the gifts he has given me to help others accomplish their God-given assignment as they also help me to fulfill God's call in my life.

Memory Verse: 2 Corinthians 5:21

"For he has made him (Jesus) to be sin for us, who knew no sin; that we might be made the righteousness of God in him."

To every family member: *"I love you; you are blessed, and you are a blessing."*
Don't forget the hugs.

January 3rd

Scripture: Proverbs 4:20-22 (AMP)

"My son, attend to my words; consent *and* submit to my sayings. Let them not depart from your sight; keep them in the center of your heart. For they are life to those who find them, healing *and* health to all their flesh."

In your prayer journal, identify in this portion of scripture a promise to receive or a command to obey.

Prayer:

God, my Father, I honor your Word today. I want to desire and delight in your Word more than anything else in my life. Help me to have a sincere love for the Word of God. Help me to think about your Word day and night and to study and meditate on your Word so that I will keep it in my heart. Let your Word change the way I think and the way I see people, circumstances and situations. May your Word be like a seed that grows in the soil of my heart to produce fruit in my life that will honor you. You said your Word is an incorruptible seed that will certainly produce what you sent it forth to do. It will not fail. As I keep your Word active in my mind this day, I will walk in life and health for you have declared it. Thank you for your faithfulness to fulfill this promise in my life today. I give you praise for these things in the wonderful name of my Lord Jesus Christ, Amen.

Proclamation:

The Word of God is an incorruptible seed that I have planted in my heart today. The Word of God is the power of God for my salvation, my healing, my provision. It will supply me the abundant life God has promised, for Jesus came to give me life and to give me life more abundantly. This is a good day, for it is the day the Lord has made, and I will rejoice and be glad in it.

Memory Verse: 2 Corinthians 5:21

"For he has made him (Jesus) to be sin for us, who knew no sin; that we might be made the righteousness of God in him."

To every family member: *"I love you; you are blessed, and you are a blessing."*
Don't forget the hugs.

January 4th

Scripture: Luke 10:19 (KJV)

"Behold, I give unto you power to tread on serpents and scorpions, and over all the power of the enemy: and nothing shall by any means hurt you."

In your prayer journal, identify in this portion of scripture a promise to receive or a command to obey.

Prayer:

My Father, I thank you for the authority that you have given to me in the name of the Lord Jesus Christ. You said that I could tread on every demonic work and have victory over all the power of the devil and his forces and nothing would by any means hurt me. Help me to live in the revelation of this truth. I do not need to fear or be anxious about anything because in everything you cause me to triumph. The devil is under my feet, and Jesus said I can bind on earth what is already bound in heaven and I can loose on earth what is already loosed in heaven. I can call forth God's will into every situation and circumstance. I can change the outcome of events through the authority that is in the name of Jesus. Lord, you said to pray that your kingdom come and your will be done on earth just like it is always done in heaven. I stand this day in the authority you have given to bind every wicked work that would attempt to rob, kill or destroy in my life the things that God has freely given me to enjoy. I declare that the will of God will be fulfilled in my life, my family, and my business this day in every way. In Jesus' name I pray, Amen.

Proclamation:

Jesus said that all authority in heaven and on earth has been given unto him. Then Jesus gave me the responsibility to enforce his will on the earth by the authority of his name. I call forth this day the will of God to be performed in those things that pertain to my life. I bind every wicked device of the enemy and declare that every assignment he has against me will fail. God's will is what will be done in my life today, and I know the things Jesus has done for me will bring me life and life more abundantly.

Memory Verse: 2 Corinthians 5:21

"For he has made him (Jesus) to be sin for us, who knew no sin; that we might be made the righteousness of God in him."

To every family member: "*I love you; you are blessed, and you are a blessing.*"
Don't forget the hugs.

January 5th

Scripture: Hebrews 2:14-15 (NKJV)

"Inasmuch then as the children have partaken of flesh and blood, He Himself likewise shared in the same, that through death He might destroy him who had the power of death, that is, the devil and release those who through fear of death were all their lifetime subject to bondage."

In your prayer journal, identify in this portion of scripture a promise to receive or a command to obey.

Prayer:

God, My Father, I give you thanks for setting me free from the fear of death. When Jesus died for me and rose again from the dead; he defeated death and the devil, who had the power of death. You destroyed the devil, rendering him idle, useless and unemployed according to your Word. I thank you that the devil has no more power in my life. I am free from fear and the power of death because the love of God has freed me from fear. You did not give me the spirit of fear, but you gave me the spirit of power and love and a sound mind. I have received the Spirit of God, and he witnesses to me that I am your child and an heir of your kingdom. I praise and thank you this day for your great grace that is poured out on me. In Jesus' name I pray, Amen.

Proclamation:

I am no longer under the bondage of fear because Jesus has set me free from the fear of death. Jesus destroyed the fear of death by defeating death at his resurrection. I will not give in or give any place to fear in my life because perfect love cast out fear. The love of God has been made perfect in me. My hope and my confidence is in God and in his great love for me. If God gave me his Son, how much more will he freely give me all things to enjoy?

Memory Verse: 2 Corinthians 5:21

"For he has made him (Jesus) to be sin for us, who knew no sin; that we might be made the righteousness of God in him."

To every family member: *"I love you; you are blessed, and you are a blessing."*
Don't forget the hugs.

January 6th

Scripture: Ephesians 4:25-28 (NLT)

"So stop telling lies. Let us tell our neighbors the truth, for we are all parts of the same body. And "don't sin by letting anger control you." Don't let the sun go down while you are still angry, for anger gives a foothold to the devil. If you are a thief, quit stealing. Instead, use your hands for good hard work, and then give generously to others in need."

In your prayer journal, identify in this portion of scripture a promise to receive or a command to obey.

Prayer:

God, my Father, I worship you today. I want my life to honor you in the words I speak and in the things I do. I will speak what is true without exaggeration. I will be honest and humble before everyone I meet today. I know that the Spirit of God has given me the love of God so that I can choose to love everyone without exception - not just those who are kind and gentle, but even those who are hard to love. Your grace gives me strength to live free from anger and walk in peace regardless of what others might do or say. I give you thanks for these things working mightily in me today. In Jesus' name I pray, Amen.

Proclamation:

I choose this day to live my life according to the incorruptible Word of God. I walk in the truth of God's Word, and I am honest and compassionate to all I meet. I do not allow anger to control my thoughts or emotions, but I put away from me every evil work and device of the devil. He has no place in my life or my family. Instead, my family and I walk in the place of God's grace and blessing.

Memory Verse: 2 Corinthians 5:21

"For he has made him (Jesus) to be sin for us, who knew no sin; that we might be made the righteousness of God in him."

To every family member: *"I love you; you are blessed, and you are a blessing."*
Don't forget the hugs.

January 7th

Scripture: Philippians 1:9-11 (NRSV)

"And this is my prayer, that your love may overflow more and more with knowledge and full insight to help you to determine what is best, so that in the day of Christ you may be pure and blameless, having produced the harvest of righteousness that comes through Jesus Christ for the glory and praise of God."

In your prayer journal, identify in this portion of scripture a promise to receive or a command to obey.

Prayer:

My Heavenly Father, I pray this day that the love of God that has been put in my heart by the Holy Spirit will grow and increase more and more so that everything I do is done because of the compassion of God within me. Help me see people and situations through the eyes of God's love and help me produce in my life a daily harvest of good fruit that many people will see and taste and experience God's goodness. I pray that every good thing that is produced through my life because of your love will bring much praise and glory to you. I pray this in the name of the Lord Jesus Christ, Amen.

Proclamation:

Today is a good day because it is the day the Lord has made. I am greatly blessed of God today because he has spread abroad in my heart his divine love. I choose to walk in love with everyone I meet. I seek to express God's love as it is described in the Scriptures declaring that love is not selfish, rude, arrogant or proud. It does not act inappropriately, but always does what is right. Love bears up in all things and causes those who choose love to be filled with hope and faith. I choose to walk in love today.

Memory Verse: 2 Corinthians 5:21

"For he has made him (Jesus) to be sin for us, who knew no sin; that we might be made the righteousness of God in him."

To every family member: *"I love you; you are blessed, and you are a blessing."*
Don't forget the hugs.

January 8th

Scripture: Proverbs 4:23-25 (GW)

"Guard your heart more than anything else, because the source of your life flows from it. Remove dishonesty from your mouth. Put deceptive speech far away from your lips. Let your eyes look straight ahead and your sight be focused in front of you."

In your prayer journal, identify in this portion of scripture a promise to receive or a command to obey.

Prayer:

Heavenly Father, you have instructed me to place a guard around my heart, my mind and thoughts. You said my heart is most important because it is out of my heart that my life flows. Help me to guard my heart and not allow anything to enter in that would defile me and pollute my way of thinking and saying and doing. May my words be filled with life and encouragement and help me to keep my eyes focused on the things of God. Jesus said that the Spirit of God within us would be a fountain of life, a river of living water that would flow out of us and bring life to everything it touches. I thank you today for that river within me. I guard my heart and do not allow anything to remain in me that would cause me to become bitter or unforgiving and thereby pollute that force of life within me. Thank you for your grace that gives me the ability to overcome every wicked device of the enemy. I praise you for the victory in Jesus' name, Amen.

Proclamation:

I declare this day that my heart is fixed, trusting in the Lord. I will not allow any words that offend or thoughts that condemn me to remain in my heart. I keep my eyes focused on the pathway as the Word of God leads me. I will not turn to the right or to the left, but I will continue walking in righteous paths that will always lead me to the place of God's fulfilled promises. This is a good day, for it is the day the Lord has made, and I will be glad and rejoice in it.

Memory Verse: 2 Corinthians 5:17

"Therefore if any man be in Christ, he is a new creature: old things are passed away; behold, all things are become new."

To every family member: *"I love you; you are blessed, and you are a blessing."*
Don't forget the hugs.

January 9th

Scripture: Hebrews 4:12-14 (NCV)

"God's word is alive and working and is sharper than a double-edged sword. It cuts all the way into us, where the soul and the spirit are joined, to the center of our joints and bones. And it judges the thoughts and feelings in our hearts. Nothing in all the world can be hidden from God. Everything is clear and lies open before him, and to him we must explain the way we have lived. Since we have a great high priest, Jesus the Son of God, who has gone into heaven, let us hold on to the faith we have."

In your prayer journal, identify in this portion of scripture
a promise to receive or a command to obey.

Prayer:

Father, you created everything by your Word. Your Word is alive and powerful. It is able to identify in my life what is spiritual and what is only of the soul. Nothing can be hidden from you. You know all things and still you love me and are working in me to do and to fulfill all of your good pleasure. Thank you for Jesus, my great high priest, who is in heaven and is seated at the right hand of God and is always interceding for me. Father, I ask you to make these things real to me today. May your Word bring forth great faith in my life. Jesus paid the price for my redemption and my forgiveness and my righteousness is not based on my works but his. I pray my faith would be strong in the grace of God today. In Jesus' name I pray, Amen.

Proclamation:

Jesus is my high priest. He has completed the work required for my redemption. He paid for my sins in full by the blood he shed on the cross. My faith is in his blood and in the work he accomplished on my behalf. As my high priest, Jesus is always declaring my righteousness because his work to give me righteousness was a perfect work that is settled forever.

Memory Verse: 2 Corinthians 5:17

"Therefore if any man be in Christ, he is a new creature:
old things are passed away; behold, all things are become new."

To every family member: *"I love you; you are blessed, and you are a blessing."*
Don't forget the hugs.

January 10th

Scripture: Ephesians 4:29-32 (NRSV)

"Let no evil talk come out of your mouths, but only what is useful for building up, as there is need, so that your words may give grace to those who hear. And do not grieve the Holy Spirit of God, with which you were marked with a seal for the day of redemption. Put away from you all bitterness and wrath and anger and wrangling and slander, together with all malice, and be kind to one another, tenderhearted, forgiving one another, as God in Christ has forgiven you."

In your prayer journal, identify in this portion of scripture a promise to receive or a command to obey.

Prayer:

God, my Father, please help me guard my tongue from speaking any words that would grieve you or would judge and condemn others. I purpose to put out of my life all bitterness and anger. I know you would have me speak to everyone today in such a way that when I leave they are encouraged. I thank you, Father, that I am forgiven because Jesus took upon himself all judgment, for not only my sin, but also the sins of all mankind. Therefore, I forgive anyone and everyone that has ever hurt me or stolen from me or wounded me in any way. I forgive them and release them from any further judgment because you have forgiven me. I receive these things now in the wonderful name of my Lord Jesus, Amen.

Proclamation:

I always speak words of life and encouragement to everyone I meet. I do not hold on to bitterness. Instead, I speak words that are filled with the love and grace of God. I don't speak down to anyone as if they were inferior, but I honor all and put the welfare of others before my own.

Memory Verse: 2 Corinthians 5:17

"Therefore if any man be in Christ, he is a new creature: old things are passed away; behold, all things are become new."

To every family member: *"I love you; you are blessed, and you are a blessing."*
Don't forget the hugs.

January 11th

Scripture: Philippians 2:1-4 (NCV)

"Does your life in Christ give you strength? Does his love comfort you? Do we share together in the spirit? Do you have mercy and kindness? If so, make me very happy by having the same thoughts, sharing the same love, and having one mind and purpose. When you do things, do not let selfishness or pride be your guide. Instead, be humble and give more honor to others than to yourselves. Do not be interested only in your own life, but be interested in the lives of others."

In your prayer journal, identify in this portion of scripture
a promise to receive or a command to obey.

Prayer:

God, my Father, you have given me your Holy Spirit who lives in me and will never leave me. You have given me your love and your life so that I can live out of the life of God within me instead of living only for myself. I call on the power of the Spirit of God to manifest in my life God's character of mercy and kindness. Father, help me today to live in that place of agreement with the Word of God and the Spirit of God. I pray that my life would give demonstration of your love so I might please you and be a blessing to my family and all those I meet today. I ask these things in the name of my Lord Jesus Christ, Amen.

Proclamation:

I choose this day to walk in agreement with the Word of God. I do not allow selfishness or pride to guide my life, but I am led by the Spirit of God. I speak only words of life and encouragement. I do not allow strife to enter any part of my life. I do not argue or become irritated with others. I lay down my life today by choosing to regard the needs of others above my own. God is with me and blesses me in everything I do. I walk in the blessings and favor of God today.

Memory Verse: 2 Corinthians 5:17

"Therefore if any man be in Christ, he is a new creature:
old things are passed away; behold, all things are become new."

To every family member: *"I love you; you are blessed, and you are a blessing."*
Don't forget the hugs.

January 12th

Scripture: Proverbs 3:1-4 (NKJV)

"My son, do not forget my law, but let your heart keep my commands; for length of days and long life and peace they will add to you. Let not mercy and truth forsake you; bind them around your neck, write them on the tablet of your heart, and so find favor and high esteem in the sight of God and man."

In your prayer journal: identify in this portion of scripture a promise to receive or a command to obey.

Prayer:

My God and Father, I take hold of your Word today. Your commandments bring me long life and peace. Give me ears to hear your Word above all other voices. Help me to recognize your voice and be quick to both hear and obey your Word. I pray your mercy and truth will remain in me. Help me wear them like a necklace and engrave them on my heart so that I will always respond to people with mercy and speak forth your Word of truth with the love of God. I thank you today for divine favor that rests upon me that I might have good success in the sight of man and in your sight. I receive these things now in Jesus' wonderful name, Amen.

Proclamation:

I keep the Word of God with me at all times. It is always before my eyes and in my heart. God's Word brings me long life and lengthens my days. I follow after the commandments of God, and because I do, I am blessed of the Lord and walk in favor and good success in everything I do.

Memory Verse: 2 Corinthians 5:17

"Therefore if any man be in Christ, he is a new creature: old things are passed away; behold, all things are become new."

To every family member: *"I love you; you are blessed, and you are a blessing."*
Don't forget the hugs.

January 13th

Scripture: Matthew 18:18-20 (AMP)

"Truly I tell you, whatever you forbid *and* declare to be improper and unlawful on earth must be what is already forbidden in heaven, and whatever you permit *and* declare proper and lawful on earth must be what is already permitted in heaven. Again I tell you, if two of you on earth agree (harmonize together, make a symphony together) about whatever [anything and everything] they may ask, it will come to pass *and* be done for them by My Father in heaven. For wherever two or three are gathered (drawn together as My followers) in (into) My name, there I Am in the midst of them."

In your prayer journal, identify in this portion of scripture a promise to receive or a command to obey.

Prayer:

My Heavenly Father, you have instructed me to forbid on the earth what you forbid in heaven and to permit on earth what you permit in heaven. You said that I am in this world but I am not of this world. You have delivered me from the authority of darkness, and you have translated me into your kingdom. I live according to the kingdom of God and not according to the kingdoms of this world. Help me to speak your Word with your authority to accomplish your will. You said that, if just two of us agree together on the earth, whatever we ask, you will do. I thank you this day for this promise. Give me wisdom to know what to permit and what to forbid. Help me walk in agreement with you and others who are called by your name so our prayers will be answered and our declarations be fulfilled. I thank you for this now. In Jesus' name I pray, Amen.

Proclamation:

I receive today the promise of God's Word that allows me to enforce his will by permitting what God permits and disallowing what God forbids.

Memory Verse: 2 Corinthians 5:17

"Therefore if any man be in Christ, he is a new creature: old things are passed away; behold, all things are become new."

To every family member: "I love you; you are blessed, and you are a blessing." Don't forget the hugs.

Faith Family Minute | 15

January 14th

Scripture: Hebrews 4:15-16 (NKJV)

"For we do not have a High Priest who cannot sympathize with our weaknesses, but was in all *points* tempted as *we are, yet* without sin. Let us therefore come boldly to the throne of grace, that we may obtain mercy and find grace to help in time of need."

In your prayer journal, identify in this portion of scripture a promise to receive or a command to obey.

Prayer:

Heavenly Father, I come to you today boldly like your Word says. I can come to you with great confidence because I know the work Jesus did for me was a perfect and complete work. Not only was he tempted in every way like I am tempted, but he is still touched with my human weaknesses. Jesus sympathizes with me, having experienced everything I will ever experience, and he successfully defeated every temptation that challenged him. I can come before the very throne of God without fear or condemnation, guilt or shame because I know you have accepted me in the beloved. Thank you for such access into your presence and the promise of obtaining mercy and finding the grace I need for this day. I give you praise, in Jesus' wonderful name, Amen.

Proclamation:

I come boldly today to the throne room of God. I have access into his glorious presence by the blood of Jesus. In this holy place, I receive mercy that helps me in every time of need. God's grace is available to me in abundance, and with God's grace I can reign in life like a king. For God has made me a king and priest to accomplish his will and to minister unto him with thanksgiving and praise, for he is worthy.

Memory Verse: 2 Corinthians 5:17

"Therefore if any man be in Christ, he is a new creature: old things are passed away; behold, all things are become new."

To every family member: *"I love you; you are blessed, and you are a blessing."*
Don't forget the hugs.

January 15th

Scripture: Ephesians 6:10-13 (NLT)

"A final word: Be strong in the Lord and in his mighty power. Put on all of God's armor so that you will be able to stand firm against all strategies of the devil. For we are not fighting against flesh-and-blood enemies, but against evil rulers and authorities of the unseen world, against mighty powers in this dark world, and against evil spirits in the heavenly places. Therefore, put on every piece of God's armor so you will be able to resist the enemy in the time of evil. Then after the battle you will still be standing firm."

In your prayer journal, identify in this portion of scripture a promise to receive or a command to obey.

Prayer:

Heavenly Father, thank you for the armor of God that protects and shields me from every evil work. My strength is in you. You cause me to stand in victory today over every temptation and crafty device of the devil. My enemies are not people but spiritual, unseen forces that oppose God's will in my life. I bind them with the authority of Jesus' name and declare God's Word that states that greater is he that is in me than he that is in the world. I have the Spirit of God within me and he leads me today in righteous paths. Father, thank you for this blessed and prosperous day, in Jesus' name I pray, Amen.

Proclamation:

God's Word declares that he gives his angels charge over me to keep me in all my ways. I am not alone today. I have the angels of heaven from without protecting me, and I am empowered by God's Holy Spirit from within who is able to teach me, and guide me, and shield me from every evil work.

Memory Verse: Philippians 4:19

"But my God shall supply all your need according to his riches in glory by Christ Jesus."

To every family member: *"I love you; you are blessed, and you are a blessing."*
Don't forget the hugs.

January 16th

Scripture: Philippians 2:5-11 (ASV)

"Have this mind in you, which was also in Christ Jesus: who, existing in the form of God, counted not the being on an equality with God a thing to be grasped, but emptied himself, taking the form of a servant, being made in the likeness of men; and being found in fashion as a man, he humbled himself, becoming obedient even unto death, yea, the death of the cross. Wherefore also God highly exalted him, and gave unto him the name which is above every name; that in the name of Jesus every knee should bow, of things in heaven and things on earth and things under the earth, and that every tongue should confess that Jesus Christ is Lord, to the glory of God the Father."

In your prayer journal, identify in this portion of scripture a promise to receive or a command to obey.

Prayer:

Heavenly Father, just as Jesus humbled himself for us and became a man who demonstrated who you are and what you are like, I ask you to help me today to also give demonstration to the life of God that is within me. Help me to have the right attitude that will serve others. Help me to be of the same mind that was in Jesus, to think the way God thinks and to speak the words God speaks and to do the things that please God as I seek to be a blessing to everyone. I ask this in the name of the Lord Jesus Christ, Amen.

Proclamation:

I have the mind of Christ because the Spirit of God abides within me today. I am a blessing to everyone I meet. I choose to lay aside my comfort and convenience if somebody else needs my help today. I am sensitive to the leading of the Holy Spirit. I listen to hear the voice of God, and I am quick to obey what he tells me. The Word of God promises me that if I humble myself before him, he will exalt me.

Memory Verse: Philippians 4:19

"But my God shall supply all your need according to his riches in glory by Christ Jesus."

To every family member: *"I love you; you are blessed, and you are a blessing."*
Don't forget the hugs.

January 17th

Scripture: Proverbs 3:5-8 (GNT)

"Trust in the Lord with all your heart. Never rely on what you think you know. Remember the Lord in everything you do, and he will show you the right way. Never let yourself think that you are wiser than you are; simply obey the Lord and refuse to do wrong. If you do, it will be like good medicine, healing your wounds and easing your pains."

In your prayer journal, identify in this portion of scripture a promise to receive or a command to obey.

Prayer:

Father, I put my trust in you today. I know you will guide me along the pathway you choose for me. You always led me in good paths where I am protected from every evil work and where I am always at the right place at the right time to receive and walk in the blessings of God. I purpose not to devise my own plans or choose my own ways because I know that my thoughts and my ways are limited, but your wisdom and your plans for me are perfect. I thank you for the power of the Holy Spirit that works mightily in me today to teach me and lead me so that I may experience, like a good medicine, health for my body and soundness for my mind. I bless your holy name and give you praise for these things in Jesus' name, Amen.

Proclamation:

I trust the Lord with all of my heart. I acknowledge him in everything I do. I desire to follow his leading because I know that my plans may fail but his plans will never fail. As I follow the Lord and do what is right in his eyes, obeying his Word and refusing to do wrong, I will experience health and walk in success in all I do.

Memory Verse: Philippians 4:19

"But my God shall supply all your need according to his riches in glory by Christ Jesus."

To every family member: *"I love you; you are blessed, and you are a blessing."*
Don't forget the hugs.

January 18th

Scripture: 1 Peter 5:8-9 (NKJV)

"Be sober, be vigilant; because your adversary the devil walks about like a roaring lion, seeking whom he may devour. Resist him, steadfast in the faith, knowing that the same sufferings are experienced by your brotherhood in the world."

In your prayer journal, identify in this portion of scripture a promise to receive or a command to obey.

Prayer:

Heavenly Father, you have equipped me and prepared me for every good work. You have given me your Holy Spirit to live in me forever and to teach me the things of God. Help me to be diligent and watchful for my adversary the devil. I know he is roaming about, looking for someone who will give him access into his or her life. I do not fear him because you have defeated him and given me victory over him and all of his wicked works. I know he has no place in my life unless I give it to him. Help me today to keep closed any door of access he might try to enter. I trust you to keep me from deception and temptation. I resist every attempt of the devil to enter my life. I draw near to God and the devil flees from me just as you said he would. Thank you for bringing to pass these things this day in Jesus' name, Amen.

Proclamation:

I am watchful and diligent to recognize and resist every crafty device of the devil. He has no place in my life or my family. Jesus has already defeated him and rendered him without power or strength to defeat me. I give him no place and command him to leave me and to take his hands off of my family and my possessions. The devil is a thief, but he is not going to steal from me. I have dominion over him and command him to get under my feet according to the word of God.

Memory Verse: Philippians 4:19

"But my God shall supply all your need according to his riches in glory by Christ Jesus."

To every family member: *"I love you; you are blessed, and you are a blessing."*
Don't forget the hugs.

January 19th

Scripture: Hebrews 10: 23-25 (KJV)

"Let us hold fast the profession of our faith without wavering; (for he is faithful that promised;) And let us consider one another to provoke unto love and to good works: Not forsaking the assembling of ourselves together, as the manner of some is; but exhorting one another: and so much the more, as ye see the day approaching."

In your prayer journal, identify in this portion of scripture a promise to receive or a command to obey.

Prayer:

My Father, I want to be filled with faith and hope so that I will never waver or let go of the promises of your Word. You tell me to hold fast, to maintain my confession of faith because you are faithful and what you have promised you will certainly perform. I want to be someone you can use to provoke others to walk in love and do good works because of the demonstration of my faith. Help me today to encourage others to walk in faith and continue to meet with other believers every time there is an opportunity. I ask you to strengthen me in my faith and cause my hope, my joyful expectations, to be fulfilled so that many will look and see in me the goodness and faithfulness of God. I thank you for these things in Jesus' name, Amen.

Proclamation:

I am filled with hope and will not cease from confessing the Word of God to everyone I meet. I know that my God is faithful to perform his Word and fulfill his promises. I will continue to encourage others to walk in love and to do good works that glorify God and to never forsake the times when the church meets together. I will encourage others, and others will encourage me to continue in the things of God, and together we will be strong and daily glorify God.

Memory Verse: Philippians 4:19

"But my God shall supply all your need according to his riches in glory by Christ Jesus."

To every family member: *"I love you; you are blessed, and you are a blessing."*
Don't forget the hugs.

January 20th

Scripture: Ephesians 6:14-18 (NKJV)

"Stand therefore, having girded your waist with truth, having put on the breastplate of righteousness, and having shod your feet with the preparation of the gospel of peace; above all, taking the shield of faith with which you will be able to quench all the fiery darts of the wicked one. And take the helmet of salvation, and the sword of the Spirit, which is the word of God; praying always with all prayer and supplication in the Spirit, being watchful to this end with all perseverance and supplication for all the saints..."

In your prayer journal, identify in this portion of scripture a promise to receive or a command to obey.

Prayer:

Father, help me today to walk in the reality that is described as the armor of God. I know that righteousness, peace, faith and salvation are mine. You have provided them for me as a free gift. I did not earn them, but I have received them by your grace. You have made me righteous and given me peace and faith that works mightily in me. I will put your Word in my mouth and speak it forth as if it were a sword that shall defeat my enemies and advance the kingdom of God. I pray today for me and my family and those who are called by your name to accomplish your will and bring forth your purpose. I pray these things in the name of my Lord Jesus Christ, Amen.

Proclamation:

I have put on the armor of God, and I am able to stand steadfast today in every circumstance of life. I will not give in or give up. I will not cast away my confidence or lose hope regarding any promise of God being fulfilled in my life. God is faithful and what he has promised, he will perform.

Memory Verse: Philippians 4:19

"But my God shall supply all your need according to his riches in glory by Christ Jesus."

To every family member: *"I love you; you are blessed, and you are a blessing."*
Don't forget the hugs.

January 21st

Scripture: Philippians 2:14-16 (KJV)

"Do all things without murmurings and disputing: That ye may be blameless and harmless, the sons of God, without rebuke, in the midst of a crooked and perverse nation, among whom ye shine as lights in the world; Holding forth the word of life; that I may rejoice in the day of Christ, that I have not run in vain, neither laboured in vain."

In your prayer journal, identify in this portion of scripture a promise to receive or a command to obey.

Prayer:

God, my Father, I desire to do your will today. I do not want to be a person who just hears and agrees with your Word, but I want to be one who obeys and does your Word. I want to live before you without complaining to you or arguing with others so that I will never bring harm to your reputation because I am called by your name. I ask you to help me be an example to everyone by making my life to be like a light that shines in the darkness of this world to reveal your love and goodness. Make me profitable and fruitful in everything that will bring glory to you. I ask all these things in Jesus' name, Amen.

Proclamation:

I give no place to strife and arguing. I do not murmur or complain, speaking or doing things in a way or with an attitude that would displease God or give anyone the opportunity to point a finger at me in judgment. Instead, I hold on to the Word of God that brings life to me and to those around me. I depend on God to always put me over and make me successful in everything I do. I am an example of one who walks in abundant life and the joy of the Lord strengthens me every day and in all my ways.

Memory Verse: Philippians 4:19

"But my God shall supply all your need according to his riches in glory by Christ Jesus."

To every family member: *"I love you; you are blessed, and you are a blessing."*
Don't forget the hugs.

January 22nd

Scripture: Philippians 3:7-9 (NLT)

"I once thought these things were valuable, but now I consider them worthless because of what Christ has done. Yes, everything else is worthless when compared with the infinite value of knowing Christ Jesus my Lord. For his sake I have discarded everything else, counting it all as garbage, so that I could gain Christ and become one with him. I no longer count on my own righteousness through obeying the law; rather, I become righteous through faith in Christ. For God's way of making us right with himself depends on faith."

In your prayer journal, identify in this portion of scripture a promise to receive or a command to obey.

Prayer:

Father, the most valuable thing in my life is my relationship with you. I know there is no way to please you by my own efforts. I cannot make myself acceptable to you by my own works but only by faith in what Jesus has done for me. My righteousness is not based on my many good works or my limited evil works. My righteousness is a gift I receive from you by simple faith. I trust you to make me acceptable because Jesus did a perfect work on my behalf. I can only receive your righteousness for it is such a precious treasure I could never have earned it by my own efforts but only received it by your grace. I give you thanks for this wonderful gift in the name of my Lord Jesus Christ, Amen.

Proclamation:

I stand this day before God having received the gift of his righteousness. I am the righteousness of God in Christ Jesus. I treasure above everything else my relationship with God. I will depend on him. I come boldly before the throne of God because I know I am accepted in his presence. I can ask whatever I will, and God my Father will do it for me because my greatest desire is to please him with my faith.

Memory Verse: Proverbs 3:5-6

"Trust in the Lord with all your heart; and lean not unto your own understanding. In all your ways acknowledge him, and he shall direct your paths."

To every family member: "I love you; you are blessed, and you are a blessing."
Don't forget the hugs.

January 23rd

Scripture: Proverbs 3:9-10 (HCSB)

"Honor the Lord with your possessions and with the first produce of your entire harvest; then your barns will be completely filled, and your vats will overflow with new wine."

In your prayer journal, identify in this portion of scripture a promise to receive or a command to obey.

Prayer:

My Heavenly Father, I honor you today in all of my ways. I know my success is not based on my ability alone, but is the result of your favor and blessing in my life. You said that as I honor you with my finances and bring to you the first fruits of all my increase that you will cause my barns, my storehouses, to be filled and the rich blessings of God will overflow in my life. I want to thank you for your faithfulness. You have promised to always watch over your Word to perform it in my life. I will be careful to bring to you the first of all my increase, and as I do you will prosper me in everything I do. I give you praise this day in Jesus' name, Amen.

Proclamation:

I know that everything I have received has come from the Lord. He is the source of my provision. He is the reason I can succeed in everything I do. I bring to him my tithes for every dollar of increase I receive. I bring my offerings that represent the increase of my business or income of any kind. For everything I receive, I return a portion to God as an acknowledgment of his blessing in my life.

Memory Verse: Proverbs 3:5-6

"Trust in the Lord with all your heart; and lean not unto your own understanding. In all your ways acknowledge him, and he shall direct your paths."

To every family member: "I love you; you are blessed, and you are a blessing." Don't forget the hugs.

January 24th

Scripture: Hebrews 10:35-39 (RSV)

"Therefore do not throw away your confidence, which has a great reward. For you have need of endurance, so that you may do the will of God and receive what is promised. "For yet a little while and the coming one shall come and shall not tarry; but my righteous one shall live by faith and if he shrinks back, my soul has no pleasure in him." But we are not of those who shrink back and are destroyed, but of those who have faith and keep their souls."

In your prayer journal, identify in this portion of scripture a promise to receive or a command to obey.

Prayer:

My Father, I praise you and thank you that today my faith is strong. I will continue to follow after you because I know that there is a great reward. The promises of your Word are certain and what you have promised you will accomplish. You said that without faith it is impossible to please you, but you reward those who diligently seek after you. Help me today to follow you without distraction. Keep me from discouragement and despair. I know that I need to be patient and keep my eyes focused on your Word to follow the leading of the Spirit of God and to see by faith the fulfillment of your promises even before they come to pass. I receive your grace to help me to do these things this day. In Jesus' name I pray, Amen.

Proclamation:

I will not cast away my confidence in God. I will stand fast in faith and keep my eyes on the promises of God's Word. I will continue to always do what is right and what is pleasing to God because I know he sees me and watches over me to bless me and bring me into my inheritance. God is faithful, and God is able to do in my life what he has promised. The grace of God rests upon me today so that I will walk in joy and great expectation of his manifest presence and power in my life.

Memory Verse: Proverbs 3:5-6

"Trust in the Lord with all your heart; and lean not unto your own understanding. In all your ways acknowledge him, and he shall direct your paths."

To every family member: *"I love you; you are blessed, and you are a blessing."*
Don't forget the hugs.

January 25th

Scripture: Philippians 3:12-14 (NLT)

"I don't mean to say that I have already achieved these things or that I have already reached perfection. But I press on to possess that perfection for which Christ Jesus first possessed me. No, dear brothers and sisters, I have not achieved it, but I focus on this one thing: Forgetting the past and looking forward to what lies ahead, I press on to reach the end of the race and receive the heavenly prize for which God, through Christ Jesus, is calling us."

In your prayer journal, identify in this portion of scripture a promise to receive or a command to obey.

Prayer:

My Heavenly Father, I am so thankful that you forget my past and do not remember my sins against me. I know that I am to also forget my past and to look ahead to what you have prepared for me. Father, empower me today not to live in the past defeats or victories I once experienced, but to look ahead to the perfect and abundant life you desire for me. Help me to continue to run in this race of life, always keeping my eyes on the prize before me. I thank you for these things now, in Jesus' name I pray, Amen.

Proclamation:

I am like an athlete running in a marathon. I do not focus my attention on the times I tripped and fell down or even when I got ahead of someone else. No, I look to the prize that awaits me at the finish line when the voice of God my Father says, "Well done, good and faithful servant." I am not afraid of what lies ahead of me because God is with me. He says, "yes" to me about every promise he has made, and he will watch over his Word to perform it in my life. I am confident that what God wants me to do in the days ahead I will do by the power of God that works mightily in me.

Memory Verse: Proverbs 3:5-6

"Trust in the Lord with all your heart; and lean not unto your own understanding. In all your ways acknowledge him, and he shall direct your paths."

To every family member: "*I love you; you are blessed, and you are a blessing.*"
Don't forget the hugs.

January 26th

Scripture: Philippians 4:4-7 (MSG)

"Celebrate God all day, every day. I mean, revel in him! Make it as clear as you can to all you meet that you're on their side, working with them and not against them. Help them see that the Master is about to arrive. He could show up any minute! Don't fret or worry. Instead of worrying, pray. Let petitions and praises shape your worries into prayers, letting God know your concerns. Before you know it, a sense of God's wholeness, everything coming together for good, will come and settle you down. It's wonderful what happens when Christ displaces worry at the center of your life."

In your prayer journal, identify in this portion of scripture a promise to receive or a command to obey.

Prayer:

Father, I praise you, I rejoice in you today. You are worthy of all praise, and I delight myself in you. Help me to honor you by how I act before everyone I meet today. Lord, make me continuously aware of your abiding presence with me. I pray I would never forget that you always see and hear everything I do and say. May I never be afraid of anything because I know you are always with me. Keep me from fear and worry, for I trust you to take care of me today. I thank you for your peace that fills my every thought and helps me guard my heart from being distracted from you. I pray this in the name of my Lord Jesus Christ, Amen.

Proclamation:

I will continuously praise God without ceasing. I will walk before him today in such a way that everyone who meets me will sense God's presence with me. I will not be filled with fear or anxiety about anything, but in everything I face today, I will pray and cast all of my worries and fears on God who is with me. And as I pray with thanksgiving, God's peace encompasses me about on every side so that my mind remains peaceful, always enjoying his presence.

Memory Verse: Proverbs 3:5-6

"Trust in the Lord with all your heart; and lean not unto your own understanding. In all your ways acknowledge him, and he shall direct your paths."

To every family member: "I love you; you are blessed, and you are a blessing."
Don't forget the hugs.

January 27th

Scripture: Proverbs 3:13-18 (NKJV)

"Happy is the man *who* finds wisdom, and the man *who* gains understanding; for her proceeds *are* better than the profits of silver, and her gain than fine gold. She is more precious than rubies, and all the things you may desire cannot compare with her. Length of days *is* in her right hand, in her left hand riches and honor. Her ways *are* ways of pleasantness, and all her paths *are* peace. She *is* a tree of life to those who take hold of her, and happy *are all* who retain her."

In your prayer journal, identify in this portion of scripture a promise to receive or a command to obey.

Prayer:

Heavenly Father, I ask you for your wisdom. You said that if I lack wisdom I could ask you and you would give me wisdom. As Paul prayed for the church to be filled with wisdom and revelation in the knowledge of God, I pray for that same wisdom to fill my life today. I want to know you. I want to receive everything you have made available for me to enjoy and to use for your glory and my blessing. Teach me wisdom so I can walk in peace and happiness, enjoying the fruit wisdom brings into my life. In Jesus' name I pray, Amen.

Proclamation:

I purpose this day to follow after the wisdom of God. The Bible declares that wisdom is better to have than silver or gold; yet if I find and follow wisdom, I will walk in ways that are pleasant and peaceful, and I will have long life and the ability to retain riches and honor. I will seek after the wisdom of God and will delight myself in his ways, and because I do, the blessings of God will come upon me and overtake me, and I will enjoy his presence all the days of my life.

Memory Verse: Proverbs 3:5-6

"Trust in the Lord with all your heart; and lean not unto your own understanding. In all your ways acknowledge him, and he shall direct your paths."

To every family member: "I love you; you are blessed, and you are a blessing."
Don't forget the hugs.

January 28th

Scripture: Philippians 4:8 (KJV)

"Finally, brethren, whatsoever things are true, whatsoever things are honest, whatsoever things are just, whatsoever things are pure, whatsoever things are lovely, whatsoever things are of good report; if there be any virtue, and if there be any praise, think on these things."

In your prayer journal, identify in this portion of scripture a promise to receive or a command to obey.

Prayer:

Heavenly Father, you have shown me how to keep my mind free of worry and fear by thinking on those things that are true and honest, just, pure, lovely and what has a good report. You have given me the power to cast down every thought and exalted imagination that would try to occupy my mind with things that bring fear, worry and visions of defeat instead of victory. I ask you to help me to always have my mouth filled with praise to you and my mind focused on the blessings of God you said belong to me. I know you will help me to establish every thought I have today to line up with your Word and to be quick to recognize every thought that does not come from you. I thank you for these things in the name of my Lord Jesus Christ, Amen.

Proclamation:

The Word of God says that I have the mind of Christ. The Spirit of God within me reveals to me the things of God. He speaks to me and shows me things that are happening right now and things that are yet to come. I do not allow thoughts and imaginations that are not of God to fill my mind. Instead, I look in the Word of God and find God's will for my life and think on those things constantly. The scriptures say that, if I will meditate in the Word of God all the time (day and night), I will know God's will and I will have faith to do his will. The result will be the blessings of God filling my life. I am greatly blessed today. My life is filled with good things, and the praise of God is always on my lips, and the peace of God rules in my life.

Memory Verse: Proverbs 3:5-6

"Trust in the Lord with all your heart; and lean not unto your own understanding. In all your ways acknowledge him, and he shall direct your paths."

To every family member: *"I love you; you are blessed, and you are a blessing."*
Don't forget the hugs.

January 29th

Scripture: Hebrews 11:1,6 (ASV)

"Now faith is assurance of things hoped for, a conviction of things not seen.... And without faith it is impossible to be well-pleasing unto him; for he that cometh to God must believe that he is, and that he is a rewarder of them that seek after him."

In your prayer journal, identify in this portion of scripture a promise to receive or a command to obey.

Prayer:

God, my Father, you have created all things by your mighty power. You have created man and ordained a way for him to live in joy and victory. I thank you for loving me and showing me how to live according to your will so that my life will give demonstration of your great love and perfect wisdom. You are my God. I believe that you made me for your pleasure, and you have said that you take pleasure in the prosperity of your servants. Let me live today in the prosperity and abundance of your joy, the richness of your love and the blessings of your kingdom. I seek after your will for my life. I desire to please you and honor you in all of my ways. I believe that you reward me as I seek you. Speak to me today by the Spirit of God and through the Word of God that I might be filled with faith and my faith would grow and be strong to glorify you. I ask these things in Jesus' name, Amen.

Proclamation:

I am filled with faith because the Word of God lives big on the inside of me. Faith comes to me by continuously hearing the Word of God. With faith I can live in great expectation of God's Word being fulfilled in my life. I look at those things that cannot be seen with my physical eyes, but I can see them clearly by the eye of faith. I see things as the Word of God declares them to be. Whatever I ask in faith believing I shall receive. Therefore I receive the things I ask for today.

Memory Verse: Hebrews 10:35-36

"Cast not away therefore your confidence, which has great recompence of reward. For you have need of patience, that after you have done the will of God, you might receive the promise."

To every family member: *"I love you; you are blessed, and you are a blessing."*
Don't forget the hugs.

January 30th

Scripture: Philippians 4:12-13 (NKJV)

"I know how to be abased, and I know how to abound. Everywhere and in all things I have learned both to be full and to be hungry, both to abound and to suffer need. I can do all things through Christ who strengthens me."

In your prayer journal, identify in this portion of scripture a promise to receive or a command to obey.

Prayer:

God, my Father, I thank you for the strength you give me today to walk in victory over every circumstance of life. Whether I have more than I can use or if there is no visible supply, you will provide for me everything I need. My provision comes from you. You said that I can come into your presence with thanksgiving and praise and boldly enter your throne room with great confidence. I know you will hear me and by faith I can access everything I have need of for today. You are my fortress and strength and like a high tower of refuge I run to you in every time of need and you lift me up above all my enemies. You are more than able to bring to me just what I need whether it be men, means or provision. You are my Jehovah Jireh, the one who sees my need long before I know about it and causes your abundant supply to show up at just the right time. I thank you for these things this day as I pray in the name of the Lord Jesus Christ, Amen.

Proclamation:

God is my helper in time of need. He rescues me from all my enemies and lifts me up into the place of his grace. He gives me strength to stand in the face of adversity. He brings me my daily bread and supplies all my needs both physical and spiritual. I can do all things through Christ who strengthens me.

Memory Verse: Hebrews 10:35-36

"Cast not away therefore your confidence, which has great recompence of reward. For you have need of patience, that after you have done the will of God, you might receive the promise."

To every family member: "I love you; you are blessed, and you are a blessing." Don't forget the hugs.

January 31st

Scripture: Philippians 4:18-19 (KJV)

"But I have all, and abound: I am full, having received of Epaphroditus the things which were sent from you, an odour of a sweet smell, a sacrifice acceptable, wellpleasing to God. But my God shall supply all your need according to his riches in glory by Christ Jesus."

In your prayer journal, identify in this portion of scripture a promise to receive or a command to obey.

Prayer:

Heavenly Father, thank you for meeting all of my needs as I also help to meet the needs of others. As Epaphroditus brought to Paul a financial offering from the Philippian Church to help supply his need, Paul, in return declared that God would meet every need of Epaphroditus and of all those who participated in this gift. You said as I give, it shall be given again unto me. Father, you also said that my giving would be like a sweet smell, an aroma that would please you. I believe you will speak to me today about what to give, how much to give and whom to give to so that my giving would also please you and bring the answer to the prayer of someone in need today. Thank you for hearing me and giving me clear direction according to your purpose for my life today. In Jesus' name I pray, Amen.

Proclamation:

My God supplies me with everything I need. All my employment needs, affairs and requirements for every occasion are abundantly supplied to me today. I am a joyful giver. I give to please God and to be a blessing to those in need. I believe my gift is like a seed that is planted in good soil that will yield an abundant harvest providing me with enough to meet all of my needs and to have much more to give to every good work. I am blessed in everything I do for the favor of God rests upon me today.

Memory Verse: Hebrews 10:35-36

"Cast not away therefore your confidence, which has great recompence of reward. For you have need of patience, that after you have done the will of God, you might receive the promise."

To every family member: "I love you; you are blessed, and you are a blessing." Don't forget the hugs.

February 1st

Scripture: 2 Chronicles 20:11-12 (NKJV)

"Here they are, rewarding us by coming to throw us out of Your possession which You have given us to inherit. O our God, will You not judge them? For we have no power against this great multitude that is coming against us; nor do we know what to do, but our eyes *are* upon You."

In your prayer journal, identify in this portion of scripture a promise to receive or a command to obey.

Prayer:

My Heavenly Father, as Jehoshaphat declared in this scripture that in times of trouble he did not know what to do, but he put his eyes upon you, let me always keep my eyes focused upon you and not on the circumstances. Thank you for helping me keep my eyes upon the promises of God instead of the problems that would come against me. Lord God, you are my help in times of trouble and you are more than able to deliver me from all my enemies. As Jehoshaphat's enemies were defeated without a fight, I know you will bring me into that place of victory today. I give you praise for this good day in Jesus' name, Amen.

Proclamation:

My heart is fixed trusting in the Lord. He is my refuge and strength and a very present help to me in times of trouble. I do not look at the giants of opposition who would rise up against me, but instead I look to the exceeding great and precious promises of God who will deliver me from my enemies, heal me of every sickness or disease and who provides for me whatever I need. My God is bigger than any problem I will ever have.

Memory Verse: Hebrews 10:35-36

"Cast not away therefore your confidence, which has great recompence of reward. For you have need of patience, that after you have done the will of God, you might receive the promise."

To every family member: "I love you; you are blessed, and you are a blessing."
Don't forget the hugs.

February 2nd

Scripture: 2 Corinthians 4:18 (ASV)

"While we look not at the things which are seen, but at the things which are not seen: for the things which are seen are temporal; but the things which are not seen are eternal."

In your prayer journal, identify in this portion of scripture a promise to receive or a command to obey.

Prayer:

I praise and magnify your great and glorious name, my God, for your kingdom is not of this world; it is eternal. Even though I cannot see the kingdom of God with my physical eyes, I can look into the kingdom of God by faith. Help me to see clearly the absolute goodness of your kingdom. Help me today to live in the kingdom of God so that it is more real to me than what my eyes can see. In your kingdom are righteousness, peace and joy. Nothing can enter into the kingdom that defiles or corrupts or destroys, but only that which is good. I walk by faith and not by sight. Lead me by the Spirit of God and show me the things I can only see by faith. Let the faith of God fill my life, my words and my eyes, I pray in the wonderful name of my Lord Jesus Christ, Amen.

Proclamation:

I will look into the Word of God today and see the things he has promised me, and I will do the things He shows me. God's Word is true. He is faithful to fulfill all of his promises to me, and I will be faithful to follow wholly after him. His word brings me life and joy beyond comprehension. God fulfills his good pleasure toward me, and he has declared that it is his good pleasure to give me his kingdom.

Memory Verse: Hebrews 10:35-36

"Cast not away therefore your confidence, which has great recompence of reward. For you have need of patience, that after you have done the will of God, you might receive the promise."

To every family member: *"I love you; you are blessed, and you are a blessing."*
Don't forget the hugs.

～ February 3rd ～

Scripture: Hebrews 12:1-3 (NASB)

"Therefore, since we have so great a cloud of witnesses surrounding us, let us also lay aside every encumbrance and the sin which so easily entangles us, and let us run with endurance the race that is set before us, fixing our eyes on Jesus, the author and perfecter of faith, who for the joy set before Him endured the cross, despising the shame, and has sat down at the right hand of the throne of God. For consider Him who has endured such hostility by sinners against Himself, so that you will not grow weary and lose heart."

In your prayer journal, identify in this portion of scripture a promise to receive or a command to obey.

Prayer:

Heavenly Father, I fix my eyes upon Jesus today because he is the author and finisher of my faith. I see in the Word of God the testimonies of multitudes who have faithfully followed after you and have successfully walked in victory even against great opposition. I will cast away from me every sin so that I will not stumble, and I will trust you to keep me from every crafty device of the devil. Help me to endure every circumstance of life with joy even as Jesus looked beyond the sufferings of the cross to the great victory he would experience of sitting at the right hand of God his Father. Thank you, Father, for strengthening me today so I will not be weary, quit or give up before I experience your will and favor fulfilled in my life. I give you praise for these things today in Jesus' name, Amen.

Proclamation:

The mighty hand of God is upon me today to strengthen me in my faith so I will not grow weary in doing what is right. I stand steadfast in the favor of God. Jesus bore my sin and shame, and after defeating death, he sat down at the right hand of God because he finished the work God gave him to do. Jesus gives me his victory. He gives me his righteousness, and he gives me faith to do and complete his will for my life.

Memory Verse: Hebrews 10:35-36

"Cast not away therefore your confidence, which has great recompence of reward. For you have need of patience, that after you have done the will of God, you might receive the promise."

To every family member: "I love you; you are blessed, and you are a blessing."
Don't forget the hugs.

February 4th

Scripture: Hebrews 12:12-15 (NLT)

"So take a new grip with your tired hands and strengthen your weak knees. Mark out a straight path for your feet so that those who are weak and lame will not fall but become strong. Work at living in peace with everyone, and work at living a holy life, for those who are not holy will not see the Lord. Look after each other so that none of you fails to receive the grace of God. Watch out that no poisonous root of bitterness grows up to trouble you, corrupting many."

In your prayer journal, identify in this portion of scripture a promise to receive or a command to obey.

Prayer:

Blessed be the wonderful name of the Lord my God. I give you praise today, my Father, for making me strong in the things of God. Strengthen me so that I will not let go of the promises of your Word or fail to continue walking in a way that pleases you. Your grace is at work within me today to keep me free from offenses and hurt feelings that wound my heart and open up the door to bitterness in my life. I receive your grace to heal me when I get wounded and to empower me to walk in forgiveness, even to bless those who count themselves my enemies. Help me today to live a holy life that is filled with the love of God that brings praise to you. I ask these things in the name of my Lord Jesus Christ, Amen.

Proclamation:

I am strong today in the power of God. The same Spirit that raised Jesus from the dead lives on the inside of me to strengthen me and give me victory in every situation of life. My hands are strong to do the will of God, and my feet walk in the paths of my inheritance. My life causes many to want to know God and follow after him because they see his love in me, and my life is enriched with God's blessings. I am blessed of the Lord, and my delight is in him.

Memory Verse: Hebrews 10:35-36

"Cast not away therefore your confidence, which has great recompence of reward. For you have need of patience, that after you have done the will of God, you might receive the promise."

To every family member: *"I love you; you are blessed, and you are a blessing."*
Don't forget the hugs.

February 5th

Scripture: Isaiah 54:14-17 (MSG)

"'You'll be built solid, grounded in righteousness, far from any trouble—nothing to fear! Far from terror—it won't even come close! If anyone attacks you, don't for a moment suppose that I sent them, and if any should attack, nothing will come of it. I create the blacksmith who fires up his forge and makes a weapon designed to kill. I also create the destroyer—but no weapon that can hurt you has ever been forged. Any accuser who takes you to court will be dismissed as a liar. This is what God's servants can expect. I'll see to it that everything works out for the best.' God's Decree."

In your prayer journal, identify in this portion of scripture a promise to receive or a command to obey.

Prayer:

My Father, you have caused me to be firmly established in righteousness. You have promised to protect me and keep me far from fear and terror. Even when trouble rises up against me, you will come to my rescue. You said that no weapon that is formed against me will succeed. Neither can any accusation against me stick. Lord my God, be a wall of fire around me and let the glory of God fill my life. Let my words honor you today and give me even a greater revelation of your love so that my faith in you will be strong. I ask you for these things now, in Jesus' name, Amen.

Proclamation:

I do not fear lack or calamity, trouble or any wicked work that would come against me today. God is my help. He is my refuge and he has decreed that every work of the enemy would fall powerless before me. I have an inheritance to walk in and that inheritance is the blessing of the Lord. I am an heir of God and a joint heir of Christ Jesus; therefore, I cannot fail, for if God is for me, who can be against me.

Memory Verse: Romans 15:13

"Now the God of hope fill you with all joy and peace in believing, that you may abound in hope, through the power of the Holy Ghost."

To every family member: *"I love you; you are blessed, and you are a blessing."*
Don't forget the hugs.

February 6th

Scripture: John 7:37-39 (NKJV)

"On the last day, that great *day* of the feast, Jesus stood and cried out, saying, 'If anyone thirsts, let him come to Me and drink. He who believes in Me, as the Scripture has said, out of his heart will flow rivers of living water.' But this He spoke concerning the Spirit, whom those believing in Him would receive; for the Holy Spirit was not yet *given*, because Jesus was not yet glorified."

In your prayer journal, identify in this portion of scripture a promise to receive or a command to obey.

Prayer:

God, My Father, I pray that you fill me with the Spirit of God today. You said if I thirst after you I will be filled. Cause my heart to always be hungry and thirsty for the things of God. May I desire your Word more than my daily bread. I believe that Jesus is the Son of God and the Savior of the world; therefore you said that rivers of living water will flow out from my life. Father, let that river flow out of me today, filling me and bringing life to everyone it touches. Because Jesus was glorified, he has given the Holy Spirit to everyone who asks him. Father, I ask you now for a fresh filling of the Spirit who gives me power and fills me with joy. I praise you for doing this for me today, in Jesus' name, Amen.

Proclamation:

The Spirit of God fills my life today. I continuously drink of the fountain of living water that flows from the very presence of God who lives in me. He refreshes me and strengthens me, and his life flows out of me to bring life to everyone I meet.

Memory Verse: Romans 15:13

"Now the God of hope fill you with all joy and peace in believing, that you may abound in hope, through the power of the Holy Ghost."

To every family member: "*I love you; you are blessed, and you are a blessing.*"
Don't forget the hugs.

February 7th

Scripture: John 1:1-5 (NLV)

"The Word (Christ) was in the beginning. The Word was with God. The Word was God. He was with God in the beginning. He made all things. Nothing was made without Him making it. Life began by Him. His Life was the Light for men. The Light shines in the darkness. The darkness has never been able to put out the Light."

In your prayer journal, identify in this portion of scripture a promise to receive or a command to obey.

Prayer:

Heavenly Father, I thank you for causing the light of God to shine in my darkness. You caused me to see that Jesus is the Son of God and the Creator of the world. His life was a perfect display of your life as he gave demonstration to your love by healing the sick, setting free the oppressed and doing miracles that met the needs of individuals and multitudes. I pray that I will always walk with the revelation of all Jesus accomplished for me. You said Jesus is the light of the world, and because I am a child of God, I am also the light of the world to show forth your love and goodness. Help me to so let my light shine that all those around me will see your greatness and glorify my Father in heaven. I give you praise for doing these things this day in Jesus' name, Amen.

Proclamation:

Jesus is the light of the world, and his light has enlightened my darkness. I have received the light of life, and because I have, I shine as a light in this world. I will not walk in darkness, but as the Scriptures say, I will arise and shine, for my light has come and the glory of the Lord has risen upon me.

Memory Verse: Romans 15:13

"Now the God of hope fill you with all joy and peace in believing, that you may abound in hope, through the power of the Holy Ghost."

To every family member: "*I love you; you are blessed, and you are a blessing.*"
Don't forget the hugs.

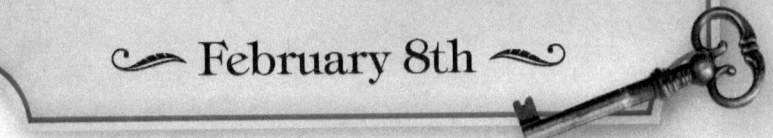

February 8th

Scripture: 1 Corinthians 2:9-12 (KJV)

"But as it is written, Eye hath not seen, nor ear heard, neither have entered into the heart of man, the things which God hath prepared for them that love him. But God hath revealed them unto us by his Spirit: for the Spirit searcheth all things, yea, the deep things of God. For what man knoweth the things of a man, save the spirit of man which is in him? Even so the things of God knoweth no man, but the Spirit of God. Now we have received, not the spirit of the world, but the spirit which is of God; that we might know the things that are freely given to us of God."

In your prayer journal, identify in this portion of scripture a promise to receive or a command to obey.

Prayer:

Father, I cannot know the things of God except by the Spirit of God that lives on the inside of me. You have given to me the Spirit of God. I ask you to speak to me today and to reveal to me the things you have freely given to me. Cause me to know what is in the heart of God. Help me to understand your will so I will not settle for less than what you have given me. Fill me with the Spirit and with knowledge, wisdom and understanding. I pray the Scriptures will transform my mind and the voice of the Holy Spirit will be made clear to me. Give me ears to hear and an understanding heart so my way will be made plain and my direction and purpose sure. I ask these things in the name of my Lord Jesus Christ, Amen.

Proclamation:

I have ears to hear what the Spirit of God says to me today. I walk in the wisdom and revelation of the knowledge of God's will. He has freely given me all things that pertain to life. I am not deficient or lacking any good thing; instead my life overflows with the goodness and purpose of God.

Memory Verse: Romans 15:13

"Now the God of hope fill you with all joy and peace in believing, that you may abound in hope, through the power of the Holy Ghost."

To every family member: *"I love you; you are blessed, and you are a blessing."*
Don't forget the hugs.

Faith Family Minute

February 9th

Scripture: 1 Corinthians 2:14-16 (MSG)

"The unspiritual self, just as it is by nature, can't receive the gifts of God's Spirit. There's no capacity for them. They seem like so much silliness. Spirit can be known only by spirit—God's Spirit and our spirits in open communion. Spiritually alive, we have access to everything God's Spirit is doing, and can't be judged by unspiritual critics. Isaiah's question, 'Is there anyone around who knows God's Spirit, anyone who knows what he is doing?' has been answered: Christ knows, and we have Christ's Spirit."

In your prayer journal, identify in this portion of scripture a promise to receive or a command to obey.

Prayer:

God, my Father, I don't want to live as a natural man who has no spiritual understanding. Help me today to live in the spirit. Help me to not dismiss the things you are leading me to do or say because those things may not make sense to my natural mind. Because the Spirit of God lives inside me I have the mind of Christ. Help me to always follow your leading and not my own reasoning because I walk by faith and not by just what I see. Father, you can show me things others cannot see. May I see and hear and understand the things of the Spirit, and because I do, I will receive all you have so freely given to me. I thank you for these things now in the name of my Lord Jesus, Amen.

Proclamation:

I do not live my life with the limitations of a natural man. Because I have received the Holy Spirit I have the mind of Christ. He lives within me. He shows me all the wonderful things God has given me. I can see and hear what others cannot because the Spirit of God reveals them to me.

Memory Verse: Romans 15:13

"Now the God of hope fill you with all joy and peace in believing, that you may abound in hope, through the power of the Holy Ghost."

To every family member: "*I love you; you are blessed, and you are a blessing.*"
Don't forget the hugs.

February 10th

Scripture: Acts 20:32 (KJV)

"And now, brethren, I commend you to God, and to the word of his grace, which is able to build you up, and to give you an inheritance among all them which are sanctified."

In your prayer journal, identify in this portion of scripture a promise to receive or a command to obey.

Prayer:

Father, I praise you for your Word of grace. Your Word edifies me and makes me strong in spirit, soul and body. Your Word is life to those who find it and it is medicine to all their flesh. Your Word reveals to me everything Jesus did for me. Your Word is the gospel, the good news declaring to me that all my sins are forgiven and I am in a right relationship with you. Your Word brings me hope in times of trouble and causes the God kind of faith to fill my life. Your Word renews my mind so that my thoughts line up with your will and you cause my plans to be profitable and succeed. I praise you for this living Word that brings me wisdom, peace and makes my way prosperous. Thank you for your Word that is able to give me the inheritance Jesus purchased for me. Help me today to live according to your Word so all my ways will please you. I ask these things in the name of Jesus, Amen.

Proclamation:

I live by the Word of God today. All scripture is profitable for me. It makes me wise in the things of God and brings me instruction in every realm of life. I meditate on the Word of God day and night. I make it a vital part of my everyday life. The Word of God speaks to me showing me what to do, what not to do and brings me the promise of God's love. I desire the Word of God and consider it more valuable than my next meal for it brings me life and life more abundantly.

Memory Verse: Romans 15:13

"Now the God of hope fill you with all joy and peace in believing, that you may abound in hope, through the power of the Holy Ghost."

To every family member: *"I love you; you are blessed, and you are a blessing."*
Don't forget the hugs.

February 11th

Scripture: Isaiah 35:3-6 (NLT)

"With this news, strengthen those who have tired hands, and encourage those who have weak knees. Say to those with fearful hearts, "Be strong, and do not fear, for your God is coming to destroy your enemies. He is coming to save you." And when he comes, he will open the eyes of the blind and unplug the ears of the deaf. The lame will leap like a deer, and those who cannot speak will sing for joy! Springs will gush forth in the wilderness, and streams will water the wasteland."

In your prayer journal, identify in this portion of scripture a promise to receive or a command to obey.

Prayer:

God, my Father, I thank you for watching over me to protect me and to keep me from all harm. When I become weary, you strengthen me and make me strong. Your love is great towards me, and you have given me authority to declare your Word boldly in every circumstance of life. You have destroyed all my enemies. You have given me authority to condemn and command to cease every evil work that would rise up against me. You heal the blind, the deaf, the lame and the mute. I thank you for your joy that springs up within me like a river of living water that heals the dry desert places in my life. Strengthen me by your Spirit and help me to walk before you today as one who is alive from the dead. I give you praise for these things this day in Jesus' name, Amen.

Proclamation:

God is my help. He protects me from all evil. He strengthens me in my weakness and encourages me in difficult times. The power of God heals my body and brings me great joy. The blessings of the Lord rest upon me today, abundantly.

Memory Verse: Romans 15:13

"Now the God of hope fill you with all joy and peace in believing, that you may abound in hope, through the power of the Holy Ghost."

To every family member: *"I love you; you are blessed, and you are a blessing."*
Don't forget the hugs.

February 12th

Scripture: Isaiah 40:28-31 (KJV)

"Hast thou not known? Hast thou not heard, that the everlasting God, the Lord, the Creator of the ends of the earth, fainteth not, neither is weary? There is no searching of his understanding. He giveth power to the faint; and to them that have no might he increaseth strength. Even the youths shall faint and be weary, and the young men shall utterly fall: But they that wait upon the Lord shall renew their strength; they shall mount up with wings as eagles; they shall run, and not be weary; and they shall walk, and not faint."

In your prayer journal, identify in this portion of scripture a promise to receive or a command to obey.

Prayer:

Heavenly Father, all might and power and strength belong to you. You are Lord and Creator of all things. No one can stand against you, and all of your enemies fall before you. You have promised to give strength to the weak, and those who are fainting and weary, you will sustain by your mighty power. As I wait upon you today, I believe that the strength of God will rise up within me. You will make me strong so that I can walk and run without stumbling and without falling. Help me today to rise up as if I had the wings of an eagle to be carried into your presence where I can behold your glory and worship at your footstool. Thank you for your mighty power that works in me today to make me strong. I receive these things now in Jesus' name, Amen.

Proclamation:

The Lord is my strength and my refuge. I trust in him to help me. He will guide me with his Word and will strengthen my body so that I can run and not be weary and I can walk and not faint. I will wait upon the Lord. I will focus my attention on him listening for his voice and obeying his every Word.

Memory Verse: Proverbs 4:20-22

"My son, attend to my words; incline your ear unto my sayings. Let them not depart from your eyes; keep them in the midst of your heart. For they are life unto those that find them, and health to all their flesh."

To every family member: "I love you; you are blessed, and you are a blessing."
Don't forget the hugs.

February 13th

Scripture: John 14:12-14 (KJV)

"Verily, verily, I say unto you, He that believeth on me, the works that I do shall he do also; and greater works than these shall he do; because I go unto my Father. And whatsoever ye shall ask in my name, that will I do, that the Father may be glorified in the Son. If ye shall ask any thing in my name, I will do it."

In your prayer journal, identify in this portion of scripture a promise to receive or a command to obey.

Prayer:

Heavenly Father, I praise and bless your holy name. I thank you for hearing me when I pray. You declare in the scripture the works that Jesus did I am also to do because he accomplished the work of my redemption, ascended into heaven and sent the Holy Spirit to live in me and empower me to do your good pleasure. You said that whatever I ask in the name of Jesus would be done. Father, this day I ask for wisdom to know what will bring glory to you. Cause me to know what to pray and what to do that will bring to pass the work of God in me and in those for whom I pray. I receive this wisdom and the working of the mighty power of God that will accomplish these things. In Jesus' name, Amen.

Proclamation:

This is a good day for it is the day the Lord has made. God has given me his Holy Spirit who abides with me forever. He will never leave me nor forsake me. The Spirit of God empowers me to boldly pray the will of God. Everything I ask in prayer that will bring glory to God the Father, Jesus will do. I pray the prayer of faith and accomplish the will of God as the works of Jesus are done through my prayer.

Memory Verse: Proverbs 4:20-22

"My son, attend to my words; incline your ear unto my sayings. Let them not depart from your eyes; keep them in the midst of your heart. For they are life unto those that find them, and health to all their flesh."

To every family member: "I love you; you are blessed, and you are a blessing."
Don't forget the hugs.

February 14th

Scripture: Ephesians 3:20-21 (KJV)

"Now unto him that is able to do exceeding abundantly above all that we ask or think, according to the power that worketh in us, Unto him be glory in the church by Christ Jesus throughout all ages, world without end, Amen."

In your prayer journal, identify in this portion of scripture a promise to receive or a command to obey.

Prayer:

My Heavenly Father, it is my greatest desire that you would be glorified in your church. You said that the mighty working power of God that is in us is able to do exceeding abundantly above all we could ask or think. There is no limit to your power that is at work within your church. Help me as a member of your church and your body to let that mighty working power operate through me as I yield to the Holy Spirit within me. I pray that your church would function in the unity of the Spirit as the Scriptures instruct us to be of one mind and to speak the same things. I will not participate in anything that would bring division or strife into your church, but I choose today to walk in the love of God. Help me to give demonstration to that love so my prayers are with power, bringing forth your will and purpose. I ask these things in the name of my Lord Jesus Christ, Amen.

Proclamation:

The unlimited power of God is within me. The same Spirit that raised Christ from the dead lives on the inside of me. I am filled with the Spirit of God today. As I pray according to the will of God I find the Spirit of God takes hold with me to release his power and bring to pass my prayer that accomplishes his will.

Memory Verse: Proverbs 4:20-22

"My son, attend to my words; incline your ear unto my sayings. Let them not depart from your eyes; keep them in the midst of your heart. For they are life unto those that find them, and health to all their flesh."

To every family member: *"I love you; you are blessed, and you are a blessing."*
Don't forget the hugs.

February 15th

Scripture: John 14:12-14 (AMP)

"You have not chosen Me, but I have chosen you and I have appointed you [I have planted you], that you might go and bear fruit *and* keep on bearing, and that your fruit may be lasting [that it may remain, abide], so that whatever you ask the Father in My Name [as presenting all that I Am], He may give it to you. This is what I command you: that you love one another."

In your prayer journal, identify in this portion of scripture a promise to receive or a command to obey.

Prayer:

Father, thank you for choosing me and ordaining me to be fruitful. I know that I am to bear the fruit of your kingdom. My life is to be fruitful and blessed in every way. The fruit of your kingdom is the fruit of answered prayer. You said anything I ask the Father in the name of Jesus you would do for me. I thank you now for hearing me. I walk in the commandment of your love, and because I do, I know I have the petitions I desire of you this day. I pray your will over my life and my family, my business and all I have. I say it is blessed and made to prosper. I increase today with the increase of God's blessings. Father, thank you for hearing me in these things, and in everything I ask you for, let me be fruitful, for my purpose is to follow the commandment of love and rejoice in the fruit of answered prayer. In Jesus' name, Amen.

Proclamation:

I am blessed of the Lord today. I am like a tree that has been planted by the river of life and nourished at the table of God's abundance. Everything I do is blessed. I prosper and increase today in every good thing. I pray the will of God and bear the fruit of answered prayer that blesses me and brings glory to God, my Father.

Memory Verse: Proverbs 4:20-22

"My son, attend to my words; incline your ear unto my sayings. Let them not depart from your eyes; keep them in the midst of your heart. For they are life unto those that find them, and health to all their flesh."

To every family member: "*I love you; you are blessed, and you are a blessing.*"
Don't forget the hugs.

February 16th

Scripture: Romans 4:18-21 (KJV)

"Who against hope believed in hope, that he might become the father of many nations, according to that which was spoken, So shall thy seed be. And being not weak in faith, he considered not his own body now dead, when he was about an hundred years old, neither yet the deadness of Sarah's womb: He staggered not at the promise of God through unbelief; but was strong in faith, giving glory to God; And being fully persuaded that, what he had promised, he was able also to perform."

In your prayer journal, identify in this portion of scripture a promise to receive or a command to obey.

Prayer:

Heavenly Father, help me to be filled with hope every day of my life just as Abraham was. I know you are able to do for me as you did for Abraham. You bring to life what is dead and call the things that are not as if they are, for with you nothing is impossible. Father, I will not reject the promises of God, but I will be strong in faith, choosing to believe what you have promised. I hold fast to your Word and will boldly declare what you have said instead of what the circumstances dictate. Lord, you are faithful. My hope is in you. I thank you today for these things in Jesus' name, Amen.

Proclamation:

Faith calls those things out of the spiritual realm into the natural realm. Faith is looking at those things that cannot be seen with the physical eye but are seen by the eye of faith as the Word of God describes them. I am strong in faith. The Word of God is working mightily in me to empower me to change the things that are contrary to the will God and bring them in line with his promises. I delight in the Lord today, and he gives me the desires of my heart. My body is healthy, my mind in strong, and I am blessed of the Lord today.

Memory Verse: Proverbs 4:20-22

"My son, attend to my words; incline your ear unto my sayings. Let them not depart from your eyes; keep them in the midst of your heart. For they are life unto those that find them, and health to all their flesh."

To every family member: "I love you; you are blessed, and you are a blessing."
Don't forget the hugs.

February 17th

Scripture: 1 Timothy 2:1-4 (NLT)

"I urge you, first of all, to pray for all people. Ask God to help them; intercede on their behalf, and give thanks for them. Pray this way for kings and all who are in authority so that we can live peaceful and quiet lives marked by godliness and dignity. This is good and pleases God our Savior, who wants everyone to be saved and to understand the truth."

In your prayer journal, identify in this portion of scripture a promise to receive or a command to obey.

Prayer:

Father, I pray today for the leaders of our nation. I pray for the President in the White House as well as every member of the Senate and House of Representatives. I pray for all the judges of our land, for governors and mayors, city and county government leaders and all those who hold a position of authority. Father, I ask you to fill them with the knowledge of your will. May every one of them have a divine encounter with you today. For those who do not yet know you, open their heart to the truth of the gospel and send them people who will be able to speak the truth into their lives. I take authority over every wicked spirit that has blinded their minds to the truth. I call that spirit bound and them loosed from all deception. Father, guide them by the Spirit of God today. Give them great wisdom to solve the difficult problems they face and to do so in a way that will honor you. I ask you for these things in the wonderful name of the Lord Jesus Christ, Amen.

Proclamation:

I declare today that every person who holds a position of authority in our government will have a willing heart that is open and desiring to do the will of God. God is at work in our leaders to reveal himself to them. They will have ears to hear what the Spirit of God speaks to them.

Memory Verse: Proverbs 4:20-22

"My son, attend to my words; incline your ear unto my sayings. Let them not depart from your eyes; keep them in the midst of your heart. For they are life unto those that find them, and health to all their flesh."

To every family member: *"I love you; you are blessed, and you are a blessing."*
Don't forget the hugs.

February 18th

Scripture: Joel 2:24-27 (NCV)

"And the threshing floors will be full of grain; the barrels will overflow with new wine and olive oil. "Though I sent my great army against you—those swarming locusts and hopping locusts, the destroying locusts and the cutting locusts that ate your crops—I will pay you back for those years of trouble. Then you will have plenty to eat and be full. You will praise the name of the Lord your God, who has done miracles for you. My people will never again be shamed. Then you will know that I am among the people of Israel, that I am the Lord your God, and there is no other God. My people will never be shamed again."

In your prayer journal, identify in this portion of scripture a promise to receive or a command to obey.

Prayer:

Father, I receive this day the promise of your Word. Though the people of Israel forsook the Word of God and experienced pestilence for their sin, you promised to restore to them all that had been destroyed. Heavenly Father, thank you for the blood of Jesus and the work of the cross to pay in full the price required for my release from guilt and shame. You don't only forgive and cleanse me, but you also heal and restore to me all I have lost. You renew my youth, settle my accounts, heal my body and restore to me and my family anything and everything the devil ever stole from me. You said if a thief be found he is to restore seven fold, even to give all of the substance of his house to repay what he robbed from others. I agree with the Word of God and say that restoration comes to me today. Overflow and plenty, abundance and joy belong to me today. Father, I give you praise for these things now in the name of my Lord Jesus Christ, Amen.

Proclamation:

I am rich in every good thing. The Lord's blessings are upon me. My mouth is satisfied with good, and I continuously rejoice in the Lord my God.

Memory Verse: Proverbs 4:20-22

"My son, attend to my words; incline your ear unto my sayings. Let them not depart from your eyes; keep them in the midst of your heart. For they are life unto those that find them, and health to all their flesh."

To every family member: *"I love you; you are blessed, and you are a blessing."*
Don't forget the hugs.

February 19th

Scripture: Matthew 7:7-8 (AMP)

"Keep on asking and it will be given you; keep on seeking and you will find; keep on knocking [reverently] and [the door] will be opened to you. For everyone who keeps on asking receives; and he who keeps on seeking finds; and to him who keeps on knocking, [the door] will be opened."

In your prayer journal, identify in this portion of scripture a promise to receive or a command to obey.

Prayer:

Father, I praise and bless your wonderful name. Thank you for your promise that, if I keep asking, seeking and knocking, I will receive. The locked doors shall be opened to me, and those things that I have not yet received will be mine. I receive your wisdom and strength and will not become discouraged. The path of least resistance is not the path of righteousness and blessing. Although obstacles are in the way of righteousness, you have given me authority to stand against every opposition with the Word of God and the name of Jesus. I receive your grace to empower me to continue to stand and hold fast to the promises of God. Thank you for every promise of God fulfilled in my life. I give you praise now in Jesus' name, Amen.

Proclamation:

I keep on looking at the Word of God. I keep on following after the will of God. I keep asking, that is, making demands of every situation that is contrary to the will of God and command those things to come in line with God's Word. He has promised me that I will find what I need, and if I continue to knock on the door that has been locked in the past, it shall be open to me. I am not willing to settle for less than God's will for me and for those for whom I pray.

Memory Verse: Matthew 7:7-8

"Ask, and it shall be given you; seek, and you shall find; knock, and it shall be opened unto you: For every one that asks receives; and he that seeks finds; and to him that knocks it shall be opened."

To every family member: "I love you; you are blessed, and you are a blessing."
Don't forget the hugs.

February 20th

Scripture: Philemon 1:4-7 (GW)

"Philemon, I always thank my God when I mention you in my prayers because I hear about your faithfulness to the Lord Jesus and your love for all of God's people. As you share the faith you have in common with others, I pray that you may come to have a complete knowledge of every blessing we have in Christ. Your love for God's people gives me a lot of joy and encouragement. You, brother, have comforted God's people."

In your prayer journal, identify in this portion of scripture a promise to receive or a command to obey.

Prayer:

Father, as Paul prayed for Philemon, so I pray for the members of the church to be faithful to the Lord Jesus Christ and walk in God's love to all people. I pray that every one of us would be filled with the knowledge of your will and recognize every good thing you have deposited in us so that we would honor you by honoring one another. You have put eternity in our hearts and filled us with the God kind of love. I pray that no one who is called by the name of the Lord would be blinded or deceived by any evil work to step out of that place of love and into strife, bitterness or offense. I choose this day to forgive any hurt I have received from others, and I receive forgiveness for any offense I have caused someone else. I receive these things now in the name of my Lord Jesus Christ, Amen.

Proclamation:

The love of God has been shed abroad in my heart by the Holy Spirit; therefore, I can walk in love to every one I meet today, even toward those who would consider me their enemy. My words bring joy and encouragement to those who hear me, and I constantly do those things that please the Lord.

Memory Verse: Matthew 7:7-8

"Ask, and it shall be given you; seek, and you shall find; knock, and it shall be opened unto you: For every one that asks receives; and he that seeks finds; and to him that knocks it shall be opened."

To every family member: *"I love you; you are blessed, and you are a blessing."*
Don't forget the hugs.

February 21th

Scripture: Proverbs 18:20-21 (CEV)

"Make your words good—you will be glad you did. Words can bring death or life! Talk too much, and you will eat everything you say."

In your prayer journal, identify in this portion of scripture a promise to receive or a command to obey.

Prayer:

Father, I bless your holy name. I give you praise and declare today your greatness. You said that even the words that come from the mouth of infants can produce praise that will silence the voice of the devil. My words are powerful. I can speak life or death. My words will set a course for my life that produces good or evil. Father, help me today to put a guard on my mouth to speak only those things that will honor you and bring blessing to me and to others. Help me to only speak words that will build up and encourage those who hear me. Cause my words to bring forth good fruit. Help me to fill my heart with good things so my mouth will be filled with praise for you and wisdom that will instruct many. I thank you for these things in Jesus' wonderful name, Amen.

Proclamation:

Death and life are in the power of my tongue. The quality of words I speak will be the quality of life I fill my life with. My words determine the direction my life takes. My words set in motion activity in both the spirit and in the natural world to release death or life, blessing or cursing. I choose today to speak the Word of God for no Word of God is without power. It will certainly bring forth the will of God, and the will of God will bless and increase and prosper me today.

Memory Verse: Matthew 7:7-8

"Ask, and it shall be given you; seek, and you shall find; knock, and it shall be opened unto you: For every one that asks receives; and he that seeks finds; and to him that knocks it shall be opened."

To every family member: *"I love you; you are blessed, and you are a blessing."*
Don't forget the hugs.

February 22th

Scripture: Matthew 20:25-28 (NLV)

"Jesus called them to Him and said, 'You know how the kings of the nations show their power to the people. Important leaders use their power over the people. It must not be that way with you. But whoever wants to be great among you, let him care for you. Whoever wants to be first among you, let him be your servant. For the Son of Man came not to be cared for. He came to care for others. He came to give His life so that many could be bought by His blood and made free from the punishment of sin.'"

In your prayer journal, identify in this portion of scripture a promise to receive or a command to obey.

Prayer:

Heavenly Father, I pray that you will help me to keep a right attitude towards others. Help me to carry in my heart the same attitude Jesus had. He came to serve others. He gave his life so that I can have life. He served his disciples even washing their feet when they were too proud to wash one another's feet. I pray for a servant's heart, a willingness to put others ahead of myself that I might accurately show the love of God to all I meet. You said a humble and contrite heart you will not despise, but you will revive and strengthen those who humble themselves before you. Father, I know you resist the proud, but you give grace to the humble. I receive your grace today in order to serve you and others with joy. I praise you for bringing to pass these things this day in my life, in Jesus' name, Amen.

Proclamation:

God resists the proud but gives grace to the humble. I humble myself under the mighty hand of God, and he will lift me up. He will exalt me in due season. My God will comfort me. He will bless me and empower me to walk in his ways and do those things that are pleasing in his sight.

Memory Verse: Matthew 7:7-8

"Ask, and it shall be given you; seek, and you shall find; knock, and it shall be opened unto you: For every one that asks receives; and he that seeks finds; and to him that knocks it shall be opened."

To every family member: "I love you; you are blessed, and you are a blessing."
Don't forget the hugs.

February 23rd

Scripture: Romans 8:1-4 (NLT)

"So now there is no condemnation for those who belong to Christ Jesus. And because you belong to him, the power of the life-giving Spirit has freed you from the power of sin that leads to death. The law of Moses was unable to save us because of the weakness of our sinful nature. So God did what the law could not do. He sent his own Son in a body like the bodies we sinners have. And in that body God declared an end to sin's control over us by giving his Son as a sacrifice for our sins. He did this so that the just requirement of the law would be fully satisfied for us, who no longer follow our sinful nature but instead follow the Spirit."

In your prayer journal, identify in this portion of scripture a promise to receive or a command to obey.

Prayer:

Father, I praise your name for you have delivered me from all condemnation, guilt and shame. You have set me free from fear. You have forgiven me and cleansed me from all sin and unrighteousness because of Jesus giving his life to be a sacrifice for me. When Jesus died for me, he fully satisfied the requirements of the law of God that demanded death for sin. Now I have passed from death to life because of what Jesus did for me. God, my Father, I receive your righteousness. I thank you that you no longer hold any sin against me, but you have removed from me all sin, iniquity and transgression. I am no longer guilty. I am free from the power of sin, and I walk in the righteousness of God as you continue to lead me by the Spirit of God. I praise you for these things now in Jesus' name, Amen.

Proclamation:

The price Jesus paid for my sin on the cross fully satisfied the righteous judgment of God the law demanded. Today, I am free from all condemnation because of the blood of Jesus.

Memory Verse: Matthew 7:7-8

"Ask, and it shall be given you; seek, and you shall find; knock, and it shall be opened unto you: For every one that asks receives; and he that seeks finds; and to him that knocks it shall be opened."

To every family member: "*I love you; you are blessed, and you are a blessing.*"
Don't forget the hugs.

February 24th

Scripture: James 3:13-18 (MSG)

"Do you want to be counted wise, to build a reputation for wisdom? Here's what you do: Live well, live wisely, live humbly. It's the way you live, not the way you talk, that counts. Mean-spirited ambition isn't wisdom. Boasting that you are wise isn't wisdom. Twisting the truth to make yourselves sound wise isn't wisdom. It's the furthest thing from wisdom—it's animal cunning, devilish conniving. Whenever you're trying to look better than others or get the better of others, things fall apart and everyone ends up at the others' throats. Real wisdom, God's wisdom, begins with a holy life and is characterized by getting along with others. It is gentle and reasonable, overflowing with mercy and blessings, not hot one day and cold the next, not two-faced. You can develop a healthy, robust community that lives right with God and enjoy its results *only* if you do the hard work of getting along with each other, treating each other with dignity and honor."

In your prayer journal, identify in this portion of scripture a promise to receive or a command to obey.

Prayer:

Thank you, Lord, for your wisdom. You said if I lack wisdom all I need to do is ask you and you will give me your wisdom. Help me to recognize what is the wisdom of God so that I will not follow after the wisdom of this world. You said the wisdom of this world is filled with bitter envy and strife and brings confusion and every evil work, but your wisdom is always pure and gentle and easy to receive. Give me a wise and understanding heart to recognize the difference and to follow after the wisdom that brings life and pleases God. I receive God's wisdom now in Jesus' name, Amen.

Proclamation:

The wisdom of this world brings death and sorrow, but the wisdom of God brings life and peace. I choose to walk in God's wisdom today.

Memory Verse: Matthew 7:7-8

"Ask, and it shall be given you; seek, and you shall find; knock, and it shall be opened unto you: For every one that asks receives; and he that seeks finds; and to him that knocks it shall be opened."

To every family member: "I love you; you are blessed, and you are a blessing."
Don't forget the hugs.

February 25th

Scripture: James 1:22-25 (NCV)

"Do what God's teaching says; when you only listen and do nothing, you are fooling yourselves. Those who hear God's teaching and do nothing are like people who look at themselves in a mirror. They see their faces and then go away and quickly forget what they looked like. But the truly happy people are those who carefully study God's perfect law that makes people free, and they continue to study it. They do not forget what they heard, but they obey what God's teaching says. Those who do this will be made happy."

In your prayer journal, identify in this portion of scripture a promise to receive or a command to obey.

Prayer:

My Lord God, you are good and your mercies endure forever. Help me today to not just hear your Word but to do your Word. You said if I would not forget your Word but be a doer of your Word I would be blessed in everything I do. I thank you for your blessings today. I look into your Word as if it were a mirror in order to see the image of God you have created me to be. Help me to remember who you have made me to be so that I will carry with me, everywhere I go, that image of God. You have changed me by giving me your Spirit who abides in me forever. You have written your Word in my heart and on my mind, and your Word speaks to me and gives me wisdom and instruction so that I always make wise choices that please you and bring your blessings to me. I thank you for these things today in Jesus' name, Amen.

Proclamation:

I am a doer of the Word of God. I am blessed because I keep before me today the Word of the living God who speaks to me and gives me clear direction for every occasion of life.

Memory Verse: Matthew 7:7-8

"Ask, and it shall be given you; seek, and you shall find; knock, and it shall be opened unto you: For every one that asks receives; and he that seeks finds; and to him that knocks it shall be opened."

To every family member: "I love you; you are blessed, and you are a blessing."
Don't forget the hugs.

February 26th

Scripture: Luke 12:27-32 (KJV)

"Consider the lilies how they grow: they toil not, they spin not; and yet I say unto you, that Solomon in all his glory was not arrayed like one of these. If then God so clothe the grass, which is to day in the field, and to morrow is cast into the oven; how much more will he clothe you, O ye of little faith? And seek not ye what ye shall eat, or what ye shall drink, neither be ye of doubtful mind. For all these things do the nations of the world seek after: and your Father knoweth that ye have need of these things. But rather seek ye the kingdom of God; and all these things shall be added unto you. Fear not, little flock; for it is your Father's good pleasure to give you the kingdom."

In your prayer journal, identify in this portion of scripture a promise to receive or a command to obey.

Prayer:

Father, you have declared in your Word that it is your good pleasure to give me the kingdom. The kingdom of God is righteousness, peace and joy that comes by the Holy Spirit. If you have given to me the kingdom of God, I have no reason to fear I will ever be deficient or wanting for anything. For in you is abundance. You have more than enough to supply all my needs. I will not fear by doubting your faithfulness to supply me with those things you know I need. I will always have an abundance of food to eat, clothes to wear and every physical requirement for me to have life and to have life more abundantly. Help me not to spend my time seeking after the things you have already promised me, but remind me that I should seek after your kingdom and those things that please you. In Jesus' name I pray, Amen.

Proclamation:

The kingdom of God abides within me. I walk in righteousness. The peace of God fills my life. The joy that is inexpressible and unexplainable fills me now. I am blessed in all my ways, every day and in every way.

Memory Verse: Romans 8:1-2

"There is therefore now no condemnation to them which are in Christ Jesus, who walk not after the flesh, but after the Spirit. For the law of the Spirit of life in Christ Jesus hath made me free from the law of sin and death."

To every family member: "I love you; you are blessed, and you are a blessing." Don't forget the hugs.

February 27th

Scripture: Joshua 1:8-9 (NIV)

"Keep this Book of the Law always on your lips; meditate on it day and night, so that you may be careful to do everything written in it. Then you will be prosperous and successful. Have I not commanded you? Be strong and courageous. Do not be afraid; do not be discouraged, for the Lord your God will be with you wherever you go."

In your prayer journal, identify in this portion of scripture a promise to receive or a command to obey.

Prayer:

Father, I thank you for your promise of being with me wherever I go. Your presence abides within me, and I know that I am never alone. I delight myself in your Word today. I meditate on it day and night, and you reveal to me wonderful things that cause me to be successful and prosperous in everything I do. Everything I set my hand to prospers because your divine favor rests on me today. I will not be afraid of anything, for in every situation of life, I know that if you are for me then who can be against me? Even if there are enemies that would rise up against me, you said they would turn and run away from me in terror because you are my help, my strength and my life. I give you thanks for bringing to pass all these things for me because you delight in me and give me the desires of my heart. Thank you, my Lord, for your great grace working in me today in Jesus' name, Amen.

Proclamation:

The Word of God abides within me. I speak God's Word that brings to pass his will and accomplishes his purpose. I do not fear but rejoice in my God.

Memory Verse: Romans 8:1-2

"There is therefore now no condemnation to them which are in Christ Jesus, who walk not after the flesh, but after the Spirit. For the law of the Spirit of life in Christ Jesus hath made me free from the law of sin and death."

To every family member: "I love you; you are blessed, and you are a blessing."
Don't forget the hugs.

February 28th

Scripture: Jeremiah 17:7-8 (KJV)

"Blessed is the man that trusteth in the Lord, and whose hope the Lord is. For he shall be as a tree planted by the waters, and that spreadeth out her roots by the river, and shall not see when heat cometh, but her leaf shall be green; and shall not be careful in the year of drought, neither shall cease from yielding fruit."

In your prayer journal, identify in this portion of scripture a promise to receive or a command to obey.

Prayer:

Blessed is the name of the Lord my God. I bless your holy name for you are good and your mercies endure forever. Father, I put my hope in you. I trust you, and I am grateful for every blessing of God. Truly, you have made me like a tree that has been planted by the river so that, even in times of drought, I will continue to flourish and bear fruit. Jesus said if I am thirsty to come to him and drink of the water of life freely. The same promise he gave the woman at the well is also good for me. I will never be thirsty, for you have placed within me a fountain of living water that springs up unto eternal life. Thank you, Father, for this abundant life in Jesus' name, Amen.

Proclamation:

My hope and trust is in the Lord my God. He has placed within me the kingdom of God. As the fountain of life in the midst of the Garden of Eden watered the garden and brought life to everything, so the Spirit of God abides within me and causes life to spring up like a fountain and flow out of my inner most being. I am full and complete in the Lord my God. He satisfies my every need according to his riches in glory through my Lord Jesus Christ.

Memory Verse: Romans 8:1-2

"There is therefore now no condemnation to them which are in Christ Jesus, who walk not after the flesh, but after the Spirit. For the law of the Spirit of life in Christ Jesus hath made me free from the law of sin and death."

To every family member: "I love you; you are blessed, and you are a blessing."
Don't forget the hugs.

March 1st

Scripture: Galatians 3:26-29 (PHILLIPS)

"For now that you have faith in Christ you are all sons of God. All of you who were baptised "into" Christ have put on the family likeness of Christ. Gone is the distinction between Jew and Greek, slave and free man, male and female—you are all one in Christ Jesus. And if you belong to Christ, you are true descendants of Abraham, you are true heirs of his promise."

In your prayer journal, identify in this portion of scripture a promise to receive or a command to obey.

Prayer:

Father, thank you for bringing to me the knowledge of your salvation. You have forgiven me and given me life. You brought me into your kingdom and gave me a great inheritance. Because I am in Christ, you have given me everything you promised to Abraham. I am an heir of God and a joint heir with Christ Jesus. I have access into your presence, I have authority in the name of Jesus, I have the abiding presence of the Holy Spirit, and you have deposited in me gifts and abilities to do your will and accomplish your purpose. I thank you, Father, for using the gifts you have placed in me to be a blessing to many. I pray these things in Jesus' name, Amen.

Proclamation:

The favor of God rests upon me today with everyone I meet. I walk in the blessings of Abraham according to the promises of God's Word. I am blessed and increased in every good thing. My life gives evidence of what God has done for me, so when people look at me, they see the goodness and blessings of God.

Memory Verse: Romans 8:1-2

"There is therefore now no condemnation to them which are in Christ Jesus, who walk not after the flesh, but after the Spirit. For the law of the Spirit of life in Christ Jesus hath made me free from the law of sin and death."

To every family member: "I love you; you are blessed, and you are a blessing."
Don't forget the hugs.

March 2nd

Scripture: Psalms 103:1-5 (NIV)

"Praise the Lord, my soul; all my inmost being, praise his holy name. Praise the Lord, my soul, and forget not all his benefits, who forgives all your sins and heals all your diseases, who redeems your life from the pit and crowns you with love and compassion, who satisfies your desires with good things so that your youth is renewed like the eagle's"

In your prayer journal, identify in this portion of scripture a promise to receive or a command to obey.

Prayer:

Father, I praise and bless your holy name. I will not forget all your many benefits. You have forgiven me and cleansed me from all unrighteousness. You have healed me of all diseases. You have redeemed my life from destruction and surrounded me with your love and compassion. You fulfill the desires of my heart and give me strength. I will praise you for all of your wonderful works that you have done for me because you love me. I thank you that I don't have to earn your love and blessings, but I only need to receive them for it is your good pleasure to see me walking happy and successful in every realm of life. I bless you for all these things this day in Jesus' name, Amen.

Proclamation:

I am blessed in everything I do. I am blessed when I rise up and when I lie down, when I go out and when I come in. The Lord my God, blesses me with health and wisdom so that I do not lack, need or want for any good thing. I am increased daily with the exceedingly great benefits of the Lord.

Memory Verse: Romans 8:1-2

"There is therefore now no condemnation to them which are in Christ Jesus, who walk not after the flesh, but after the Spirit. For the law of the Spirit of life in Christ Jesus hath made me free from the law of sin and death."

To every family member: *"I love you; you are blessed, and you are a blessing."*
Don't forget the hugs.

March 3rd

Scripture: 1 Peter 5:5-7 (RSV)

"Likewise you that are younger be subject to the elders. Clothe yourselves, all of you, with humility toward one another, for 'God opposes the proud, but gives grace to the humble.' Humble yourselves therefore under the mighty hand of God, that in due time he may exalt you. Cast all your anxieties on him, for he cares about you."

In your prayer journal, identify in this portion of scripture a promise to receive or a command to obey.

Prayer:

God, my Father, I am so thankful for your goodness and mercies in my life. You have given me an abundance of promises from your Word, showing me your desire to bless me. You have put people in my life to teach me wisdom and show me how to walk in faith so that I might please you and be fruitful in everything I do. I do not despise those you have given me to teach me the things of God. I choose to humble myself before you and receive from those who are older and mature in the knowledge of God. I know there will be a time when you will exalt me and position me to also teach and lead others according to your unique purpose for my life. I do not worry or fret or walk in fear and uncertainty, but instead I cast all of my fears and worries and concerns upon you today because I know you love me. I praise you for all these things in Jesus' name, Amen.

Proclamation:

God resists the proud, but gives grace to the humble. I humble myself before God, and I receive his grace. I know that I cannot fix the problems I face, but I can cast the care and worry of them on the Lord. I do not need to walk in fear because I know God loves me, is with me and will help me to receive from him directly and through those he puts in my life to overcome every difficulty.

Memory Verse: Romans 8:1-2

"There is therefore now no condemnation to them which are in Christ Jesus, who walk not after the flesh, but after the Spirit. For the law of the Spirit of life in Christ Jesus hath made me free from the law of sin and death."

To every family member: *"I love you; you are blessed, and you are a blessing."*
Don't forget the hugs.

March 4th

Scripture: Ecclesiastes 5:19-20 (HCSB)

"God has also given riches and wealth to every man and He has allowed him to enjoy them, take his reward, and rejoice in his labor. This is a gift of God, for he does not often consider the days of his life because God keeps him occupied with the joy of his heart."

In your prayer journal, identify in this portion of scripture a promise to receive or a command to obey.

Prayer:

Thank you, Father, for your blessings in my life. You give me wealth and riches that cause me to rejoice and celebrate your goodness towards me. You bless and prosper me so I can be a blessing to my family and to others. Your blessings show the world your goodness. Your blessings bring glory to you for every blessing is a gift from God. I know that riches and wealth, increase and prosperity are the will of God for everyone who follows after you with a pure heart. I don't have time to spend wondering and worrying about the things of this life because you keep me occupied with those things that bring joy to my heart. I thank you for prospering me in every good way today in Jesus' name, Amen.

Proclamation:

I give to others secretly, and God rewards me openly. I give what I have, and God gives me what he has. I give to bless others, and God gives to bless me. God gives me power to get wealth that I might partner with him in establishing his covenant in the earth.

Memory Verse: Romans 8:1-2

"There is therefore now no condemnation to them which are in Christ Jesus, who walk not after the flesh, but after the Spirit. For the law of the Spirit of life in Christ Jesus hath made me free from the law of sin and death."

To every family member: *"I love you; you are blessed, and you are a blessing."* Don't forget the hugs.

March 5th

Scripture: 1 Corinthians 13:1-7 (NET)

"If I speak in the tongues of men and of angels, but I do not have love, I am a noisy gong or a clanging cymbal. And if I have prophecy, and know all mysteries and all knowledge, and if I have all faith so that I can remove mountains, but do not have love, I am nothing. If I give away everything I own, and if I give over my body in order to boast, but do not have love, I receive no benefit. Love is patient, love is kind, it is not envious. Love does not brag, it is not puffed up. It is not rude, it is not self-serving, it is not easily angered or resentful. It is not glad about injustice, but rejoices in the truth. It bears all things, believes all things, hopes all things, endures all things."

In your prayer journal, identify in this portion of scripture a promise to receive or a command to obey.

Prayer:

Heavenly Father, help me to walk in your love. I know that anything I do that is not motivated by the love of God has no real value. There is no lasting benefit to anything outside of love. You have commanded us to love one another. I choose this day to show the love of God to everyone, not just those who are easy to love, but also those who are difficult to love. You showed great love towards us even when we were your enemies and did not understand your love. Now your love abides within us because the Holy Spirit dwells there. He empowers us to stay in love when others won't. I thank you today for your grace that strengthens me to love the unlovely as well as the lovely. Help me to express your love as your Word describes it. I ask this in Jesus' name, Amen.

Proclamation:

The love of God has filled my heart because the Spirit of God is the Spirit of love and he lives on the inside of me. God is described as love. What God does is what love does.

Memory Verse: Acts 1:8

"But you shall receive power, after that the Holy Ghost is come upon you: and you shall be witnesses unto me both in Jerusalem, and in all Judaea, and in Samaria, and unto the uttermost part of the earth."

To every family member: *"I love you; you are blessed, and you are a blessing."*
Don't forget the hugs.

March 6th

Scripture: Nehemiah 8:6,10 (KJV)

"And Ezra blessed the Lord, the great God. And all the people answered, Amen, Amen, with lifting up their hands: and they bowed their heads, and worshipped the Lord with their faces to the ground."

"Then he said unto them, Go your way, eat the fat, and drink the sweet, and send portions unto them for whom nothing is prepared: for this day is holy unto our Lord: neither be ye sorry; for the joy of the Lord is your strength."

In your prayer journal, identify in this portion of scripture a promise to receive or a command to obey.

Prayer:

Heavenly Father, it is my desire to worship you. I acknowledge your presence with me now. As I begin to pray, I know you invite me into your holy place. You have told me to come boldly to your throne room, and I will find grace and mercy to help me in every time of need. I lift up holy hands in your name as I worship at your footstool. Thank you for hearing me and instructing me to receive all you have prepared for me today. You have said that I can eat of the fatness of your table and drink of the river of your pleasures. I know your Word is like food for me, and the Spirit of God is as a river of living water. This river will quench my spiritual thirst and heal everything it touches. I believe I receive from you everything I need. I can take of what you have given me and send a portion to others in need so that we all might eat and drink of your supply and rejoice in you, for the joy of the Lord is our strength. Thank you today for this exceeding great joy. In Jesus' name, Amen.

Proclamation:

I will rejoice in the Lord today. I am strong in the Lord and in the power of his might because his joy is my strength.

Memory Verse: Acts 1:8

"But you shall receive power, after that the Holy Ghost is come upon you: and you shall be witnesses unto me both in Jerusalem, and in all Judaea, and in Samaria, and unto the uttermost part of the earth."

To every family member: *"I love you; you are blessed, and you are a blessing."*
Don't forget the hugs.

March 7th

Scripture: Galatians 3:13-14 (KJV)

"Christ hath redeemed us from the curse of the law, being made a curse for us: for it is written, Cursed is every one that hangeth on a tree: That the blessing of Abraham might come on the Gentiles through Jesus Christ; that we might receive the promise of the Spirit through faith."

In your prayer journal, identify in this portion of scripture a promise to receive or a command to obey.

Prayer:

Heavenly Father, I thank you for making me free from the curse of the law that required death for my sin. Help me to understand just how much you love me and what Jesus really did for me when he died in my place. You not only delivered me from death, but you blessed me with the same blessings you promised Abraham. You have promised to bless me with increase and favor and with your divine protection. Your loving kindness and tender mercies rest upon me today. Thank you for this great demonstration of your love. I will daily give you praise, for I am thankful for your great grace. I receive these things in Jesus' wonderful name, Amen.

Proclamation:

I am blessed of the Lord for he has redeemed my life from destruction. He has paid my debt and given me an inheritance of righteousness, peace and joy that comes from the abiding presence of the Holy Spirit. I walk in the blessings of God today. I am called by his name, and I rest in his love. I am rich and increased with every good thing. My life is greatly blessed of the Lord.

Memory Verse: Acts 1:8

"But you shall receive power, after that the Holy Ghost is come upon you: and you shall be witnesses unto me both in Jerusalem, and in all Judaea, and in Samaria, and unto the uttermost part of the earth."

To every family member: *"I love you; you are blessed, and you are a blessing."*
Don't forget the hugs.

March 8th

Scripture: John 10:7-11 (NKJV)

"Then Jesus said to them again, 'Most assuredly, I say to you, I am the door of the sheep. All who *ever* came before Me are thieves and robbers, but the sheep did not hear them. I am the door. If anyone enters by Me, he will be saved, and will go in and out and find pasture. The thief does not come except to steal, and to kill, and to destroy. I have come that they may have life, and that they may have *it* more abundantly. I am the good shepherd. The good shepherd gives His life for the sheep.'"

In your prayer journal, identify in this portion of scripture a promise to receive or a command to obey.

Prayer:

I bless the name of the Lord my God for he is worthy of praise. Thank you, Lord, for coming to me that I might have life and life more abundantly. I have entered into your sheep-fold through Jesus. You have promised to lead me by still waters and into green pastures. You supply all my need, watching over me, as a shepherd watches for the welfare of his sheep. You protect me from those who steal and kill, keeping me safe. You are my shepherd, and I hear your voice, and you lead me in the paths of righteousness. Thank you for your faithfulness. I never need to fear the threats of the enemy, for you are with me. You are my shield and my strength; you protect me from all evil and bless me with every good thing. May I bring praise to your holy and wonderful name today. In Jesus' name I pray, Amen.

Proclamation:

My God is my protector, my defender, my savior and my life. I am filled with life because of the one who gave his life so I might have life in abundance. I call upon the name of the Lord, and he hears me; he saves me and delivers me from all distress. He surrounds me like a wall of fire without and fills me with his glory within. I am blessed of the Lord.

Memory Verse: Acts 1:8

"But you shall receive power, after that the Holy Ghost is come upon you: and you shall be witnesses unto me both in Jerusalem, and in all Judaea, and in Samaria, and unto the uttermost part of the earth."

To every family member: "*I love you; you are blessed, and you are a blessing.*"
Don't forget the hugs.

March 9th

Scripture: Jude 1:24-25 (KJV)

"Now unto him that is able to keep you from falling, and to present you faultless before the presence of his glory with exceeding joy, To the only wise God our Saviour, be glory and majesty, dominion and power, both now and ever. Amen."

In your prayer journal, identify in this portion of scripture a promise to receive or a command to obey.

Prayer:

Heavenly Father, I come to you today with praise and thanksgiving for all of the wonderful things you have done for me. I am greatly blessed of the Lord. You are able to keep me from falling when I am weak. You lift me up and sustain me with your strength. I thank you for your promise to preserve me in all my ways and lead me by your Holy Spirit. Father, you bring me into your glory and declare that I am faultless. It is your joy to come to me and comfort me. I ask you to help me walk before you with clean hands and a pure heart. I want to please you in all my ways. I put away from me everything that would dishonor or displease you, and I receive afresh the power of your presence. You are at work within me causing me to will and to do your good pleasure. Thank you for this good day and your grace that makes me fruitful and successful in every good work. I declare these things in Jesus' mighty name, Amen.

Proclamation:

I am the righteousness of God in Christ Jesus because he is able to keep me from falling. He presents me as one who is faultless in his glorious presence and fills me with exceeding joy.

Memory Verse: Acts 1:8

"But you shall receive power, after that the Holy Ghost is come upon you: and you shall be witnesses unto me both in Jerusalem, and in all Judaea, and in Samaria, and unto the uttermost part of the earth."

To every family member: *"I love you; you are blessed, and you are a blessing."*
Don't forget the hugs.

March 10th

Scripture: 1 John 5:1-5 (HCSB)

"Everyone who believes that Jesus is the Messiah has been born of God, and everyone who loves the Father also loves the one born of Him. This is how we know that we love God's children when we love God and obey His commands. For this is what love for God is: to keep His commands. Now His commands are not a burden, because whatever has been born of God conquers the world. This is the victory that has conquered the world: our faith. And who is the one who conquers the world but the one who believes that Jesus is the Son of God?"

In your prayer journal, identify in this portion of scripture
a promise to receive or a command to obey.

Prayer:

Heavenly Father, you are great and greatly to be praised. You are worthy of honor and glory for all might and dominion belong to you. You have given us victory over the world through our Lord Jesus Christ. I thank you for your Word and promise to me that I have overcome the world. I believe that Jesus is the Son of God; therefore, I am a world overcomer. Lord, I ask you to give me wisdom and understanding that I would make wise choices and righteous decisions that would glorify you and bring your blessings to me and my family. Your commandment is for us to love one another. As I walk in your love today and demonstrate that love, I will not be overcome with the things of the world. Thank you for the victory that is mine in Jesus' name, Amen.

Proclamation:

The world has no power over me. All that is in the world is the lust of the eyes, the lust of the flesh and the pride of life, but I do not follow after the world. I follow after the things of the kingdom of God, and the kingdom of God has overcome all that is in this world.

Memory Verse: Acts 1:8

"But you shall receive power, after that the Holy Ghost is come upon you: and you shall be witnesses unto me both in Jerusalem, and in all Judaea, and in Samaria, and unto the uttermost part of the earth."

To every family member: *"I love you; you are blessed, and you are a blessing."*
Don't forget the hugs.

March 11th

Scripture: Matthew 21:21-22 (NKJV)

"So Jesus answered and said to them, 'Assuredly, I say to you, if you have faith and do not doubt, you will not only do what was done to the fig tree, but also if you say to this mountain, "Be removed and be cast into the sea," it will be done. And whatever things you ask in prayer, believing, you will receive.'"

In your prayer journal, identify in this portion of scripture a promise to receive or a command to obey.

Prayer:

Heavenly Father, You are mighty and nothing is impossible with you. You have created all things with your Word, and by your Word you have shown me that I can speak to fig trees or mountains or anything that exists and command it to come in line with the will of God. You have given me power to change the course of events by my words and set in motion your will in the earth. Thank you for the power of my words and help me to guard my tongue to only speak words that will produce good things. Let my words bring honor to your great name. Keep me from speaking death and cursing instead of life and blessings. I commit all my ways unto you today. Establish my thoughts to conform to your will so the words I speak and the plans I follow would come from you. I give you praise for these things this day, in Jesus' name, Amen.

Proclamation:

I choose this day to speak words of life and blessing. I know my words are powerful and they have the potential to produce whatever I say. I will fill my heart with the Word of God because my mouth will speak out whatever my heart is filled with. My words will be filled with life to encourage and bless all who hear.

Memory Verse: Acts 1:8

"But you shall receive power, after that the Holy Ghost is come upon you: and you shall be witnesses unto me both in Jerusalem, and in all Judaea, and in Samaria, and unto the uttermost part of the earth."

To every family member: "I love you; you are blessed, and you are a blessing."
Don't forget the hugs.

March 12th

Scripture: 1 Samuel 17:45-47 (MSG)

"David answered, 'You come at me with sword and spear and battle-ax. I come at you in the name of God-of-the-Angel-Armies, the God of Israel's troops, whom you curse and mock. This very day God is handing you over to me. I'm about to kill you, cut off your head, and serve up your body and the bodies of your Philistine buddies to the crows and coyotes. The whole earth will know that there's an extraordinary God in Israel. And everyone gathered here will learn that God doesn't save by means of sword or spear. The battle belongs to God—he's handing you to us on a platter!'"

In your prayer journal, identify in this portion of scripture a promise to receive or a command to obey.

Prayer:

God, my Father, I ask you to help me to be bold like your servant David was when he faced the giant Goliath. I want to always remember you are my strength, you are my defender, and you are the one I depend on to give me victory over all of those things that seem to be so big and impossible to defeat. You have already defeated the devil and given me authority over him through the name of the Lord Jesus Christ. You, Lord God are Almighty and All Powerful and there is nothing too hard for you. I do not war against people, but against spiritual powers you have already defeated. You stripped the devil of his authority and ability to defeat me, and as I submit myself to you, the devil runs from me in terror, for you are with me. All of the armies of Heaven are on my side. The victory is mine because the battle belongs to the Lord. Thank you for the victory that is mine every time. In Jesus' name I pray, Amen.

Proclamation:

I cannot be defeated, for if God is for me, then who can be against me?

Memory Verse: Philippians 4:13
"I can do all things through Christ which strengthens me."

To every family member: *"I love you; you are blessed, and you are a blessing."*
Don't forget the hugs.

March 13th

Scripture: Psalms 36:5-9 (GW)

"O Lord, your mercy reaches to the heavens, your faithfulness to the skies. Your righteousness is like the mountains of God, your judgments like the deep ocean. You save people and animals, O Lord. Your mercy is so precious, O God, that Adam's descendants take refuge in the shadow of your wings. They are refreshed with the rich foods in your house, and you make them drink from the river of your pleasure. Indeed, the fountain of life is with you. In your light we see light."

In your prayer journal, identify in this portion of scripture a promise to receive or a command to obey.

Prayer:

My Father, you are glorious in majesty and great in mercy. You are great and greatly are you to be praised. I thank you today for your faithfulness to me because you love me. You have redeemed my life from ruin and brought me into your kingdom. You give me richly all the things to enjoy that are in your house. I drink of the river of your pleasure, which satisfies me and strengthens me and gives me peace. I have the light (the revelation) of who you are and what you have done for me. I pray you will fill me more and more with understanding of your greatness and your love for me. I thank you for all these things in Jesus' name, Amen.

Proclamation:

I walk in God's favor today. Everything I set my hand to prospers and brings me good success. I walk with the confidence that God is my Father and he loves me and delights in me. I am his favorite. He watches over me to keep me safe in all my ways. He sends his angels to minister to me and fills me with his Holy Spirit who empowers me to do his will and to walk in his blessings. I am greatly blessed today.

Memory Verse: Philippians 4:13

"I can do all things through Christ which strengthens me."

To every family member: "*I love you; you are blessed, and you are a blessing.*"
Don't forget the hugs.

March 14th

Scripture: 1 Corinthians 4:17-20 (KJV)

"For this cause have I sent unto you Timotheus, who is my beloved son, and faithful in the Lord, who shall bring you into remembrance of my ways which be in Christ, as I teach every where in every church. Now some are puffed up, as though I would not come to you. But I will come to you shortly, if the Lord will, and will know, not the speech of them which are puffed up, but the power. For the kingdom of God is not in word, but in power."

In your prayer journal, identify in this portion of scripture a promise to receive or a command to obey.

Prayer:

Heavenly Father, I thank you for those faithful followers of the Lord whom you have raised up to teach the churches about the things of God. I pray that the Kingdom of God comes and the will of God is done on earth just as it is always done in Heaven. I pray that all the churches will give evidence of your power working in them through signs and wonders and miracles that glorify the Lord Jesus. Your Kingdom is not limited to words and ideas and philosophies of men, but your Word is confirmed by the miraculous working power of God. This power gives demonstration to the resurrection of Christ from the dead. Jesus is alive, and he is building his church that will endure forever. Thank you for helping me grow in faith and in the knowledge of your will. Fill me with the Spirit of God so I will live in the power of God and bring praise and glory to you. I ask these things now in Jesus' name, Amen.

Proclamation:

I am filled with the Spirit of God. The power of God works in me today. I can pray and declare the will of God, and God will answer my prayer and accomplish his purpose.

Memory Verse: Philippians 4:13
"I can do all things through Christ which strengtheneth me."

To every family member: *"I love you; you are blessed, and you are a blessing."*
Don't forget the hugs.

March 15th

Scripture: John 3:3-8 (NLT)

"Jesus replied, 'I tell you the truth, unless you are born again, you cannot see the Kingdom of God.' 'What do you mean?' exclaimed Nicodemus. 'How can an old man go back into his mother's womb and be born again?' Jesus replied, 'I assure you, no one can enter the Kingdom of God without being born of water and the Spirit. Humans can reproduce only human life, but the Holy Spirit gives birth to spiritual life. So don't be surprised when I say, 'You must be born again.' The wind blows wherever it wants. Just as you can hear the wind but can't tell where it comes from or where it is going, so you can't explain how people are born of the Spirit.'"

In your prayer journal, identify in this portion of scripture a promise to receive or a command to obey.

Prayer:

Heavenly Father, I am so thankful that you brought to me the gospel of the Lord Jesus Christ. You opened my heart to believe, and the Spirit of God came into my life and gave me a new life I never had before. When the Spirit of God came into me and joined Himself with my human spirit, I was born again. Thank you for your life that now abides in me because of the Spirit of God who lives in me. He will never leave me or abandon me. Help me to live out of the new spiritual life that is in me instead of the old natural life I used to live by. Father, may the Spirit of God speak to me and lead me today that I might live in and walk in the Kingdom of God. I ask you, Father, for these things in Jesus' name, Amen.

Proclamation:

I have been born of the Spirit of God, and the life of God dwells in me. God lives in me. I have entered the Kingdom of God. His righteousness, peace and joy are mine today.

Memory Verse: Philippians 4:13

"I can do all things through Christ which strengthens me."

To every family member: *"I love you; you are blessed, and you are a blessing."*
Don't forget the hugs.

March 16th

Scripture: Genesis 1:26-28 (MSG)

"God spoke: 'Let us make human beings in our image, make them reflecting our nature So they can be responsible for the fish in the sea, the birds in the air, the cattle, and, yes, Earth itself, and every animal that moves on the face of Earth.' God created human beings; he created them godlike, reflecting God's nature. He created them male and female. God blessed them: 'Prosper! Reproduce! Fill Earth! Take charge! Be responsible for fish in the sea and birds in the air, for every living thing that moves on the face of Earth.'"

In your prayer journal, identify in this portion of scripture a promise to receive or a command to obey.

Prayer:

Heavenly Father, you have created all things. You gave man authority and dominion to rule the earth, to see that every good thing grew and multiplied according to your will. Even when man sinned and lost the ability to reflect your image, you sent Jesus to redeem us and restore us. I pray I will operate in the authority and dominion you ordained for me to walk in. Help me to speak to the things that need to be changed in order to bring them in line with your will. I thank you for the power to bind on earth what you have declared to be bound in heaven and to loose on the earth, that is to declare legal and lawful those things that are according to your will in heaven. Your authority and dominion have been given to me to declare your will and to accomplish your purpose. I give you thanks for these things today in Jesus' name, Amen.

Proclamation:

I am made in God's image and after his likeness. I have authority to execute his will in the earth by the authority of the name of Jesus. I speak words that carry the will of God, and when I speak, God watches over his Word to perform it.

Memory Verse: Philippians 4:13
"I can do all things through Christ which strengthens me."

To every family member: *"I love you; you are blessed, and you are a blessing."*
Don't forget the hugs.

March 17th

Scripture: Psalms 19:7-11 (NASB)

"The law of the Lord is perfect, restoring the soul; the testimony of the Lord is sure, making wise the simple. The precepts of the Lord are right, rejoicing the heart; the commandment of the Lord is pure, enlightening the eyes. The fear of the Lord is clean, enduring forever; the judgments of the Lord are true; they are righteous altogether. They are more desirable than gold, yes, than much fine gold; Sweeter also than honey and the drippings of the honeycomb. Moreover, by them Your servant is warned; in keeping them there is great reward."

In your prayer journal, identify in this portion of scripture a promise to receive or a command to obey.

Prayer:

God, my Father, I worship your holy name, for you are worthy of all praise. You have given me all things that pertain to this life that I might be successful in everything I do and to do everything in such a way that it brings glory to you. Your Word is perfect. Every precept and every declaration of your Word brings me wisdom and enlightens me. As I honor your Word, following everything you have said, I will find that your Word is more desirable than gold and sweeter than honey. I have a great reward as I follow after your Word. I pray that I will first of all seek the guidance and counsel of your Word for every decision I must make. Father, speak to me by your Word today and make me wise with the wisdom your Word brings me. Help me to love your Word and to see that it truly has more value than gold and is more necessary than my next meal. I thank you for opening my ears to your voice as I seek after you in the Word of God. In Jesus' name I pray, Amen.

Proclamation:

The Word of God is alive. It is living and full of life. By the incorruptible seed of the Word of God, I have been born again. By hearing the Word of God, I am filled with faith. And by the Word of God, I have a great reward.

Memory Verse: Philippians 4:13

"I can do all things through Christ which strengthens me."

To every family member: *"I love you; you are blessed, and you are a blessing."*
Don't forget the hugs.

March 18th

Scripture: Isaiah 55:8-11 (HCSB)

"'For My thoughts are not your thoughts and your ways are not My ways.' This is the Lord's declaration. 'For as heaven is higher than earth so My ways are higher than your ways and My thoughts than your thoughts. For just as rain and snow fall from heaven and do not return there without saturating the earth and making it germinate and sprout and providing seed to sow and food to eat, so My word that comes from My mouth will not return to Me empty, but it will accomplish what I please and will prosper in what I send it to do.'"

In your prayer journal, identify in this portion of scripture a promise to receive or a command to obey.

Prayer:

Heavenly Father, you are above all. There is no one like you. You have created all things by your Word and for your pleasure. Everything is sustained by your Word and held together by what you have declared. I know your Word will accomplish its purpose; it will not return to you unfulfilled. Help me today to be transformed by renewing my mind with your Word. I want to think your thoughts and speak words that are in agreement with what you have said, for it is your Word that will stand. As the rain causes the earth to bud and produce good fruit, so your Word causes good things to be produced in me. I thank you for your Word and what it accomplishes today as I believe it, speak it and stand in agreement with it. Blessings of increase, protection and peace will be added to me today. I give you praise for these things now, in Jesus' name, Amen.

Proclamation:

The blessings of the Lord come upon me and overtake me today, for God's Word is at work in my life. I am blessed in all my ways, daily harvesting the good fruit of God's Word that is sown in my life.

Memory Verse: Philippians 4:13

"I can do all things through Christ which strengthens me."

To every family member: *"I love you; you are blessed, and you are a blessing."*
Don't forget the hugs.

March 19th

Scripture: John 12:44-47 (KJV)

"Jesus cried and said, He that believeth on me, believeth not on me, but on him that sent me. And he that seeth me seeth him that sent me. I am come a light into the world, that whosoever believeth on me should not abide in darkness. And if any man hear my words, and believe not, I judge him not: for I came not to judge the world, but to save the world."

In your prayer journal, identify in this portion of scripture a promise to receive or a command to obey.

Prayer:

My Father, I thank you today for your great love for me. I know who you are and what you are like by looking at Jesus. He showed me your love for he perfectly demonstrated your compassion and power. If I see Jesus, I see you. You sent Jesus to save me and not to condemn me. Jesus healed the sick and set the oppressed free. He forgave sinners and supplied the needs of the multitudes. Because he did those things for them, I know he has done the same for me, for God is no respecter of people. Jesus died in my place so I can live in abundant life. Jesus brought me out of darkness and misery into the light of salvation. I praise you Father that I no longer walk in the darkness of fear and confusion but in the light of your life. Thank you for this amazing work of your grace in me today. In Jesus' name I pray, Amen.

Proclamation:

I have been delivered from the fear of judgment, guilt and condemnation. I am free and free indeed because of what Jesus has done for me. My confidence is in God and Jesus, the one he sent to show me his love and mercy.

Memory Verse: Romans 10:9-10

"...if you shall confess with your mouth the Lord Jesus, and shall believe in your heart that God has raised him from the dead, you shall be saved. For with the heart man believes unto righteousness; and with the mouth confession is made unto salvation."

To every family member: "I love you; you are blessed, and you are a blessing."
Don't forget the hugs.

March 20th

Scripture: Isaiah 2:2-4 (NLT)

"In the last days, the mountain of the Lord's house will be the highest of all—the most important place on earth. It will be raised above the other hills, and people from all over the world will stream there to worship. People from many nations will come and say, 'Come, let us go up to the mountain of the Lord to the house of Jacob's God. There he will teach us his ways and we will walk in his paths.' For the Lord's teaching will go out from Zion; his word will go out from Jerusalem. The Lord will mediate between nations and will settle international disputes. They will hammer their swords into plowshares and their spears into pruning hooks. Nation will no longer fight against nation nor train for war anymore."

In your prayer journal, identify in this portion of scripture
a promise to receive or a command to obey.

Prayer:

God, my Father, I thank you for your promise that the day will come when the kingdoms of this world will become the kingdoms of our God. Your kingdom will be above all, and all people will come to Zion, your church, to learn your ways. The Word of the Lord will settle disputes between nations, and the military budgets of nations will be used for the harvest of souls. Help me today to stand in my place in your kingdom as it is advancing around the world, bringing salvation to all who hear. I pray for the leaders of nations to bow their knees to the name of the Lord Jesus Christ. I pray for the wind of the Spirit of God to blow across the borders of all lands, touching the hearts of the people and drawing them by the love of God. Lord of the Harvest, I ask you to send laborers into all the harvest fields that are ready to be reaped. In Jesus' name, Amen.

Proclamation:

The glory of the Lord will cover all the earth.

Memory Verse: Romans 10:9-10

"...if you shall confess with your mouth the Lord Jesus, and shall believe in your heart that God has raised him from the dead, you shall be saved. For with the heart man believes unto righteousness; and with the mouth confession is made unto salvation."

To every family member: *"I love you; you are blessed, and you are a blessing."*
Don't forget the hugs.

March 21st

Scripture: Colossians 2:8-10 (MSG)

"Watch out for people who try to dazzle you with big words and intellectual double-talk. They want to drag you off into endless arguments that never amount to anything. They spread their ideas through the empty traditions of human beings and the empty superstitions of spirit beings. But that's not the way of Christ. Everything of God gets expressed in him, so you can see and hear him clearly. You don't need a telescope, a microscope, or a horoscope to realize the fullness of Christ, and the emptiness of the universe without him. When you come to him, that fullness comes together for you, too. His power extends over everything."

In your prayer journal, identify in this portion of scripture a promise to receive or a command to obey.

Prayer:

God, my Father, I am greatly blessed this day because of what Jesus did for me. Everything about God is found in what Jesus did and what he said. He is the full expression of God. Father, I ask you to keep me from the empty philosophies of men and empty traditions that some would hold to be more important than Jesus. I am complete in Jesus. He made me righteous, he healed my broken heart and body, and he has made me whole. I do not have to try to be loved or accepted because, if I am in Christ, I have been accepted as the beloved of God. God approves everything in Christ, because Jesus perfectly fulfilled the will of God. Father, I thank you for this abundant grace that fills me with joy and peace today. In Jesus' name, Amen.

Proclamation:

I am complete, not wanting or lacking any good thing because I am in Christ Jesus, and in him I am complete, satisfied and fulfilled.

Memory Verse: Romans 10:9-10

"...if you shall confess with your mouth the Lord Jesus, and shall believe in your heart that God has raised him from the dead, you shall be saved. For with the heart man believes unto righteousness; and with the mouth confession is made unto salvation."

To every family member: *"I love you; you are blessed, and you are a blessing."*
Don't forget the hugs.

March 22nd

Scripture: Isaiah 43:1-3a (NKJV)

"But now, thus says the Lord, who created you, O Jacob, and He who formed you, O Israel: 'Fear not, for I have redeemed you; I have called *you* by your name; you *are* Mine. When you pass through the waters, I *will* be with you; and through the rivers, they shall not overflow you. When you walk through the fire, you shall not be burned, nor shall the flame scorch you. For I *am* the Lord your God, the Holy One of Israel, your Savior;'"

In your prayer journal, identify in this portion of scripture a promise to receive or a command to obey.

Prayer:

My Father, you are my strength and my protector. You have created me. You have redeemed me and given me a promise of your abiding presence and protection. You will keep me from the floods of water or the flames of fire or any other thing that would come against me to destroy me. You are the All Mighty and nothing is too difficult for you. I put my trust in you today. Thank you, Father, for showing me your great love and your mighty power. I am greatly blessed because you are with me. No enemy can overcome me, defeat or destroy me. I give you praise for all your promises today, in Jesus' name, Amen.

Proclamation:

Because God is for me, there is no one or no thing that can defeat me. Jesus has redeemed me from the curse of sin by becoming accursed for me. He took my place in judgment so I can take his place in righteousness. He took my sickness and disease so I can take hold of his healing and health. I am whole because he was broken. I am complete in him this day.

Memory Verse: Romans 10:9-10

"...if you shall confess with your mouth the Lord Jesus, and shall believe in your heart that God has raised him from the dead, you shall be saved. For with the heart man believes unto righteousness; and with the mouth confession is made unto salvation."

To every family member: *"I love you; you are blessed, and you are a blessing."*
Don't forget the hugs.

March 23rd

Scripture: John 6:26-27 (MSG)

"Jesus answered, 'You've come looking for me not because you saw God in my actions but because I fed you, filled your stomachs—and for free. Don't waste your energy striving for perishable food like that. Work for the food that sticks with you, food that nourishes your lasting life, food the Son of Man provides. He and what he does are guaranteed by God the Father to last.'"

In your prayer journal, identify in this portion of scripture a promise to receive or a command to obey.

Prayer:

Heavenly Father, I thank you for providing for all of my needs both physical and spiritual. You fed the multitudes, not because they were starving, but just because you loved them and wanted to bless them. When they sought after you the next day, you showed them their heart. You showed them their need to seek after you was much greater than just another meal. Help me today to seek after you for the things that last forever and not for the things that are only temporary. You said you would meet all of my need according to your riches in glory. You have everything I will ever need for my spirit, soul and body. I thank you for all these things, in Jesus' name, Amen.

Proclamation:

The Lord is my provider; therefore, I will not want for anything. He supplies all my needs and satisfies me with good things. Every good and perfect gift comes from God. He will sustain me and strengthen me, and he even sees what I will have need of long before I need it, and he makes provision for me ahead of time. I am greatly blessed of the Lord. The economies may crash and currencies may fail; trouble and difficulties may arise for many, but my God watches over me. He will sustain me and cause me to be like a tree with deep roots nourished by unseen waters that cause me to continually flourish and be fruitful.

Memory Verse: Romans 10:9-10

"...if you shall confess with your mouth the Lord Jesus, and shall believe in your heart that God has raised him from the dead, you shall be saved. For with the heart man believes unto righteousness; and with the mouth confession is made unto salvation."

To every family member: "I love you; you are blessed, and you are a blessing."
Don't forget the hugs.

March 24th

Scripture: James 4:6-7 (AMP)

"But He gives us more and more grace power of the Holy Spirit, to meet this evil tendency and all others fully. That is why He says, God sets Himself against the proud and haughty, but gives grace [continually] to the lowly (those who are humble enough to receive it). So be subject to God. Resist the devil [stand firm against him], and he will flee from you."

In your prayer journal, identify in this portion of scripture a promise to receive or a command to obey.

Prayer:

Father, thank you today for the grace that empowers me to stand against every temptation the devil would bring my way. You give me more and more grace to overcome every crafty device of the enemy. I choose this day to submit myself unto the Lord Jesus Christ. I humble myself before him because I know that without him I cannot succeed on my own. Jesus empowers me by the Holy Spirit of God to resist the devil, and because I do, the devil runs from me. All authority in heaven and in earth belongs to the Lord Jesus Christ. His name is above every name. Every name in heaven, in the earth and beneath the earth must bow to the name of the Lord Jesus. God, my Father, I thank you for the mighty name of Jesus, and it is by the authority of his name I pray, Amen.

Proclamation:

The grace of God belongs to me today. By his grace, I am more than a conqueror. The devil runs from me in terror as I humble myself before the Lord and submit myself to him.

Memory Verse: Romans 10:9-10

"...if you shall confess with your mouth the Lord Jesus, and shall believe in your heart that God has raised him from the dead, you shall be saved. For with the heart man believes unto righteousness; and with the mouth confession is made unto salvation."

To every family member: *"I love you; you are blessed, and you are a blessing."*
Don't forget the hugs.

March 25th

Scripture: 3 John 1:2-4 (KJV)

"Beloved, I wish above all things that thou mayest prosper and be in health, even as thy soul prospereth. For I rejoiced greatly, when the brethren came and testified of the truth that is in thee, even as thou walkest in the truth. I have no greater joy than to hear that my children walk in truth."

In your prayer journal, identify in this portion of scripture a promise to receive or a command to obey.

Prayer:

My Father, it is my desire to walk in the truth. You said that your Word is truth. As I renew my mind to think according to your Word, I will make my soul prosperous in the ways of God. Help me today to hear, to understand and to obey your Word. Lord, I do not want to just hear and obey your Word because I know I should, but I want to have my whole life so conformed and so transformed to your Word that I think and act and speak in perfect agreement with your Word. I know, when my life becomes conformed to your truth, I will naturally see things the way you see them and do things as you would do them, and I will prosper in everything I do, and my life will bring glory to you. I believe that you, Lord, are at work in me, bringing to pass these things this day, in Jesus' name, Amen.

Proclamation:

My ways are prosperous, and I have good success in all I do and set my hands to today. I choose to walk in the truth as the Word of God directs me and the Spirit of God empowers me so that I please God in all my ways.

Memory Verse: Romans 10:9-10

"...if you shall confess with your mouth the Lord Jesus, and shall believe in your heart that God has raised him from the dead, you shall be saved. For with the heart man believes unto righteousness; and with the mouth confession is made unto salvation."

To every family member: *"I love you; you are blessed, and you are a blessing."*
Don't forget the hugs.

March 26th

Scripture: Colossians 2:13-17 (NIV)

"When you were dead in your sins and in the uncircumcision of your flesh, God made you alive with Christ. He forgave us all our sins, having canceled the charge of our legal indebtedness, which stood against us and condemned us; he has taken it away, nailing it to the cross. And having disarmed the powers and authorities, he made a public spectacle of them, triumphing over them by the cross. Therefore do not let anyone judge you by what you eat or drink, or with regard to a religious festival, a New Moon celebration or a Sabbath day. These are a shadow of the things that were to come; the reality, however, is found in Christ."

In your prayer journal, identify in this portion of scripture a promise to receive or a command to obey.

Prayer:

Father, thank you for forgiving me and removing from me all judgment that was against me because of my sin. The righteous demands of your perfect law condemned me, and I was guilty, but when Jesus was nailed to the cross; the law requiring my death was nailed there with him. He paid the price for my indebtedness, and therefore, removed it from me. Lord, you disarmed all my enemies by taking away from them any right to accuse me. Thank you, Lord, that I stand before you cleansed of all sin and free from all guilt. I am no longer required to keep the ordinances of religious festivals and Sabbath days, for all those things were fulfilled in the Lord Jesus. He is my Sabbath. He released me from the works of the law to rest in the finished work of Christ. Thank you, Father, that I am free and free indeed, in Jesus' name I pray, Amen.

Proclamation:

He whom the Son sets free is free indeed. Jesus set me free from the judgments of the law so I would be free from guilt and shame. I am the righteousness of God in Christ because of his works and not because of mine.

Memory Verse: Acts 10:38

"How God anointed Jesus of Nazareth with the Holy Ghost and with power: who went about doing good, and healing all that were oppressed of the devil; for God was with him."

To every family member: *"I love you; you are blessed, and you are a blessing."*
Don't forget the hugs.

March 27th

Scripture: Jeremiah 29:11-13 (KJV)

"For I know the thoughts that I think toward you, saith the Lord, thoughts of peace, and not of evil, to give you an expected end. Then shall ye call upon me, and ye shall go and pray unto me, and I will hearken unto you. And ye shall seek me, and find me, when ye shall search for me with all your heart."

In your prayer journal, identify in this portion of scripture a promise to receive or a command to obey.

Prayer:

Heavenly Father, the psalmist declared that your thoughts for me are more than could be numbered. I thank you, Lord, that my life and my circumstances are not hidden from you. You know all about me. You know my struggles and my fears, my sins and my desires. There is nothing in my life that you are unaware of. You think good things about me, and your plans for me are plans of good. You are not ignoring the challenges I am facing, but instead you have given me wisdom and power to overcome every difficulty and to receive the provision for every need. I am greatly blessed this day because you love me and are watching over me to help me in times of trouble. I am filled with joy because my hope is in you, and you are faithful to fulfill your good plans for me. I give you praise for these things this day, in Jesus' name, Amen.

Proclamation:

The Lord is on my side. I will not fear or be anxious about anything because my God watches over me to direct me, to bless me and to keep me from all evil and to prosper me in everything I do.

Memory Verse: Acts 10:38

"How God anointed Jesus of Nazareth with the Holy Ghost and with power: who went about doing good, and healing all that were oppressed of the devil; for God was with him."

To every family member: *"I love you; you are blessed, and you are a blessing."*
Don't forget the hugs.

March 28th

Scripture: Proverbs 16:1-3 (AMP)

"The plans of the mind *and* orderly thinking belong to man, but from the Lord comes the [wise] answer of the tongue. All the ways of a man are pure in his own eyes, but the Lord weighs the spirits (the thoughts and intents of the heart). Roll your works upon the Lord [commit and trust them wholly to Him; He will cause your thoughts to become agreeable to His will, and] so shall your plans be established and succeed."

In your prayer journal, identify in this portion of scripture a promise to receive or a command to obey.

Prayer:

Heavenly Father, you are perfect in all your ways. I worship you this day for you are good and your mercies endure forever. I ask you to establish my thoughts. I commit to you the works of this day. Cause me to think your thoughts so the plans I make really come from the heart of God. Father, bless the works of my hands and let the meditations of my heart be pleasing to you. You have done a great work in me because you love me. I ask you to make me fruitful in every good work that I do this day. Prosper me and increase me and cause me to find favor with everyone I meet, even with those who would hear my name. Grant me wisdom so that I do not waste my time or resources on empty works. May all my works be done with excellence. May everyone see that my success is only because of the knowledge and understanding you bring me. I thank you for hearing me and bringing to pass these things this day, in Jesus' name, Amen.

Proclamation:

My thoughts come from the Lord. He establishes my going out and my coming in and all that I do so I succeed and prosper in all my ways.

Memory Verse: Acts 10:38

"How God anointed Jesus of Nazareth with the Holy Ghost and with power: who went about doing good, and healing all that were oppressed of the devil; for God was with him."

To every family member: *"I love you; you are blessed, and you are a blessing."* Don't forget the hugs.

March 29th

Scripture: Psalms 112:5-10 (NRSV)

"It is well with those who deal generously and lend, who conduct their affairs with justice. For the righteous will never be moved; they will be remembered forever. They are not afraid of evil tidings; their hearts are firm, secure in the Lord. Their hearts are steady, they will not be afraid; in the end they will look in triumph on their foes. They have distributed freely, they have given to the poor; their righteousness endures forever; their horn is exalted in honor. The wicked see it and are angry; they gnash their teeth and melt away; the desire of the wicked comes to nothing."

In your prayer journal, identify in this portion of scripture a promise to receive or a command to obey.

Prayer:

Father, I delight in your Word and in your ways. Help me to be generous and do all things in a manner that would please you and be right in your eyes. I will not allow an evil report to cause me to fear because I know you are with me and will help me overcome every evil work. My trust is in you. I ask you today to cause me to increase and have plenty so I can freely distribute to those in need. Help me to help the poor, the widows and orphans and those who need your special care. Give me a word of encouragement for those who are discouraged and make all my words right for every occasion and spoken at just the right time. Thank you for your grace that works mightily in me today, in Jesus' name, Amen.

Proclamation:

I am greatly blessed this day. The hand of the Lord rests upon me, and I receive his grace and power to accomplish his will and establish his purpose. I am equipped with everything I need just when I need it.

Memory Verse: Acts 10:38

"How God anointed Jesus of Nazareth with the Holy Ghost and with power: who went about doing good, and healing all that were oppressed of the devil; for God was with him."

To every family member: *"I love you; you are blessed, and you are a blessing."*
Don't forget the hugs.

March 30th

Scripture: Revelation 22:1-5 (PHILLIPS)

"Then he showed me the river of the water of life, sparkling like crystal as it flowed from the throne of God and of the Lamb. In the middle of the street of the city and on either bank of the river grew the tree of life, bearing twelve fruits, a different kind for each month. The leaves of the tree were for the healing of the nations. Nothing that has cursed mankind shall exist any longer; the throne of God and of the Lamb shall be within the city. His servants shall worship him; they shall see his face, and his name will be upon their foreheads. Night shall be no more; they have no more need for either lamplight or sunlight, for the Lord God will shed his light upon them and they shall reign as kings for timeless ages."

In your prayer journal, identify in this portion of scripture a promise to receive or a command to obey.

Prayer:

God, my Father, you are holy in all your works and perfect in all your ways. Everything you do is good and righteous and what you have prepared for us who love you is beyond our ability to perceive. You have described the place where we will live forever. It is a place of great joy because of your presence. It is a place of beauty and abundance where there is nothing that can hurt or offend or bring pain or sorrow, for none of those things are allowed in your presence. Help me today to live with a realization that everything here is temporary and what lies ahead is eternal. I praise you for the ability you give us to see the things that cannot be seen and reign in life both now and forever. In Jesus' name I pray, Amen.

Proclamation:

I am not discouraged or afraid. My God has shown me his glorious presence and the place where he dwells. I will drink of the fountain of living water and eat of the table of God's provision. My life is blessed beyond measure, and my joy is full, for he has made me complete in him who is the head of all, and his mercies toward me endure forever.

Memory Verse: Acts 10:38

"How God anointed Jesus of Nazareth with the Holy Ghost and with power: who went about doing good, and healing all that were oppressed of the devil; for God was with him."

To every family member: *"I love you; you are blessed, and you are a blessing."*
Don't forget the hugs.

March 31st

Scripture: Matthew 28:18-20 (NLT)

"Jesus came and told his disciples, 'I have been given all authority in heaven and on earth. Therefore, go and make disciples of all the nations, baptizing them in the name of the Father and the Son and the Holy Spirit. Teach these new disciples to obey all the commands I have given you. And be sure of this: I am with you always, even to the end of the age.'"

In your prayer journal, identify in this portion of scripture a promise to receive or a command to obey.

Prayer:

My Father, you are able to do all things, for there is nothing too hard for you. As you anointed Jesus by the power of the Holy Spirit to heal the sick and to cast out demons and set the oppressed free, so you have anointed me. You have sent me to do the same works that Jesus did, and he has promised me that he will be with me wherever I go. I know that I cannot do anything in my own strength or ability. I am dependent on you. You commanded me to be filled with the Spirit of God and to go in that power and do your will. I choose to obey your Word and to do your works this day. Fill me with the Spirit of God, so I can obey your Word. Help me to make disciples who will follow after you with all their hearts and will also do everything you have commanded. I thank you for these things in Jesus' name, Amen.

Proclamation:

The Spirit of the Lord is within me, and he empowers me to accomplish the will of God today. The things I do are not by my might or by my power but by the Spirit of God who strengthens me.

Memory Verse: Acts 10:38

"How God anointed Jesus of Nazareth with the Holy Ghost and with power: who went about doing good, and healing all that were oppressed of the devil; for God was with him."

To every family member: "I love you; you are blessed, and you are a blessing."
Don't forget the hugs.

April 1st

Scripture: John 15:9-12 (GW)

"'I have loved you the same way the Father has loved me. So live in my love. If you obey my commandments, you will live in my love. I have obeyed my Father's commandments, and in that way I live in his love. I have told you this so that you will be as joyful as I am, and your joy will be complete. Love each other as I have loved you. This is what I'm commanding you to do.'"

In your prayer journal, identify in this portion of scripture a promise to receive or a command to obey.

Prayer:

My Father, I stand before you today amazed at your great love for me. Thank you for loving me. I desire to live in your love and to keep your commandments that instruct me to love you and to love others. Thank you for the fullness of your joy that fills my life because I walk in your love. In your love there is abundant life and perfect peace because where the love of God abides is where the presence of God dwells. Lord, help me walk in your love so everyone will know that I am one of your disciples. Thank you, Father, for these things working in me today, in Jesus' name, Amen.

Proclamation:

I love God, and because I do, the love of God is at work in me to empower me to keep his commandments. I do not labor to keep the commandments of God out of fear, but instead his commandments remove all fear from my life. The commandments God requires me to keep are not the ten commandments of the law but the two commandments Jesus declared: to love God and to love one another. Today I choose life, and I choose the love of God.

Memory Verse: Acts 10:38

"How God anointed Jesus of Nazareth with the Holy Ghost and with power: who went about doing good, and healing all that were oppressed of the devil; for God was with him."

To every family member: "I love you; you are blessed, and you are a blessing."
Don't forget the hugs.

April 2nd

Scripture: Rom. 1:16-17 (HCSB)

"For I am not ashamed of the gospel, because it is God's power for salvation to everyone who believes, first to the Jew, and also to the Greek. For in it God's righteousness is revealed from faith to faith, just as it is written: The righteous will live by faith."

In your prayer journal, identify in this portion of scripture a promise to receive or a command to obey.

Prayer:

Heavenly Father, you are great and worthy of all praise. You have redeemed my life from destruction and blessed me with every good thing. Your grace and favor rest on me today, and I worship and bless your holy name. Thank you for the gospel of the Lord Jesus Christ, the good news that brings me your salvation. The good news that announces my forgiveness, your love for me and the full and abundant life you want me to enjoy. I am not ashamed of the gospel of the Lord Jesus Christ, for it is the power of God for my salvation I receive this day by faith. I have been made righteous before God by faith in what Jesus did for me. He took upon himself the judgment for my sins and carried away my curse. I praise you, Lord, for these things now in Jesus' wonderful name, Amen.

Proclamation:

I will proudly declare the gospel of the Lord Jesus Christ for it is the power of God for salvation to everyone who will believe it. Jesus accomplished for me what I could never accomplish for myself. I am forgiven. I am accepted in the beloved. I am healed and whole in my body, sound in my mind and enjoying the peace of God that rules in my heart. I am blessed.

Memory Verse: Mark 11:23

"For verily I say unto you, that whosoever shall say unto this mountain, Be removed, and be cast into the sea and shall not doubt in his heart, but shall believe that those things which he says shall come to pass, he shall have whatsoever he says."

To every family member: *"I love you; you are blessed, and you are a blessing."*
Don't forget the hugs.

April 3rd

Scripture: Deuteronomy 30:19-20 (NKJV)

"'I call heaven and earth as witnesses today against you, that I have set before you life and death, blessing and cursing; therefore choose life, that both you and your descendants may live; that you may love the Lord your God, that you may obey His voice, and that you may cling to Him, for He is your life and the length of your days; and that you may dwell in the land which the Lord swore to your fathers, to Abraham, Isaac, and Jacob, to give them.'"

In your prayer journal, identify in this portion of scripture a promise to receive or a command to obey.

Prayer:

Father, you are Lord of all, and there is nothing impossible with you. You have created all things for your glory. You have called me to follow after you, to love you and to cling to you, for you are my life and every good thing I could ever desire is with you. You have instructed me to choose life and blessing so that I might live and prosper. Father, you said heaven and earth would bear record of the choices I make and would see to it that the blessings that are found only in your presence or the curses that are the result of your absence would be mine. I choose life today. Help me to always recognize what is of God and what is not. Help me choose what is righteous and good in your eyes so my family and I experience the blessings of living in your promises. I thank you for these things now in Jesus' name, Amen.

Proclamation:

I choose to follow after the Lord with all my heart. He has given me the power to choose what will fill my life. Life or death, blessing or cursing is mine for the choosing. I choose life and blessings because I choose to love the Lord my God and to seek after him.

Memory Verse: Mark 11:23

"For verily I say unto you, that whosoever shall say unto this mountain, Be removed, and be cast into the sea and shall not doubt in his heart, but shall believe that those things which he says shall come to pass, he shall have whatsoever he says."

To every family member: *"I love you; you are blessed, and you are a blessing."*
Don't forget the hugs.

April 4th

Scripture: James 1:16-20 (NLT)

"So don't be misled, my dear brothers and sisters. Whatever is good and perfect comes down to us from God our Father, who created all the lights in the heavens. He never changes or casts a shifting shadow. He chose to give birth to us by giving us his true word. And we, out of all creation, became his prized possession. Understand this, my dear brothers and sisters: You must all be quick to listen, slow to speak, and slow to get angry. Human anger does not produce the righteousness God desires."

In your prayer journal, identify in this portion of scripture a promise to receive or a command to obey.

Prayer:

Heavenly Father, with the power of your Word, you have created all things. You spoke and it was done. You declared a thing, and it was accomplished according to your good pleasure. All your works are good, for you only do that which is good and perfect and righteous. Thank you for your faithfulness. I can be sure you will always love me and treat me with love and mercy. Lord, you never change. Help me to walk in the knowledge of your love for me. I thank you for it now in Jesus' name, Amen.

Proclamation:

God is good, and his mercies endure forever. He will continually bless me with his goodness. Every good and perfect gift comes to me from my heavenly Father. He lavishes on me his goodness and calls me by name. He brings me out of darkness into his marvelous light. He satisfies my mouth with good things and watches over me for my good. I thank him for this wonderful grace that fills my life today.

Memory Verse: Mark 11:23

"For verily I say unto you, that whosoever shall say unto this mountain, Be removed, and be cast into the sea and shall not doubt in his heart, but shall believe that those things which he says shall come to pass, he shall have whatsoever he says."

To every family member: "I love you; you are blessed, and you are a blessing."
Don't forget the hugs.

April 5th

Scripture: Luke 6:46-49 (NASB)

"'Why do you call Me, "Lord, Lord," and do not do what I say? Everyone who comes to Me and hears My words and acts on them, I will show you whom he is like: he is like a man building a house, who dug deep and laid a foundation on the rock; and when a flood occurred, the torrent burst against that house and could not shake it, because it had been well built. But the one who has heard and has not acted *accordingly*, is like a man who built a house on the ground without any foundation; and the torrent burst against it and immediately it collapsed, and the ruin of that house was great.'"

In your prayer journal, identify in this portion of scripture a promise to receive or a command to obey.

Prayer:

Heavenly Father, Jesus is the Lord of my life, and because he is, I will hear and obey his Word. Jesus is the solid foundation upon which I can build my life. As I follow your Word, I am building my house, my life, upon that which is certain and everlasting. Help me to daily follow your Word by hearing, speaking and doing it so that I will stand steadfast and immovable on the foundation that never changes. Even if the storms of life are all around me I know the power of the Holy Spirit is working in me mightily. Thank you, my Lord, for your great grace is mine today, in Jesus' name I pray, Amen.

Proclamation:

The Word of the Lord is forever settled in Heaven. The Word of the Lord is a lamp to my feet and a light unto my pathway. God's Word is certain and true. The Word of God's power created everything and everything is sustained through the power of his Word. I stand upon that certain and unmovable foundation this day.

Memory Verse: Mark 11:23

"For verily I say unto you, that whosoever shall say unto this mountain, Be removed, and be cast into the sea and shall not doubt in his heart, but shall believe that those things which he says shall come to pass, he shall have whatsoever he says."

To every family member: "*I love you; you are blessed, and you are a blessing.*"
Don't forget the hugs.

April 6th

Scripture: Psalms 15 (MSG)

"God, who gets invited to dinner at your place? How do we get on your guest list? 'Walk straight, act right, tell the truth.' 'Don't hurt your friend, don't blame your neighbor; despise the despicable.' 'Keep your word even when it costs you, make an honest living, never take a bribe.' 'You'll never get blacklisted if you live like this.'"

In your prayer journal, identify in this portion of scripture a promise to receive or a command to obey.

Prayer:

God, my Father, I bless your holy name. I thank you for your goodness and mercy that is mine today. You invite me to come boldly into your presence. You set a place at your table for me to come and dine with you. You said I could eat of the fatness of your table and drink from the rivers of your pleasure. Father, I want to be like you. You made me in your image. Help me to act like you do, to be honest and truthful and to keep my word at all costs, for in doing these things, I show others who you are and what you are like so their hope and trust are in you. I ask you for these things this day, in Jesus' name, Amen.

Proclamation:

I honor the Lord with my words and in everything I do. I don't blame others or do things that would hurt or offend them. I give freely and help those in need. I speak the truth and stand behind my word. I please God with my faith, and I don't pretend to know everything or how to do anything apart from God. I am strong in the Lord and in the power of his might. I love God, and the divine favor of God rests on me today.

Memory Verse: Mark 11:23

"For verily I say unto you, that whosoever shall say unto this mountain, Be removed, and be cast into the sea and shall not doubt in his heart, but shall believe that those things which he says shall come to pass, he shall have whatsoever he says."

To every family member: *"I love you; you are blessed, and you are a blessing."*
Don't forget the hugs.

April 7th

Scripture: Luke 6:36-38 (PHILLIPS)

"'You must be merciful, as your father in Heaven is merciful.' 'Don't judge other people and you will not be judged yourselves. Don't condemn and you will not be condemned. Make allowances for others and people will make allowances for you. Give and men will give to you—yes, good measure, pressed down, shaken together and running over will they pour into your lap. For whatever measure you use with other people, they will use in their dealings with you.'"

In your prayer journal, identify in this portion of scripture
a promise to receive or a command to obey.

Prayer:

Father, you have forgiven me of all sin. You do not condemn me or judge me, but instead, you pour out your blessings upon me and fill my life with every good thing. I delight myself in you, for you give me the desires of my heart. Father, I receive from you now the grace I need to treat others like you treat me. As you have given to me abundantly, I give to others liberally. Help me to always notice those who need my help, to recognize those you have sent to me so I can be a blessing to them in your name. Father, I thank you for your promise that says, when I give to others it shall be given again to me and I will receive more than I gave. I see in your Word that, by this giving and receiving again with increase, I can always have enough to meet my own needs and to have more than enough to help meet the needs of others. I praise you for these things, in Jesus' name, Amen.

Proclamation:

I forgive because I have been forgiven. I will not judge or condemn others because God does not judge or condemn me. I do not know what is in the heart of another person because I only see the outside, but God looks in their heart. I give freely and abundantly to those in need and to those whom God directs me.

Memory Verse: Mark 11:23

"For verily I say unto you, that whosoever shall say unto this mountain, Be removed, and be cast into the sea and shall not doubt in his heart, but shall believe that those things which he says shall come to pass, he shall have whatsoever he says."

To every family member: *"I love you; you are blessed, and you are a blessing."*
Don't forget the hugs.

April 8th

Scripture: Hebrews 13:1-5 (PHILLIPS)

"Never let your brotherly love fail, nor refuse to extend your hospitality to strangers—sometimes men have entertained angels unawares. Think constantly of those in prison as if you were prisoners at their side. Think too of all who suffer as if you shared their pain. Both honourable marriage and chastity should be respected by all of you. God himself will judge those who traffic in the bodies of others or defile the relationship of marriage. Keep your lives free from the lust for money: be content with what you have. God has said: 'I will never leave you nor forsake you'."

In your prayer journal, identify in this portion of scripture a promise to receive or a command to obey.

Prayer:

Father, I rejoice in you this day. Your great love is poured out on me, and I am blessed more than I know how to express with words. You send me both people and angels to help me in times of need, and sometimes I may not be able to tell the difference. Show me how I can be hospitable to every one and remind me about those who are suffering in prison or pain so I will pray for them and bring a powerful effect in their lives and see them delivered, released and healed. Lord I desire to be honorable in everything I do, and in every relationship, I want to respect you by doing what is righteous and good in your eyes. Keep me from temptations of every kind. I trust you to preserve me and keep me because you have promised to never leave nor forsake me. I thank you for these things now in Jesus' name, Amen.

Proclamation:

All the resources of heaven are available to me today. The riches of glory and the host of angels will supply all I need and the power to accomplish the will of God. I am complete and whole, prosperous and blessed in all my ways.

Memory Verse: Mark 11:23

"For verily I say unto you, that whosoever shall say unto this mountain, Be removed, and be cast into the sea and shall not doubt in his heart, but shall believe that those things which he says shall come to pass, he shall have whatsoever he says."

To every family member: *"I love you; you are blessed, and you are a blessing."*
Don't forget the hugs.

April 9th

Scripture: Matthew 13:33-35 (KJV)

"Another parable spake he unto them; The kingdom of heaven is like unto leaven, which a woman took, and hid in three measures of meal, till the whole was leavened. All these things spake Jesus unto the multitude in parables; and without a parable spake he not unto them: That it might be fulfilled which was spoken by the prophet, saying, I will open my mouth in parables; I will utter things which have been kept secret from the foundation of the world."

In your prayer journal, identify in this portion of scripture a promise to receive or a command to obey.

Prayer:

Father, your kingdom is an everlasting kingdom, and your dominion reaches to the ends of the earth. You are above all, and all might and power belong to you. Your kingdom is hidden from many because it is not seen with physical eyes. Help me today to recognize and walk in your kingdom of righteousness, peace and joy in the Holy Spirit. Lord, my God, thank you for your promise that, as leaven permeates all it is put in, so your kingdom will fill all the earth. You said the kingdom of God is within me and because it is it will completely fill my life. I choose this day to submit myself to the Lord Jesus Christ, the king of the kingdom, and to the work of the Holy Spirit, who enlightens me and empowers me to do the work of the kingdom until the knowledge of your salvation covers all the earth. I believe the good work you have started in me will continue and be completed for your glory and my blessing. I thank you for these things in Jesus' name, Amen.

Proclamation:

I live in this world, but I am not of this world because I am a citizen of the kingdom of God. The kingdom of God is in me, and I live in the kingdom of righteousness, peace and joy in the Holy Spirit.

Memory Verse: Ephesians 6:10-11

"Finally, my brethren, be strong in the Lord, and in the power of his might. Put on the whole armor of God, that you may be able to stand against the wiles of the devil."

To every family member: *"I love you; you are blessed, and you are a blessing."* Don't forget the hugs.

April 10th

Scripture: 1 John 4:16-18 (NKJV)

"And we have known and believed the love that God has for us. God is love, and he who abides in love abides in God, and God in him. Love has been perfected among us in this: that we may have boldness in the day of judgment; because as He is, so are we in this world. There is no fear in love; but perfect love casts out fear, because fear involves torment. But he who fears has not been made perfect in love."

In your prayer journal, identify in this portion of scripture a promise to receive or a command to obey.

Prayer:

Heavenly Father, I thank you for your great love for me. Out of all the people in this world, you have revealed your love to me. You opened my heart to receive both forgiveness and righteousness. I thank you Lord Jesus for your great love that took the judgment for my sin upon the cross and carried my sin away, never again to be found. Lord, you have placed your love within me so I will never be afraid. I ask you today for boldness and strength to stand in the face of any opposition without fear. I will declare your Word over every situation in my life, for you are my God. You will help me and make me to be more than a conqueror. I praise you for your mighty work that works in me today. In Jesus' name I pray, Amen.

Proclamation:

I am the blessed of the Lord. He has forgiven me of all sin, and he has given me his righteousness. I will not fear, for God is with me. I am bold to declare the Word of the Lord because his Word endures forever.

Memory Verse: Ephesians 6:10-11

"Finally, my brethren, be strong in the Lord, and in the power of his might. Put on the whole armor of God, that you may be able to stand against the wiles of the devil."

To every family member: "I love you; you are blessed, and you are a blessing." Don't forget the hugs.

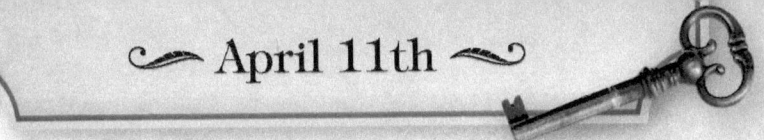

April 11th

Scripture: Psalms 81:13-16 (NIV)

"If my people would only listen to me, if Israel would only follow my ways, how quickly I would subdue their enemies and turn my hand against their foes! Those who hate the Lord would cringe before him and their punishment would last forever. But you would be fed with the finest of wheat; with honey from the rock I would satisfy you."

In your prayer journal, identify in this portion of scripture a promise to receive or a command to obey.

Prayer:

Father, I worship you and bless your holy name. I ask you to give me ears to hear your voice that I might follow after you with all my heart. You will subdue all my enemies by your power and might. You will cause me to walk in victory and dominion over every obstacle and adversary. Give me wisdom and strength to declare your Word with authority and see results that will bring honor to you according to your good pleasure. Thank you for every good thing that comes to me today in abundance. I am greatly blessed, for you hear and answer my prayers. Father, you give me power and authority to accomplish your will and to establish your kingdom. I call forth the will of God to be done today on earth, even as it is always done in heaven. I declare these things now in Jesus' name, Amen.

Proclamation:

Today I will follow after the Lord by seeking his ways and not my own. God subdues every enemy, every thought of condemnation, inferiority, fear and failure under my feet. I am blessed of the Lord. He satisfies my every need and fills my life with every good thing.

Memory Verse: Ephesians 6:10-11

"Finally, my brethren, be strong in the Lord, and in the power of his might. Put on the whole armor of God, that you may be able to stand against the wiles of the devil."

To every family member: *"I love you; you are blessed, and you are a blessing."*
Don't forget the hugs.

April 12th

Scripture: Romans 8:31-35 (VOICE)

"So what should we say about all of this? If God is on our side, *then tell me*: whom should we fear? If He did not spare His own Son, but handed Him over on our account, then *don't you think that* He will graciously give us all things with Him? Can anyone be so bold as to level a charge against God's chosen? *Especially since* God's "*not guilty*" verdict is already declared. Who has the authority to condemn? Jesus the Anointed who died, but *more importantly, conquered death when He* was raised to sit at the right hand of God where He pleads on our behalf. So who can separate us? What can come between us and the love of God's Anointed? Can troubles, hardships, persecution, hunger, poverty, danger, or even death? *The answer is, absolutely nothing.*"

In your prayer journal, identify in this portion of scripture a promise to receive or a command to obey.

Prayer:

My Father, your love for me is greater than I can imagine. You have forgiven me of all sin and given me everything. You have declared me "not guilty" and you refuse to consider any accusation against me. You gave your Son Jesus to carry my guilt far away on the cross. You gave him victory over death, and now he gives me his victory and lives in your presence to represent me before your throne. I thank you that no enemy will defeat me and no opposition or trouble will ever cause you to give up on me. Help me to walk in the confidence of your great love. Help me to stand boldly in the face of all adversity because, if you are for me and you are with me, nothing can ever harm me. I give you thanks for these things, in Jesus' name, Amen.

Proclamation:

I am greatly loved by God. He has done a work for me and is doing a work in me. He daily loads me down with his blessings and his kindness never ends.

Memory Verse: Ephesians 6:10-11

"Finally, my brethren, be strong in the Lord, and in the power of his might. Put on the whole armor of God, that you may be able to stand against the wiles of the devil."

To every family member: "*I love you; you are blessed, and you are a blessing.*"
Don't forget the hugs.

April 13th

Scripture: Proverbs 3:21-26 (MSG)

"Dear friend, guard Clear Thinking and Common Sense with your life; don't for a minute lose sight of them. They'll keep your soul alive and well, they'll keep you fit and attractive. You'll travel safely, you'll neither tire nor trip. You'll take afternoon naps without a worry, you'll enjoy a good night's sleep. No need to panic over alarms or surprises, or predictions that doomsday's just around the corner, because God will be right there with you; He'll keep you safe and sound."

In your prayer journal, identify in this portion of scripture a promise to receive or a command to obey.

Prayer:

Father, you have not given me a spirit of fear, but you have given me love, peace and a sound mind. I ask you to establish my thoughts and my plans so I will honor you in all my ways and walk in success in everything I do today. Your grace is sufficient for me today. You strengthen me with your power and you grant me your wisdom so I can make wise choices and righteous decisions that will bring me good results. Your presence will keep me from all worry and fear and I will walk in the knowledge of your will. Help me to recognize the devil's devices that would draw my attention away from you. I will walk in confidence, knowing the promises you give me in your Word. Help me to live in your peace so that peace will be what rules in my heart. I receive these things now, in Jesus' name, Amen.

Proclamation:

I will not be confused or troubled, fearing what someone might say or do to me. God is my strength. He abides with me, and the anointing of God is on me to teach me what I need to know and to lead me in the way I should go.

Memory Verse: Ephesians 6:10-11

"Finally, my brethren, be strong in the Lord, and in the power of his might. Put on the whole armor of God, that you may be able to stand against the wiles of the devil."

To every family member: *"I love you; you are blessed, and you are a blessing."*
Don't forget the hugs.

April 14th

Scripture: Romans 8:5-9 (NLV)

"Those who let their sinful old selves tell them what to do live under that power of their sinful old selves. But those who let the Holy Spirit tell them what to do are under His power. If your sinful old self is the boss over your mind, it leads to death. But if the Holy Spirit is the boss over your mind, it leads to life and peace. The mind that thinks only of ways to please the sinful old self is fighting against God. It is not able to obey God's Laws. It never can. Those who do what their sinful old selves want to do cannot please God."

In your prayer journal, identify in this portion of scripture a promise to receive or a command to obey.

Prayer:

Heavenly Father, you have set me free from the power of sin. You have delivered me from the realm of darkness and brought me into your kingdom. I praise you for your marvelous love and the work you have done in me, giving me new life. By your grace, I will no longer walk according to my old way of thinking, but according to the Word of God and the leading of the Holy Spirit who lives in me. Help me to renew my mind so my thoughts line up with your Word. You said your Word is truth and if I know the truth it will set me free from lies and deception. I know things are not always as they appear to be. I trust you to show me how things really are. Lord give me an understanding heart and wisdom to do the things that please you. In Jesus' name I pray, Amen.

Proclamation:

I do not make decisions and come to conclusions based on what I see and the way I feel. I am not ruled by my flesh and senses. I am not limited by the world's systems of getting things done. God is my helper. His Word gives me answers and his Spirit leads me into all truth.

Memory Verse: Ephesians 6:10-11

"Finally, my brethren, be strong in the Lord, and in the power of his might. Put on the whole armor of God, that you may be able to stand against the wiles of the devil."

To every family member: *"I love you; you are blessed, and you are a blessing."*
Don't forget the hugs.

April 15th

Scripture: Ephesians 2:8-10 (NLT)

"God saved you by his grace when you believed. And you can't take credit for this; it is a gift from God. Salvation is not a reward for the good things we have done, so none of us can boast about it. For we are God's masterpiece. He has created us anew in Christ Jesus, so we can do the good things he planned for us long ago."

In your prayer journal, identify in this portion of scripture a promise to receive or a command to obey.

Prayer:

Lord, you are great, and all praise and glory belong to you. You are above all. I worship you this day. I thank you for this great salvation you have given me. My sins are forgiven, and you have made me a brand new person that never existed before I came to Jesus. You have done a work in me because you love me. I ask you, Father, to help me to accomplish today the works you have before ordained for me to do. Make me fruitful in every good work. Prosper me, and bless the works of my hands, and cause my thoughts to be ordered by you so at the end of this day my works would bring pleasure to you and others know of your greatness. I ask these things now, in Jesus' name, Amen.

Proclamation:

I am a new creation in the Lord Jesus Christ. On the day I was born-again, I received a new life. Beginning that day, I had no more history than a brand new baby has. My old life is gone, and I walk in a new life in a relationship with God I never knew before. I have abundant life, and joy beyond measure. I am truly blessed of the Lord.

Memory Verse: Ephesians 6:10-11

"Finally, my brethren, be strong in the Lord, and in the power of his might. Put on the whole armor of God, that you may be able to stand against the wiles of the devil."

To every family member: *"I love you; you are blessed, and you are a blessing."*
Don't forget the hugs.

April 16th

Scripture: Matthew 5:13-16 (NCV)

"You are the salt of the earth. But if the salt loses its salty taste, it cannot be made salty again. It is good for nothing, except to be thrown out and walked on. You are the light that gives light to the world. A city that is built on a hill cannot be hidden. And people don't hide a light under a bowl. They put it on a lampstand so the light shines for all the people in the house. In the same way, you should be a light for other people. Live so that they will see the good things you do and will praise your Father in heaven."

In your prayer journal, identify in this portion of scripture a promise to receive or a command to obey.

Prayer:

Heavenly Father, you have made me in your image and likeness. I pray I will glorify you by what I say and what I do. As light reveals what would otherwise be hidden in the dark, let my life bring revelation to others of the goodness and grace of God. May your glory shine through me today. As a city that is situated on a high hill is easy to see, help me reveal to the world who God is and what you are like as you reveal yourself through me. You said I am to go in your name and do your works so people see who you are and put their trust in you. I thank you for the power and the life of the Holy Spirit who abides in me and empowers me to shine in such a way that many would believe. I ask this now in Jesus' name, Amen.

Proclamation:

In God there is light, and in him there is no darkness at all. Everything God does is good. He is the Father of lights, and every good and perfect gift comes from him. He has revealed his light in the life of the Lord Jesus Christ. I will arise and shine, for my light has come and the glory of God has risen upon me.

Memory Verse: Philippians 4:6-7

"Be anxious for nothing, but in everything by prayer and supplication, with thanksgiving, let your requests be made known to God; and the peace of God, which surpasses all understanding, will guard your hearts and minds through Christ Jesus."

To every family member: "I love you; you are blessed, and you are a blessing."
Don't forget the hugs.

April 17th

Scripture: Jeremiah 17:5-8 (NIV)

"This is what the Lord says: 'Cursed is the one who trusts in man, who draws strength from mere flesh and whose heart turns away from the Lord. That person will be like a bush in the wastelands; they will not see prosperity when it comes. They will dwell in the parched places of the desert, in a salt land where no one lives. But blessed is the one who trusts in the Lord, whose confidence is in him. They will be like a tree planted by the water that sends out its roots by the stream. It does not fear when heat comes; its leaves are always green. It has no worries in a year of drought and never fails to bear fruit.'"

In your prayer journal, identify in this portion of scripture a promise to receive or a command to obey.

Prayer:

Father, I put my trust in you. My confidence is not in man but in the living God who freely gives me all things. I will not live in empty, fruitless places but instead I will prosper, abound in the blessings of the Lord. You supply all I need. Even in times of lack, I have abundance. You make me like a tree planted by the river that is continuously supplied and always stays green. You said poverty, want and lack are the results of the curse that is in the earth because of sin. I thank you that Jesus paid the price for my sin and has delivered me from the curse. He became accursed for me on the cross so that I might receive the blessings of God. I thank you Father that I live free of worry and fear because my confidence is in you. I praise you for your blessings shown to me today in Jesus' name, Amen.

Proclamation:

I dwell in the blessings of God. My trust is in him because I know God loves me and he will provide for all my need. He will prosper me and make me fruitful and satisfied with every good thing. I am greatly blessed of the Lord.

Memory Verse: Philippians 4:6-7

"Be anxious for nothing, but in everything by prayer and supplication, with thanksgiving, let your requests be made known to God; and the peace of God, which surpasses all understanding, will guard your hearts and minds through Christ Jesus."

To every family member: *"I love you; you are blessed, and you are a blessing."*
Don't forget the hugs.

April 18th

Scripture: Matthew 6:31-34 (PHILLIPS)

"So don't worry and don't keep saying, 'What shall we eat, what shall we drink or what shall we wear?! That is what pagans are always looking for; your Heavenly Father knows that you need them all. Set your heart on the kingdom and his goodness, and all these things will come to you as a matter of course. "Don't worry at all then about tomorrow. Tomorrow can take care of itself! One day's trouble is enough for one day."

In your prayer journal, identify in this portion of scripture
a promise to receive or a command to obey.

Prayer:

Lord, my God, I praise you today, for you are the source of all my supply. Whatever I need you will give me, for my trust is in you. Help me to seek the Kingdom of God above all else. Keep me from being distracted by the things in the world that trouble so many people. I would seek what is right and good in your eyes, and because I do, your peace will rule in my life and over my mind. My clothes will be finer than Solomon's, and my food will be abundant, for you watch over me and take care of me, so I will not fear shortage, famine, war or trouble. You are more than enough; you are the Lord God Almighty, and you are my God, and there is nothing impossible with you. I praise you for all these things in Jesus' name, Amen.

Proclamation:

The name of the Lord is above all names. He is my life, and he is my help. He takes care of me and causes me to live with a joyful anticipation of his presence and power working in me today.

Memory Verse: Philippians 4:6-7

"Be anxious for nothing, but in everything by prayer and supplication, with thanksgiving, let your requests be made known to God; and the peace of God, which surpasses all understanding, will guard your hearts and minds through Christ Jesus."

To every family member: "I love you; you are blessed, and you are a blessing."
Don't forget the hugs.

April 19th

Scripture: Psalms 91:9-14 (MSG)

"Yes, because God's your refuge, the High God your very own home, evil can't get close to you, harm can't get through the door. He ordered his angels to guard you wherever you go. If you stumble, they'll catch you; their job is to keep you from falling. You'll walk unharmed among lions and snakes and kick young lions and serpents from the path. 'If you'll hold on to me for dear life,' says God, 'I'll get you out of any trouble. I'll give you the best of care if you'll only get to know and trust me.'"

In your prayer journal, identify in this portion of scripture a promise to receive or a command to obey.

Prayer:

Heavenly Father, you are my refuge and strength. You keep me from all harm. I thank you for your Word that declares that the angels of God have been sent to me to protect and to preserve me. I am sheltered from all harm in your presence. Cause me to recognize your presence and help me to run to you in times of trouble. Father, I want to know you so I will trust you fully. I call upon you, and you said you would answer me and be with me in times of trouble and would deliver me and honor me and with long life you would satisfy me and show me your salvation. I thank you for hearing me and answering me now in Jesus' name, Amen.

Proclamation:

I have set my love upon the Lord, and he keeps me from all trouble. No weapon of the enemy can defeat me, and no evil work can conquer me. For God lifts me up out of the reach of the adversary and keeps me safe in his presence.

Memory Verse: Philippians 4:6-7

"Be anxious for nothing, but in everything by prayer and supplication, with thanksgiving, let your requests be made known to God; and the peace of God, which surpasses all understanding, will guard your hearts and minds through Christ Jesus."

To every family member: *"I love you; you are blessed, and you are a blessing."*
Don't forget the hugs.

April 20th

Scripture: Romans 12:1-2 (NASB)

"Therefore I urge you, brethren, by the mercies of God, to present your bodies a living and holy sacrifice, acceptable to God, which is your spiritual service of worship. And do not be conformed to this world, but be transformed by the renewing of your mind, so that you may prove what the will of God is, that which is good and acceptable and perfect."

In your prayer journal, identify in this portion of scripture a promise to receive or a command to obey.

Prayer:

Father, it is my desire to please you and to follow you by obeying your Word. I present my body to you today as a living sacrifice. I yield my members to the will of God, refusing to allow my body to rule me and do what is comfortable and enjoyable to the flesh instead of doing what pleases God. My body is the temple of the Holy Spirit who lives in me. Help me to honor you by the things I do and to never grieve the Spirit of God. I will renew my mind by the Word of God so I will always be able to recognize the will of God. Your Word will teach me what is good and what is acceptable and pleasing to you. You said the good work you have started in me you would continue until the day I see Jesus face to face. Help me today to be willing to perform your will and your good pleasure. I believe you are at work within me bringing these things to pass, and I thank you for that good work in Jesus' name, Amen.

Proclamation:

The Word of God is working mightily in me to renew my mind to think thoughts that are in line with God's will. This same Word will strengthen me in my inner man so I will not follow after the lusts of my flesh but after those things that please God and bring honor to him.

Memory Verse: Philippians 4:6-7

"Be anxious for nothing, but in everything by prayer and supplication, with thanksgiving, let your requests be made known to God; and the peace of God, which surpasses all understanding, will guard your hearts and minds through Christ Jesus."

To every family member: *"I love you; you are blessed, and you are a blessing."*
Don't forget the hugs.

April 21st

Scripture: Proverbs 11:24-25 (NASB)

"Some give freely, yet grow all the richer; others withhold what is due, and only suffer want. A generous person will be enriched and one who gives water will get water."

In your prayer journal, identify in this portion of scripture a promise to receive or a command to obey.

Prayer:

Father, you teach us in your Word the spiritual laws of giving and receiving. You said whatever any one gives is what the giver will receive again and it will be returned in a measure that far exceeds what was given. It is my joy to honor you with my money and with my possessions by giving to others when they have a need. I know that everything I have has come from you. You are the creator and the owner of everything. You said the silver is yours and the gold is also yours. Anything I give to anyone has come from you. I trust you today with my finances. I will honor you by giving to others as you direct me. I thank you for the promises you have given me. You promised to bless me and multiply what I have given and to cause me to increase and be fruitful in every good work. The devourer will not eat up my crops or steal my increase, but I will walk in the blessings of the Lord, always having enough to meet my own needs and to give to every good work. I thank you for this promise now, in Jesus' name, Amen.

Proclamation:

The blessing of the Lord makes me rich and adds no sorrow with it. I am blessed in all my ways, and I increase from day to day. I give liberally and without reservation and the Lord multiplies what I have given and returns it again unto me, good measure, pressed down, shaken together and running over.

Memory Verse: Philippians 4:6-7

"Be anxious for nothing, but in everything by prayer and supplication, with thanksgiving, let your requests be made known to God; and the peace of God, which surpasses all understanding, will guard your hearts and minds through Christ Jesus."

To every family member: *"I love you; you are blessed, and you are a blessing."*
Don't forget the hugs.

April 22nd

Scripture: Luke 4:16-21 (NIV)

"He went to Nazareth, where he had been brought up, and on the Sabbath day he went into the synagogue, as was his custom. He stood up to read, and the scroll of the prophet Isaiah was handed to him. Unrolling it, he found the place where it is written: 'The Spirit of the Lord is on me, because he has anointed me to proclaim good news to the poor. He has sent me to proclaim freedom for the prisoners and recovery of sight for the blind, to set the oppressed free, to proclaim the year of the Lord's favor.' Then he rolled up the scroll, gave it back to the attendant and sat down. The eyes of everyone in the synagogue were fastened on him. He began by saying to them, 'Today this scripture is fulfilled in your hearing.'"

In your prayer journal, identify in this portion of scripture a promise to receive or a command to obey.

Prayer:

Heavenly Father, I worship you and praise your holy name. I thank you for the things Jesus accomplished for me. I have heard the good news that my sins are forgiven. I am no longer a prisoner to sin. You have given me spiritual sight to see and understand things that cannot be seen with only physical eyes. I am free from oppression and fear. I receive the promise of the jubilee that Jesus purchased for me. Thank you for my inheritance of the kingdom of God to bring me righteousness, peace and joy that comes by the Holy Spirit. I am greatly blessed today, walking in the fulfilled promises of the Lord. The work is finished, and I have entered into a new realm of spiritual life you have given me. Help me to continue to increase in wisdom and understanding of all the wonderful things Jesus has done for me. I praise you now, in Jesus' name, Amen.

Proclamation:

Jesus lived a perfect and sinless life in order to give me his righteousness. Jesus died, taking the judgment for my sin and the resulting curse so I can live free of guilt, shame and the power of death.

Memory Verse: Philippians 4:6-7

"Be anxious for nothing, but in everything by prayer and supplication, with thanksgiving, let your requests be made known to God; and the peace of God, which surpasses all understanding, will guard your hearts and minds through Christ Jesus."

To every family member: "*I love you; you are blessed, and you are a blessing.*"
Don't forget the hugs.

April 23rd

Scripture: 1 John 4:3-6 (NKJV)

"And every spirit that does not confess that Jesus Christ has come in the flesh is not of God. And this is the *spirit* of the Antichrist, which you have heard was coming, and is now already in the world. You are of God, little children, and have overcome them, because He who is in you is greater than he who is in the world. They are of the world. Therefore they speak *as* of the world, and the world hears them. We are of God. He who knows God hears us; he who is not of God does not hear us. By this we know the spirit of truth and the spirit of error."

In your prayer journal, identify in this portion of scripture a promise to receive or a command to obey.

Prayer:

My Father, I am so thankful for the Spirit of God who abides in me and teaches me the truth. He keeps me from deception and reveals the things of God to me. I will not be deceived because greater is the one who lives in me than the spirit of antichrist that is in the world. Father, give me ears to hear what the Spirit of God says to me and cause me to recognize the things that are true, as well as things that are not true. Help me know what is of God so I will follow after every Word of God. You said you are the Good Shepherd and your sheep hear your voice and follow after you and will not follow the voice of the stranger. I pray for wisdom and understanding to measure everything I hear with the Word of God so my path is straight and I am not led astray. Thank you for making my way plain. I pray in Jesus' name, Amen.

Proclamation:

I do not live according to the most popular trends or persuasive arguments of man, but I live by every Word that proceeds from the mouth of God.

Memory Verse: Jude 1:24-25

"Now unto him that is able to keep you from falling, and to present you faultless before the presence of his glory with exceeding joy, to the only wise God our Savior, be glory and majesty, dominion and power, both now and forever. Amen."

To every family member: *"I love you; you are blessed, and you are a blessing."*
Don't forget the hugs.

April 24th

Scripture: Mark 11:22-24 (NKJV)

"So Jesus answered and said to them, 'Have faith in God. For assuredly, I say to you, whoever says to this mountain, "Be removed and be cast into the sea," and does not doubt in his heart, but believes that those things he says will be done, he will have whatever he says. Therefore I say to you, whatever things you ask when you pray, believe that you receive *them*, and you will have *them*.'"

In your prayer journal, identify in this portion of scripture a promise to receive or a command to obey.

Prayer:

Thank you, Father, for the Word of God that teaches me and reveals to me the power of prayer. You said whatever I ask for in prayer believing I "will" receive. You said the effective, fervent prayer of the righteous has great force and power. I do not pray ignorantly. I pray according to your will. Therefore, I call forth the kingdom of God to come and the will of God to be done on earth just as your will is always done in heaven. I speak to every mountain of opposition and command it to move out of my way so the will of God can be performed in my life. I speak to sickness and disease, poverty and fear and all of the devices of the enemy, and I command them to cease their work, for they have no power or might over me. I am more than a conqueror in Christ Jesus, and I have dominion over every wicked work and command it to get under my feet. Jesus is my Lord, therefore, I will not be defeated. In Jesus' name, Amen.

Proclamation:

I do not fight against people, but against spiritual works of darkness. Jesus destroyed the works of the devil, and in the name of Jesus, I will always succeed.

Memory Verse: Jude 1:24-25

"Now unto him that is able to keep you from falling, and to present you faultless before the presence of his glory with exceeding joy, to the only wise God our Savior, be glory and majesty, dominion and power, both now and forever. Amen."

To every family member: "*I love you; you are blessed, and you are a blessing.*"
Don't forget the hugs.

April 25th

Scripture: 1 John 4:7-13 (NLV)

"Dear friends, let us love each other, because love comes from God. Those who love are God's children and they know God. Those who do not love do not know God because God is love. God has shown His love to us by sending His only Son into the world. God did this so we might have life through Christ. This is love! It is not that we loved God but that He loved us. For God sent His Son to pay for our sins with His own blood. Dear friends, if God loved us that much, then we should love each other. No person has ever seen God at any time. If we love each other, God lives in us. His love is made perfect in us. He has given us His Spirit. This is how we live by His help and He lives in us."

In your prayer journal, identify in this portion of scripture a promise to receive or a command to obey.

Prayer:

Father, your love lives in me by the Holy Spirit. Thank you for loving me. I ask you to continue to reveal your love to me so I respond to all those I meet today with the love of God. Just as Jesus was moved by compassion and healed the sick and provided for those in need, help me to remain tenderhearted and compassionate. Faith works by love, and I desire to be filled with faith that I might do the works of God. Father, you said that without faith it is impossible to please you; therefore, I thank you for the power of your love that never fails and the works of faith that your love produces. May the works of love be demonstrated in me today so you are revealed to the world. I pray in Jesus' name, Amen.

Proclamation:

The love of God abounds in me more and more day by day. His love motivates me and guides me to speak his Word, to do his works and to glorify the Lord.

Memory Verse: Jude 1:24-25

"Now unto him that is able to keep you from falling, and to present you faultless before the presence of his glory with exceeding joy, to the only wise God our Savior, be glory and majesty, dominion and power, both now and forever. Amen."

To every family member: *"I love you; you are blessed, and you are a blessing."*
Don't forget the hugs.

April 26th

Scripture: Psalms 23:1-6 (NIV)

"The Lord is my shepherd, I lack nothing. He makes me lie down in green pastures, he leads me beside quiet waters, he refreshes my soul. He guides me along the right paths for his name's sake. Even though I walk through the darkest valley, I will fear no evil, for you are with me; your rod and your staff, they comfort me. You prepare a table before me in the presence of my enemies. You anoint my head with oil; my cup overflows. Surely your goodness and love will follow me all the days of my life and I will dwell in the house of the Lord forever."

In your prayer journal, identify in this portion of scripture a promise to receive or a command to obey.

Prayer:

God, my Father, you are faithful to watch over me and keep and protect me from all harm. You supply all my needs and cause me to be refreshed in your presence. Thank you for preserving me from every evil work. You defend and protect me from the devices of the enemy. You have not given me the spirit of fear, but you have given me the Spirit of God who reveals to me what you have freely given me. I rejoice in your mercy. I celebrate your goodness because your love and mercy chase me down and overtake me. I thank you for your amazing grace that is at work in me today, adjusting me, equipping me and preparing me for every good work. Bless the work of my hands, and may the meditation of my heart be pleasing to you, I pray in Jesus' name, Amen.

Proclamation:

I celebrate the goodness of God. I will bless his name, for he is good and his mercies endure forever. He is my fortress and my strong tower. I run into the safety of his presence and dwell in the secret place of his love.

Memory Verse: Jude 1:24-25

"Now unto him that is able to keep you from falling, and to present you faultless before the presence of his glory with exceeding joy, to the only wise God our Savior, be glory and majesty, dominion and power, both now and forever. Amen."

To every family member: *"I love you; you are blessed, and you are a blessing."*
Don't forget the hugs.

April 27th

Scripture: Lamentations 3:22-26 (KJV)

"It is of the Lord's mercies that we are not consumed, because his compassions fail not. They are new every morning: great is thy faithfulness. The Lord is my portion, saith my soul; therefore will I hope in him. The Lord is good unto them that wait for him, to the soul that seeketh him. It is good that a man should both hope and quietly wait for the salvation of the Lord."

In your prayer journal, identify in this portion of scripture a promise to receive or a command to obey.

Prayer:

Father, I purpose today to draw aside from the busyness of my day to come into the secret place of your presence and wait to hear your voice. I will seek after you today. You are my portion, my life and my hope is in you. You will show me your salvation and I will rejoice in you. Thank you, Lord, for your faithfulness. When I call upon you, you answer me and show me great and mighty things. You hear my prayer, and your Word declares that if you hear me I can be certain that I have the petitions I have desired. As I boldly declare your Word today, you will watch over it and quickly perform it because you are faithful, and the spoken Word of God will accomplish what it was sent to do, and it will prosper in its purpose. I will humble myself under your mighty hand and worship you for you are worthy. Thank you for hearing me and helping me live beyond my physical senses to abide in your glorious presence. In Jesus' name I pray, Amen.

Proclamation:

I am not limited to what I can see and hear and how I feel. I live in this world, but I am not of this world because the kingdom of God lives in me. It is my Father's good pleasure to give me the kingdom. I eat of the fatness of his table and drink of the river of his pleasures. I am blessed of the Lord.

Memory Verse: Jude 1:24-25

"Now unto him that is able to keep you from falling, and to present you faultless before the presence of his glory with exceeding joy, to the only wise God our Savior, be glory and majesty, dominion and power, both now and forever. Amen."

To every family member: *"I love you; you are blessed, and you are a blessing."*
Don't forget the hugs.

April 28th

Scripture: Romans 15:4-6 (HCSB)

"For whatever was written in the past was written for our instruction, so that we may have hope through endurance and through the encouragement from the Scriptures. Now may the God who gives endurance and encouragement allow you to live in harmony with one another, according to the command of Christ Jesus, so that you may glorify the God and Father of our Lord Jesus Christ with a united mind and voice."

In your prayer journal, identify in this portion of scripture a promise to receive or a command to obey.

Prayer:

Father, I thank you for the power of the Spirit of God who lives in me. You have not left me alone, but you sent the Holy Spirit to abide with me forever. I do not live by my own wisdom or strength but by the power of the Spirit and the knowledge of your Word. Reveal to me the things you have prepared for those who love you and seek to know you. Help all of us who are called by your name to live in agreement, loving one another and honoring one another that we would be of one mind and with one voice glorify you. As the scriptures revealed your power and faithfulness to previous generations, help us to demonstrate to our generation that you are the same today as you were in times past. Father, I ask you to do mighty works and show this generation your mighty power. Glorify your great name through your church, I pray in Jesus' name, Amen.

Proclamation:

Jesus is the same yesterday, today and forever. The works he did in days past, he will do today. Jesus was moved with compassion and healed the sick and set free the oppressed. The same compassion moves him today to touch this generation with his love and power.

Memory Verse: Jude 1:24-25

"Now unto him that is able to keep you from falling, and to present you faultless before the presence of his glory with exceeding joy, to the only wise God our Savior, be glory and majesty, dominion and power, both now and forever. Amen."

To every family member: *"I love you; you are blessed, and you are a blessing."*
Don't forget the hugs.

April 29th

Scripture: Galatians 6:7-9 (RSV)

"Do not be deceived; God is not mocked, for whatever a man sows, that he will also reap. For he who sows to his own flesh will from the flesh reap corruption; but he who sows to the Spirit will from the Spirit reap eternal life. And let us not grow weary in well-doing, for in due season we shall reap, if we do not lose heart. So then, as we have opportunity, let us do good to all men, and especially to those who are of the household of faith."

In your prayer journal, identify in this portion of scripture a promise to receive or a command to obey.

Prayer:

Heavenly Father, I pray for the kind of strength that will cause me to be strong in the Lord and in the power of his might. I pray that I will take hold of the Word of God by faith. Keep me from growing weary in well doing so I will not faint and give up when the harvest seems far away. Your unchangeable Word declares that I will reap as I have sown so the promise of harvest is sure. Help me to sow to the spirit and not to the things of the flesh. I do not want to reap that which is corrupt but that which brings life and life more abundantly. Help me to sow the seed of the incorruptible Word of God, to proclaim what you have said, because if you have spoken it you will bring it to pass. Your Word will not return to you empty or powerless, but it will accomplish its purpose. Whatever I give shall be given again unto me. Cause me to be aware of the needs of those about me so I can sow into their lives what you have given me, and as I do, I know it shall be given back to me good measure, pressed down, shaken together and running over. I thank you for these things now, in Jesus' name, Amen.

Proclamation:

I have purposed to sow into the lives of others words of encouragement, kindness, mercy, finances and faith. I will reap in due season.

Memory Verse: Jude 1:24-25

"Now unto him that is able to keep you from falling, and to present you faultless before the presence of his glory with exceeding joy, to the only wise God our Savior, be glory and majesty, dominion and power, both now and forever. Amen."

To every family member: "I love you; you are blessed, and you are a blessing." Don't forget the hugs.

April 30th

Scripture: 2 Timothy 3:16-17 (NKJV)

"All Scripture *is* given by inspiration of God, and *is* profitable for doctrine, for reproof, for correction, for instruction in righteousness, that the man of God may be complete, thoroughly equipped for every good work."

In your prayer journal, identify in this portion of scripture a promise to receive or a command to obey.

Prayer:

My Heavenly Father, your Word is forever settled in heaven. I pray you will help me keep your Word in my heart. I will not allow the devil to steal it away from me. I will treat it as a valuable treasure that is able to save my soul. I want to be equipped and prepared for every work you would have me to do. Your Word will comfort me and teach me, correct me and instruct me so I will walk in righteousness. I pray the Spirit of God will constantly remind me of the Word of God and reveal to me those wonderful truths that will transform my thinking so I will know and do your will. I ask you to give me ears to hear what the Word of God is saying to me today and cause it to be engraved upon my heart that I might always glorify you and be fruitful and prosperous in all I do. In Jesus' name I pray, Amen.

Proclamation:

The Word of God is able to build us up and to give us an inheritance. The Word of God is the power of God unto salvation. The Word of God is mighty, and when I pray the Word of God, I am calling forth the will of God to be done. I treasure the Word of God more than my daily food, and it feeds me and strengthens me and causes me to prosper and triumph in every good work.

Memory Verse: 1 John 4:4

"You are of God, little children, and have overcome them because greater is he that is in you than he that is in the world."

To every family member: *"I love you; you are blessed, and you are a blessing."*
Don't forget the hugs.

May 1st

Scripture: Zephaniah 3:17 (NRSV)

"The Lord, your God, is in your midst, a warrior who gives victory; he will rejoice over you with gladness, he will renew you in his love; he will exult over you with loud singing."

In your prayer journal, identify in this portion of scripture a promise to receive or a command to obey.

Prayer:

My Father, I praise your holy name. You have defeated all my enemies and given me victory. You shout for gladness and sing over me with songs of joy because you delight in me. This is a day of great blessing. This is a day of great joy because you take pleasure in my safety and in my success. You will not leave me alone or without help. I thank you for your favor and anointing that rests on me today. Father, give me wisdom and understanding that I might truly know you and how much you delight in me. It is in the name of my Lord Jesus I pray, Amen.

Proclamation:

I am accepted in God's beloved. I am greatly loved by God. He has freely given to me the kingdom of God, which abides within me. I am the apple of his eye and one he so delights in that he sings out loud with joy and rejoices over me. My God takes pleasure in my success and prosperity. He will continually reveal to me his great love and the wonderful things he has prepared for me because I love him.

Memory Verse: 1 John 4:4

"You are of God, little children, and have overcome them because greater is he that is in you than he that is in the world."

To every family member: *"I love you; you are blessed, and you are a blessing."* Don't forget the hugs.

May 2nd

Scripture: Acts 26:15-18 (PHILLIPS)

"'Who are you, Lord?' I said. And the Lord said to me, 'I am Jesus whom you are persecuting. Now get up and stand on your feet for I have shown myself to you for a reason—you are chosen to be my servant and a witness to what you have seen of me today, and of other visions of myself which I will give you. I will keep you safe from both your own people and from the Gentiles to whom I now send you. I send you to open their eyes, to turn them from darkness to light, from the power of Satan to God himself, so that they may know forgiveness of their sins and take their place with all those who are made holy by their faith in me.'"

In your prayer journal, identify in this portion of scripture a promise to receive or a command to obey.

Prayer:

Heavenly Father, reveal yourself to me today so I have a clear vision of your call and purpose for my life. Open my spiritual eyes so I will see that you have brought me out of darkness and into your marvelous light. You, Lord, have delivered me from the power of Satan and have brought me into your kingdom. Thank you for forgiving me of all sin and giving to me a place in your presence with all those who have put their trust in you. By faith I take hold of all those things that are a part of my inheritance that you have given me in Christ Jesus. I thank you for supplying all my needs and giving me both favor and wisdom and the skillful abilities I need to accomplish all of your will for me. I thank you for these things now in Jesus' name, Amen.

Proclamation:

With God nothing is impossible. God is able to accomplish anything and everything. There is no good thing he will withhold from those who walk uprightly before him.

Memory Verse: 1 John 4:4

"You are of God, little children, and have overcome them because greater is he that is in you than he that is in the world."

To every family member: "I love you; you are blessed, and you are a blessing." Don't forget the hugs.

May 3rd

Scripture: 1 Peter 4:10-11 (EXB)

"Each of you has received a gift to use to serve others. Be good servants [stewards; managers] of God's various gifts of grace. Anyone who speaks should speak words from God [or oracles from God; or as one bringing God's message]. Anyone who serves should serve with the strength God gives so that in everything God will be praised [glorified] through Jesus Christ. Glory and power belong to him forever and ever. Amen."

In your prayer journal, identify in this portion of scripture a promise to receive or a command to obey.

Prayer:

My Father, I know by your Word that you have given me gifts. The anointing of the Holy Spirit rests upon me to empower me to use these gifts for the blessing and benefit of others. You have deposited within me gifts and talents and skillful abilities to be used for your glory and for the blessing of many. Help me to recognize what you have given me and to become skillful in using these gifts. My time is not my own, and what you have given me, I will not withhold from others. I will not despise what you have given me or treat it as small or insignificant. Help me to function in the Body of Christ, as you have carefully and purposefully placed me as a vital member of your Church. I thank you that the good work you have begun in me you will continue so I will be fruitful in every good work that will bring praise to you. In Jesus' name I pray, Amen.

Proclamation:

I will not neglect the gift of God within me. I am a vital member of the Body of Christ, and the Spirit of God rests upon me to do and to accomplish his good pleasure.

Memory Verse: 1 John 4:4

"You are of God, little children, and have overcome them because greater is he that is in you than he that is in the world."

To every family member: *"I love you; you are blessed, and you are a blessing."*
Don't forget the hugs.

May 4th

Scripture: Colossians 3:1-3 (NKJV)

"If then you were raised with Christ, seek those things which are above, where Christ is, sitting at the right hand of God. Set your mind on things above, not on things on the earth. For you died, and your life is hidden with Christ in God. When Christ *who is* our life appears, then you also will appear with Him in glory."

In your prayer journal, identify in this portion of scripture a promise to receive or a command to obey.

Prayer:

Father, I seek after you today. When Jesus died for me, my old self died also. When Jesus rose again from the dead with victory over death and the grave, I was also raised up with him. When he ascended to heaven and was seated at the right hand of God, I was seated with him in heavenly places. Help me today to set my affections on those things that have to do with my salvation. Give me a revelation of both my position with Christ in heavenly places and the authority to pray and declare your will to be done on earth just like it is done in heaven. I pray that I live today with the realization of my identification with the Lord Jesus. I thank you that I have received his life, his righteousness, the authority of his name and the knowledge of his will. I praise you for these things now, in Jesus' name, Amen.

Proclamation:

I am in Christ, and he is in me. He did not leave me alone, but he gave me the Spirit of God to reveal to me all the things he has prepared for me and the power to accomplish his will.

Memory Verse: 1 John 4:4

"You are of God, little children, and have overcome them because greater is he that is in you than he that is in the world."

To every family member: *"I love you; you are blessed, and you are a blessing."*
Don't forget the hugs.

~ May 5th ~

Scripture: Galatians 4:4-6 (AMP)

"But when the proper time had fully come, God sent His Son, born of a woman, born subject to [the regulations of] the Law, To purchase the freedom of (to ransom, to redeem, to atone for) those who were subject to the Law, that we might be adopted *and* have sonship conferred upon us [and be recognized as God's sons]. And because you [really] are [His] sons, God has sent the [Holy] Spirit of His Son into our hearts, crying, Abba (Father)! Father!"

In your prayer journal, identify in this portion of scripture
a promise to receive or a command to obey.

Prayer:

Heavenly Father, you have made me your child. You chose me for adoption into your family. I have been given your name and made an heir of your kingdom. Thank you for loving me and giving me access into your presence. You invite me to come and fellowship with you, to rejoice in your presence and to declare your goodness. Jesus paid, in full, my debt of sin and ransomed me from the consequences of breaking the law of God. I stand before you today to thank you for giving me the Holy Spirit who leads me, teaches me and bears witness with me that I am a child of God. I can call you Abba, Daddy because you have made me to be, not a servant, but your child. You delivered me from the slavery of sin and have translated me into your kingdom of love. I give you thanks for all these things, in Jesus' name, Amen.

Proclamation:

I am a child of God. I have been born of the Spirit of God by the incorruptible seed of the Word of God. I am not only born of the Spirit, but the Lord has adopted me as his very own child. He gave me his name. He calls me his own. God's goodness and merciful kindness have been poured out on me in abundance.

Memory Verse: 1 John 4:4

"You are of God, little children, and have overcome them because greater is he that is in you than he that is in the world."

To every family member: "I love you; you are blessed, and you are a blessing."
Don't forget the hugs.

May 6th

Scripture: John 4:13-14 (KJV)

"Jesus answered and said unto her, Whosoever drinketh of this water shall thirst again: But whosoever drinketh of the water that I shall give him shall never thirst; but the water that I shall give him shall be in him a well of water springing up into everlasting life."

In your prayer journal, identify in this portion of scripture a promise to receive or a command to obey.

Prayer:

My Heavenly Father I worship you and give you praise. You are worthy of all glory, honor, might and dominion. Every good gift comes from you, and you satisfy the desire of every living thing. I thank you today for the living water of life that flows from the throne of God. The river in Eden watered the garden, and the river from the rock supplied the Israelites in the desert. You have placed a river within me to supply my needs and satisfy my thirst. I pray the river that flows out of me today will bring life to everyone it touches. I thank you today for feeding me from the fatness of your table and causing me to drink of the river of your pleasure. May my life overflow with the love and grace of God to bring glory to your great name. It is in Jesus' name I pray, Amen.

Proclamation:

Jesus said if anyone thirsts to come to him, and he will give them the kind of water that satisfies their thirst forever. I will drink today from that fountain of living water. Out of my innermost being shall flow rivers of life that will bring life and gladness to everyone it touches.

Memory Verse: 1 John 4:4

"You are of God, little children, and have overcome them because greater is he that is in you than he that is in the world."

To every family member: "I love you; you are blessed, and you are a blessing." Don't forget the hugs.

May 7th

Scripture: Deuteronomy 8:17-18 (AMP)

"And beware lest you say in your [mind and] heart, My power and the might of my hand have gotten me this wealth. But you shall [earnestly] remember the Lord your God, for it is He Who gives you power to get wealth, that He may establish His covenant which He swore to your fathers, as it is this day."

In your prayer journal, identify in this portion of scripture a promise to receive or a command to obey.

Prayer:

My Father, you are faithful to fulfill all of your promises. I thank you today for the promises in your Word and the desire you have for me to receive every one of those promises. You were not pleased with that first generation of people you brought out of Egypt because they failed to enter into the land of their inheritance. They refused to believe that you would help them receive what you had told them was theirs. I ask you today to show me everything you promised to do for me and through me in your Word. Help me not to back down or shy away from believing you and pleasing you. You gave Israel power to obtain great wealth for the purpose of establishing your covenant. You also empower me to receive wealth and riches not only to bless me and my family but to be a blessing to multitudes of people by using wealth to declare your Word and establish your covenant. Father, I bless your wonderful name. I believe you are at work today to help me receive wisdom and provision to accomplish your purpose. I thank you for it now, in Jesus' name, Amen.

Proclamation:

I am greatly blessed of the Lord. He blesses the works of my hands and the meditations of my heart. He fills me with faith to receive every promise of his Word so I will walk in the inheritance he has given to me.

Memory Verse: Luke 12:15

"And he said unto them, 'Take heed, and beware of covetousness; for a man's life consists not in the abundance of the things which he possesses.'"

To every family member: *"I love you; you are blessed, and you are a blessing."*
Don't forget the hugs.

May 8th

Scripture: Exodus 23:24-25 (NKJV)

"You shall not bow down to their gods, nor serve them, nor do according to their works; but you shall utterly overthrow them and completely break down their sacred pillars. "So you shall serve the Lord your God, and He will bless your bread and your water. And I will take sickness away from the midst of you."

In your prayer journal, identify in this portion of scripture a promise to receive or a command to obey.

Prayer:

Father, you are good and your mercies endure forever. You have set before us life and death, blessing and cursing. You have implored us to choose life and walk in your blessings by rejecting every evil work and doing what is righteous and good in your eyes. You have promised to bless our food and water and remove sickness and disease from us. Help us today to walk with the understanding that your greatest desire for us is to have life and to have it more abundantly. Keep us from every evil work and draw us to yourself by the Holy Spirit. It is your blessings that lead us to repentance, and it is your unconditional love that follows after us all the days of our lives. Thank you for your unrelenting pursuit to bring us into your Kingdom. In Jesus' name I thank you, Amen.

Proclamation:

The Lord is my strength and my salvation. I will seek after him with all my heart and I will delight in his Word. I will lift up my voice to praise his name. I will yield to the leading of the Holy Spirit and will declare that my paths are made plain and God blesses all the works of my hands this day.

Memory Verse: Luke 12:15

"And he said unto them, 'Take heed, and beware of covetousness; for a man's life consists not in the abundance of the things which he possesses.'"

To every family member: *"I love you; you are blessed, and you are a blessing."*
Don't forget the hugs.

May 9th

Scripture: Colossians 2:2-4 (NIV)

"My goal is that they may be encouraged in heart and united in love, so that they may have the full riches of complete understanding, in order that they may know the mystery of God, namely, Christ, in whom are hidden all the treasures of wisdom and knowledge. I tell you this so that no one may deceive you by fine-sounding arguments."

In your prayer journal, identify in this portion of scripture a promise to receive or a command to obey.

Prayer:

My Father, I thank you today for your great love for me and your desire for me to know the hidden treasures of wisdom and knowledge that are found in the Lord Jesus Christ. Jesus is the truth that reveals the greatness of God and his purpose for me. He is the one who brings me life and life in great abundance. I ask you to keep me from deception and the lies of the enemy so I will rightly discern every circumstance of life and choose what is righteous and good in your sight. Help me to live free from discouragement and united in love with everyone who is called by your name. In the wonderful name of Jesus I pray, Amen.

Proclamation:

The truth of the Lord will endure forever. He will guide me to walk in paths of righteousness. He will reveal to me his great goodness. I will follow after the Lord all the days of my life, and I will dwell in the house of the Lord forever.

Memory Verse: Luke 12:15

"And he said unto them, 'Take heed, and beware of covetousness; for a man's life consists not in the abundance of the things which he possesses.'"

To every family member: "*I love you; you are blessed, and you are a blessing.*"
Don't forget the hugs.

May 10th

Scripture: Psalms 84:10-12 (KJV)

"For a day in thy courts is better than a thousand. I had rather be a doorkeeper in the house of my God, than to dwell in the tents of wickedness. For the Lord God is a sun and shield: the Lord will give grace and glory: no good thing will he withhold from them that walk uprightly. O Lord of hosts, blessed is the man that trusteth in thee."

In your prayer journal, identify in this portion of scripture a promise to receive or a command to obey.

Prayer:

Heavenly Father, I bless your holy name. I thank you for your abiding presence in my life today. You invite me to come into your presence. You give me access to the throne of God. I can pray, and I know you hear me. I can praise and sing to you with thanksgiving for all the wonderful things you have done for me, and I know you listen to me. Lord, you are a sun and shield to me, for you give me light and protection. I do not stumble in the darkness because, when I abide in your presence, there is only light. For in God, there is no darkness at all. Thank you for protecting me and giving me grace and covering me with your glory. There is nothing you will not do for me because you love me. Father, I put my trust in you today. Thank you for hearing me. Make me to be always aware of your presence in my life. In Jesus' name I pray, Amen.

Proclamation:

The Lord is forever with me. He will not leave me or ignore me. He is aware of everything that has to do with me today. He is touched with the feelings of my weaknesses, and he strengthens me for every good work. He protects me from all evil. He gives his angels assignments to keep me in all my ways. The Lord lights my path and makes my way plain.

Memory Verse: Luke 12:15

"And he said unto them, 'Take heed, and beware of covetousness; for a man's life consists not in the abundance of the things which he possesses.'"

To every family member: "I love you; you are blessed, and you are a blessing."
Don't forget the hugs.

May 11th

Scripture: Mark 10:42-45 (HCSB)

"Jesus called them over and said to them, 'You know that those who are regarded as rulers of the Gentiles dominate them, and their men of high positions exercise power over them. But it must not be like that among you. On the contrary, whoever wants to become great among you must be your servant, and whoever wants to be first among you must be a slave to all. For even the Son of Man did not come to be served, but to serve, and to give His life a ransom for many.'"

In your prayer journal, identify in this portion of scripture a promise to receive or a command to obey.

Prayer:

Father, my prayer is that I would honor you in all of my ways. Help me today to walk in humility and kindness. Put a guard over my mouth so I only speak those things that encourage and bless those who hear me. Give me a right heart that I would not just be obedient but willing to serve others. You, have given to me and to all who are born-again of the Spirit of God great power and authority in your name to speak your Word and to accomplish your will. You have given me this authority to serve you and others. Help me today to follow the example of Jesus and become a living sacrifice that would bless many and glorify the Lord. In Jesus' name I pray, Amen.

Proclamation:

I will follow the example of Jesus and humble myself and purpose to serve those I meet today. I will not use the authority the Lord has given me to rule over people but to serve them. I am sowing good seed into the lives of people in need so the fruit of the Spirit of God will grow in their lives.

Memory Verse: Luke 12:15

"And he said unto them, 'Take heed, and beware of covetousness; for a man's life consists not in the abundance of the things which he possesses.'"

To every family member: *"I love you; you are blessed, and you are a blessing."*
Don't forget the hugs.

May 12th

Scripture: Isaiah 32:17-18 (KJV)

"And the work of righteousness shall be peace; and the effect of righteousness quietness and assurance for ever. And my people shall dwell in a peaceable habitation, and in sure dwellings, and in quiet resting places."

In your prayer journal, identify in this portion of scripture a promise to receive or a command to obey.

Prayer:

Father, I thank you today for your righteousness. Jesus took what was unrighteous out of my life and has given me his righteousness. Your righteousness has brought me peace, and I rest in quiet assurance. I will not fear. I will put my trust in you. You will help me see those things that my physical eyes are unable to see, and you will cause me to hear, by the Spirit of God, your voice. Your peace is what abides in my house. I have a quiet resting place that is undisturbed by the chaos of the world. Lord, you have given me your peace that is unlike the peace this world has because you have overcome the world and all the tribulation and pressures it brings. The peace of God rules in my heart and mind, and I will praise your name forever and ever. In Jesus' name I pray, Amen.

Proclamation:

I am not afraid because my heart is fixed trusting in the Lord. My heart is established in righteousness. I will not be moved by the chaos of this world, for I have overcome the world by my faith in the Lord Jesus Christ. I live in quiet resting places, and the peace of God rules over me today.

Memory Verse: Luke 12:15

"And he said unto them, 'Take heed, and beware of covetousness; for a man's life consists not in the abundance of the things which he possesses.'"

To every family member: *"I love you; you are blessed, and you are a blessing."*
Don't forget the hugs.

May 13th

Scripture: Psalms 67 (NKJV)

"God be merciful to us and bless us, and cause His face to shine upon us, Selah that Your way may be known on earth, your salvation among all nations. Let the peoples praise You, O God; let all the peoples praise You. Oh, let the nations be glad and sing for joy! For You shall judge the people righteously, and govern the nations on earth. Selah. Let the peoples praise You, O God; let all the peoples praise You. Then the earth shall yield her increase; God, our own God, shall bless us. God shall bless us, and all the ends of the earth shall fear Him."

In your prayer journal, identify in this portion of scripture a promise to receive or a command to obey.

Prayer:

My Father, I pray that your ways would be known upon the earth, your desire for all nations. I pray for the leaders of nations, for kings and presidents, prime ministers and leaders on all levels of government. I ask you to open their hearts to the truth of the gospel and send them people to whom they will listen. I take authority over every wicked spirit of deception and unbelief that would hold these men and women in captivity to the lies of false gods and false prophets. I bind that wicked spirit, and I loose the minds of people from its deceptive work. Lord, cause the light of the glorious gospel of Christ to shine in their hearts and give them the knowledge of your salvation in Christ Jesus. I pray for the knowledge of the glory of God to cover all the earth so that all nations praise you, for then the earth shall bring forth great increase and the blessings of the Lord upon all nations. I declare these things this day in Jesus' name, Amen.

Proclamation:

The God and Father of my Lord Jesus Christ is the Lord of all the nations. Kings and rulers will come and bow down before him. They will come to the church and ask us to teach them of God's ways so they can walk in his paths. The glory of the Lord will cover all the earth even as the waters cover the seas.

Memory Verse: Luke 12:15

"And he said unto them, 'Take heed, and beware of covetousness; for a man's life consists not in the abundance of the things which he possesses.'"

To every family member: *"I love you; you are blessed, and you are a blessing."*
Don't forget the hugs.

May 14th

Scripture: 2 Corinthians 2:14-17 (MSG)

"In the Messiah, in Christ, God leads us from place to place in one perpetual victory parade. Through us, he brings knowledge of Christ. Everywhere we go, people breathe in the exquisite fragrance. Because of Christ, we give off a sweet scent rising to God, which is recognized by those on the way of salvation—an aroma redolent with life. But those on the way to destruction treat us more like the stench from a rotting corpse. This is a terrific responsibility. Is anyone competent to take it on? No—but at least we don't take God's Word, water it down, and then take it to the streets to sell it cheap. We stand in Christ's presence when we speak; God looks us in the face. We get what we say straight from God and say it as honestly as we can."

In your prayer journal, identify in this portion of scripture a promise to receive or a command to obey.

Prayer:

Father, I thank you for the perpetual victory that is mine in Christ Jesus. You have made my life sweet with the fragrance of the love of God. Others, who know you, recognize the fragrance and celebrate with me. I pray for those who are repelled by your presence because they don't know your love for them. I pray they will not run from you for fear of judgment, but they will run to you to receive your forgiveness and life. Help me today to speak your Word in such a way that all who hear it are drawn to you. I thank you for your indescribable love in Jesus' name, Amen.

Proclamation:

I walk from victory to victory as I follow after the Lord. He causes me to speak his Word and to reveal his love. Many will hear and come to the Lord.

Memory Verse: James 4:7-8a

"Submit yourselves therefore to God. Resist the devil, and he will flee from you. Draw nigh to God, and he will draw nigh to you."

To every family member: "I love you; you are blessed, and you are a blessing." Don't forget the hugs.

May 15th

Scripture: Mark 10:49-52 (NLT)

"When Jesus heard him, he stopped and said, "Tell him to come here." So they called the blind man. "Cheer up," they said. "Come on, he's calling you!" Bartimaeus threw aside his coat, jumped up, and came to Jesus. "What do you want me to do for you?" Jesus asked. "My rabbi," the blind man said, "I want to see!" And Jesus said to him, "Go, for your faith has healed you." Instantly the man could see, and he followed Jesus down the road."

In your prayer journal, identify in this portion of scripture a promise to receive or a command to obey.

Prayer:

Father, I pray that I would walk in faith and give demonstration to the power of God in my life. Bartimaeus recognized you, called out to you, and cast away the garment that caused people to identify him as a blind man. Help me to recognize the leading of the Holy Spirit and to pray and seek you for direction and wisdom in every circumstance of life. I will cast aside every thing that would identify me with the world, putting away the things of the old man and putting on the new man whom you have created to live in righteousness and true holiness. I thank you for faith that causes me to trust you for everything and to walk in the blessings of God today. In Jesus' name I pray, Amen.

Proclamation:

I walk by faith and not by sight. I will lay aside every thing that would weigh me down so I can run this race of life unhindered and without distraction, following after the things of God.

Memory Verse: James 4:7-8a

"Submit yourselves therefore to God. Resist the devil, and he will flee from you. Draw nigh to God, and he will draw nigh to you."

To every family member: *"I love you; you are blessed, and you are a blessing."*
Don't forget the hugs.

May 16th

Scripture: Psalms 33:8-12 (KJV)

"Let all the earth fear the Lord: let all the inhabitants of the world stand in awe of him. For he spake, and it was done; he commanded, and it stood fast. The Lord bringeth the counsel of the heathen to nought: he maketh the devices of the people of none effect. The counsel of the Lord standeth for ever, the thoughts of his heart to all generations. Blessed is the nation whose God is the Lord; and the people whom he hath chosen for his own inheritance."

In your prayer journal, identify in this portion of scripture a promise to receive or a command to obey.

Prayer:

Lord, my God, you have created all things by the power of your Word. You spoke the universe into existence. There is nothing too hard for you. You confuse the plans of those who are against you and make all of their devices to fail. I thank you today for your counsel, your wisdom that will never fail. Keep me from the confusion of man's ideas that stand in opposition to you. Give me your counsel and cause me to live in your inheritance. Speak to me today and establish my every path so that I am always at the right place at the right time, doing the right thing and receiving the favor and blessings of God. I ask these things this day in Jesus' name, Amen.

Proclamation:

The Lord made the heavens and earth and all that is in them. He spoke a word and brought it to pass. God is able to do all things and nothing is too hard for him. He makes my way plain and prospers me in all I do. I am greatly blessed of the Lord today.

Memory Verse: James 4:7-8a

"Submit yourselves therefore to God. Resist the devil, and he will flee from you. Draw nigh to God, and he will draw nigh to you."

To every family member: "*I love you; you are blessed, and you are a blessing.*"
Don't forget the hugs.

May 17th

Scripture: 2 Corinthians 9:6-8 (AMP)

"[Remember] this: he who sows sparingly *and* grudgingly will also reap sparingly *and* grudgingly, and he who sows generously [that blessings may come to someone] will also reap generously *and* with blessings. Let each one [give] as he has made up his own mind *and* purposed in his heart, not reluctantly *or* sorrowfully or under compulsion, for God loves (He takes pleasure in, prizes above other things, and is unwilling to abandon or to do without) a cheerful (joyous, "prompt to do it") giver [whose heart is in his giving]. And God is able to make all grace (every favor and earthly blessing) come to you in abundance, so that you may always *and* under all circumstances *and* whatever the need be self-sufficient [possessing enough to require no aid or support and furnished in abundance for every good work and charitable donation]."

In your prayer journal, identify in this portion of scripture a promise to receive or a command to obey.

Prayer:

Heavenly Father, thank you for your abundant blessings in my life today. I am richly blessed with every good thing. You said if I sow sparingly I will reap sparingly, but if I give generously I will reap generously. Lord, help me to follow the direction of the Holy Spirit so I will never miss an opportunity to give and give with a right heart and pure motives. I know your kingdom functions according to the parable of the seed and the sower, so help me sow into good ground that will bear much fruit. You are able to return to me such abundance that I will always have all sufficiency to meet my needs and to give unto every good work. I thank you for the grace of God to give generously and to reap abundantly and to honor you in all my giving and receiving. It is in Jesus' name I pray, Amen.

Proclamation:

It is a joy to give to those in need and to support the work of the ministry. I give joyfully and abundantly. I reap much, and I daily increase. I am never without supply to meet my own need and to give to every good work.

Memory Verse: James 4:7-8a

"Submit yourselves therefore to God. Resist the devil, and he will flee from you. Draw nigh to God, and he will draw nigh to you."

To every family member: *"I love you; you are blessed, and you are a blessing."*
Don't forget the hugs.

May 18th

Scripture: Isaiah 9:6-7 (KJV)

"For unto us a child is born, unto us a son is given: and the government shall be upon his shoulder: and his name shall be called Wonderful, Counsellor, The mighty God, The everlasting Father, The Prince of Peace. Of the increase of his government and peace there shall be no end, upon the throne of David, and upon his kingdom, to order it, and to establish it with judgment and with justice from henceforth even for ever. The zeal of the Lord of hosts will perform this."

In your prayer journal, identify in this portion of scripture a promise to receive or a command to obey.

Prayer:

Father, your government rests upon the shoulders of the Lord Jesus Christ. He is the Wonderful Counselor, the Mighty God, the Everlasting Father and the Prince of Peace. There is none like him, who has defeated our enemy and carried away our sin. He suffered, died, and rose again to declare his victory over death and the grave. I thank you for this great salvation. You have delivered us from the captivity of sin and death and have translated us into the kingdom of your Son. You are establishing judgment and justice to the ends of the earth. I thank you that there will be no end of your glorious kingdom. Help me to walk with the constant realization of your abiding presence and the expansion of your kingdom until righteousness covers all the earth. In Jesus' name, I thank you for this amazing grace and your wondrous love, Amen.

Proclamation:

God's kingdom is an everlasting kingdom, and his dominion covers all the earth. He will reign forever. He has seated me with Christ and promised me I share in the inheritance of the kingdom. The Lord has given me a crown of righteousness that I might reign in life through Christ Jesus my Lord.

Memory Verse: James 4:7-8a

"Submit yourselves therefore to God. Resist the devil, and he will flee from you. Draw nigh to God, and he will draw nigh to you."

To every family member: *"I love you; you are blessed, and you are a blessing."*
Don't forget the hugs.

May 19th

Scripture: 2 Corinthians 10:3-5 (EXB)

"[For] Although we live in the world [walk in the flesh], we do not fight [wage war] in the same way the world fights [according to the flesh]. We fight with weapons that are different from those the world uses [not merely human weapons; not of the flesh]. Our weapons have power from God that can destroy the enemy's strong places [strongholds; fortresses]. We destroy people's arguments [human reasoning; sophistries] and every proud thing [pretension; exalted opinion; high thing] that raises itself against the knowledge of God. We capture every thought and make it obey Christ."

In your prayer journal, identify in this portion of scripture a promise to receive or a command to obey.

Prayer:

My Father, I pray that you would cause me to always recognize the devices of the enemy. I know I do not engage the devil with my own ideas and opinions or some worldly weapon. You have given me spiritual weapons that always defeat the works of the devil. I will cast down every thought and imagination that is contrary to the truth of your Word. I will speak your Word and demand that every opposing power or work or any such thing will come into agreement with the Word of God. You have said that I am healed, you have promised to abide with me forever, and you have accepted me into your family as a child of God. Therefore, every sign and symptom of sickness and disease, I command to leave my body; every thought of being isolated and alone, I refuse; and every thought of unworthiness or shame I reject in the name of my Lord Jesus Christ. You will strengthen me and help me to always stand strong in the face of all opposition. I receive your help in every time of my need in Jesus' name, Amen.

Proclamation:

The Lord, my God is with me. He is my fortress and my defense. I will not fear, for I have superior weapons to defeat every work of the devil.

Memory Verse: James 4:7-8a

"Submit yourselves therefore to God. Resist the devil, and he will flee from you. Draw nigh to God, and he will draw nigh to you."

To every family member: *"I love you; you are blessed, and you are a blessing."* Don't forget the hugs.

May 20th

Scripture: Hebrews 13:15 (KJV)

"By him therefore let us offer the sacrifice of praise to God continually, that is, the fruit of our lips giving thanks to his name."

In your prayer journal, identify in this portion of scripture a promise to receive or a command to obey.

Prayer:

Father, your greatness is without measure. Your goodness is beyond my comprehension. I bless your wonderful name and thank you for your faithfulness and your blessings that abound toward me this day. I offer unto you the sacrifice of praise for all you have done for me, because you love me. You have delivered me from destruction and crowned me with your loving kindness and tender mercies. I am richly blessed of the Lord. I will praise your name in the morning, and at night I will lift up my hands to thank you for your abiding presence and your grace; because you sustain me and strengthen me and make me to succeed in everything I do. You said a humble and contrite heart you would not despise. Therefore, I humble myself before you today. I place myself under the mighty hand of God who leads me where I should go and who blesses the works of my hands and the meditations of my heart. You are my delight. I put my trust in you and give you praise. In Jesus' name I pray, Amen.

Proclamation:

I choose to follow after the Lord today with all my heart. I put my trust in him for he loves me and is able to prosper me in all I do. He will make my way plain. He will comfort my heart and strengthen me in faith so I will be strong in the Lord and in the power of his might.

Memory Verse: James 4:7-8a

"Submit yourselves therefore to God. Resist the devil, and he will flee from you. Draw nigh to God, and he will draw nigh to you."

To every family member: *"I love you; you are blessed, and you are a blessing."*
Don't forget the hugs.

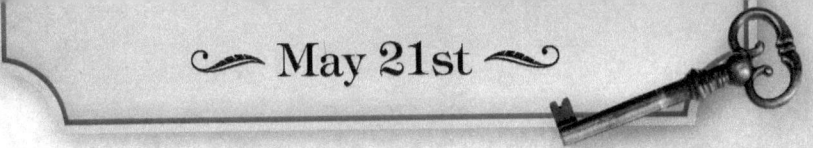

May 21st

Scripture: Romans 8:37-39 (KJV)

"Nay, in all these things we are more than conquerors through him that loved us. For I am persuaded, that neither death, nor life, nor angels, nor principalities, nor powers, nor things present, nor things to come, nor height, nor depth, nor any other creature, shall be able to separate us from the love of God, which is in Christ Jesus our Lord."

In your prayer journal, identify in this portion of scripture a promise to receive or a command to obey.

Prayer:

Father, I thank you for your great love for me. Your promise to never leave me is certain. You have declared that you will not, certainly not, not at any time will you ever leave me or forsake me. You have given me the Spirit of God who lives in me and the innumerable heavenly host of angels have been sent to minister for me, an heir of salvation. I know there is nothing that can separate me from your love and because you are with me and for me, I will not fail to experience your love, and to walk in your blessings. Your love is higher and greater than I have the capacity to understand. I believe your Word, and I thank you for making me more than a conqueror today. I praise your wonderful name and give you thanks. In Jesus' name I pray, Amen.

Proclamation:

Because God is for me, I cannot fail. He will lead me in righteousness, and he will sustain me with abundant provision. God is on my side, and my trust and confidence are in him. He will not fail me. He will not forsake me or leave me without help. He will equip me and prepare me with everything I need to succeed.

Memory Verse: 2 Timothy 2:15

"Study to show yourself approved unto God, a workman that needs not to be ashamed, rightly dividing the word of truth."

To every family member: *"I love you; you are blessed, and you are a blessing."*
Don't forget the hugs.

May 22nd

Scripture: James 1:12-14 (NLT)

"God blesses those who patiently endure testing and temptation. Afterward they will receive the crown of life that God has promised to those who love him. And remember, when you are being tempted, do not say, 'God is tempting me.' God is never tempted to do wrong, and he never tempts anyone else. Temptation comes from our own desires, which entice us and drag us away."

In your prayer journal, identify in this portion of scripture a promise to receive or a command to obey.

Prayer:

Father, I pray today for your wisdom and strength to keep me from every temptation. I know you do not tempt me with evil. You do not test me with trouble and calamities or accidents and hardships, but you are faithful to always make a way to escape every temptation that comes to me today. I ask you to help me guard my heart from offenses others would bring or carnal desires that would lead me into wrong decisions or ungodly actions. Keep me by your power and cause me to recognize the wicked devices of the devil who would try to bring a snare into my life. You have promised me a crown of life when I rule over temptations and tribulations the devil tries to bring against me. Thank you for keeping me by your mighty power and helping me to remain free from the snares bitterness or unforgiveness bring. I give you thanks for all these things in Jesus' name, Amen.

Proclamation:

I walk in the love of God today. God's love has been deposited in my heart by the Holy Spirit. I choose to walk in forgiveness. I choose to walk in peace. I will not retaliate against another for a wrong done to me. I bless my enemies, and I give no place to the devil. He will not trap me with temptation, but I will rule in life by the power of God.

Memory Verse: 2 Timothy 2:15

"Study to show yourself approved unto God, a workman that needs not to be ashamed, rightly dividing the word of truth."

To every family member: "I love you; you are blessed, and you are a blessing." Don't forget the hugs.

May 23rd

Scripture: Genesis 26:12-14 (AMP)

"Then Isaac sowed seed in that land and received in the same year a hundred times as much as he had planted, and the Lord favored him with blessings. And the man became great and gained more and more until he became very wealthy and distinguished; He owned flocks, herds, and a great supply of servants, and the Philistines envied him."

In your prayer journal, identify in this portion of scripture a promise to receive or a command to obey.

Prayer:

My Heavenly Father, I praise your glorious name this day. Thank you for the promises of your Word. The Scriptures were written for me to see how your will was accomplished in the lives of people like Isaac. I can, therefore, be assured that the same promises and blessings are for me today. You have promised increase when I sow and favor to make me so rich even the ungodly and unbeliever will envy me for your goodness and they will desire to know you. I believe you will prosper me and cause me to be increased daily, so I will always have enough to meet my needs and to give to every good work. Help me not to consider the conditions of drought or famine that may be all around me, but to consider your promises and your faithfulness to fulfill your Word. Give me the ability to hear your voice clearly and the willingness to obey you quickly so every aspect of my life will bring praises to you. In Jesus' name I pray, Amen.

Proclamation:

I am greatly blessed of the Lord today. His will is accomplished in me. I give freely, and I reap abundantly. God's divine favor rests on me, and I am the envy of many, for the blessings of God come upon me and overtake me everyday and in every way.

Memory Verse: 2 Timothy 2:15

"Study to show yourself approved unto God, a workman that needs not to be ashamed, rightly dividing the word of truth."

To every family member: *"I love you; you are blessed, and you are a blessing."*
Don't forget the hugs.

May 24th

Scripture: Psalms 119:49-50 (NLT)
"Remember your promise to me; it is my only hope.
Your promise revives me; it comforts me in all my troubles"

In your prayer journal, identify in this portion of scripture a promise to receive or a command to obey.

Prayer:

Heavenly Father, I rejoice in you today. You are my hope, and in you I put my trust. I will not forget your promises because they encourage me. Your Word strengthens me and causes me to rise up in times of trouble. I speak your Word with all boldness. Enemies who come against me will run in fear from me, scattering in every direction because you are with me. Troubles might come against me, but you will deliver me out of them all. Your Word revives me when I am weak. Your Word comforts me if I am distressed because your Word is spirit and life to me. Father, I delight myself in you. Help me to always fill my mouth with your words. I will not complain of problems, but I will declare your solutions, for you are the Lord, the God of all flesh, and nothing is to hard for you. I give you thanks and praise you for hearing me, helping me, and delivering me out of every trial, every trouble, and tribulation. In Jesus' name I pray, Amen.

Proclamation:
The Word of the Lord helps me, guides me, and brings me comfort in every circumstance of life. My hope is in the promises of God, because God is faithful and what he has said will surely come to pass.

Memory Verse: 2 Timothy 2:15
"Study to show yourself approved unto God, a workman that needs not to be ashamed, rightly dividing the word of truth."

To every family member: *"I love you; you are blessed, and you are a blessing."*
Don't forget the hugs.

May 25th

Scripture: Matthew 14:28-32 (NKJV)

"And Peter answered Him and said, 'Lord, if it is You, command me to come to You on the water.' So He said, 'Come.' And when Peter had come down out of the boat, he walked on the water to go to Jesus. But when he saw that the wind was boisterous, he was afraid; and beginning to sink he cried out, saying, 'Lord, save me!' And immediately Jesus stretched out His hand and caught him, and said to him, 'O you of little faith, why did you doubt?' And when they got into the boat, the wind ceased."

In your prayer journal, identify in this portion of scripture a promise to receive or a command to obey.

Prayer:

Father, I thank you for your willingness to give us the desires of our heart. There was no reason for Peter to walk on the water except he desired to. You granted him his bold request and helped him, even when his answered prayer got him in trouble. I ask you to help me be bold today to ask in faith, not just for the things I need, but also for the things that would satisfy my heart's desire. I ask you for outrageous faith that will not falter even in the middle of a storm. Help me to keep my eyes on you and my trust in your Word, to do the things that cannot be done except by the power of God. I thank you for hearing and answering me today in Jesus' name, Amen.

Proclamation:

I have faith to remove mountains, to quench the fiery arrows of the enemy, to curse fruitless fig trees, and quiet storms. I will see the wounded healed, the broken hearted restored to faith, and the foundations of ancient ruins restored. I live in the kingdom of God, and just a mustard seed amount of faith will bring to pass the will of God.

Memory Verse: 2 Timothy 2:15

"Study to show yourself approved unto God, a workman that needs not to be ashamed, rightly dividing the word of truth."

To every family member: *"I love you; you are blessed, and you are a blessing."*
Don't forget the hugs.

Faith Family Minute | 147

May 26th

Scripture: Luke 16:10-13 (PHILLIPS)

"'The man who is faithful in the little things will be faithful in the big things, and the man who cheats in the little things will cheat in the big things too. So that if you are not fit to be trusted to deal with the wicked wealth of this world, who will trust you with the true riches? And if you are not trustworthy with someone else's property, who will give you property of your own? No servant can serve two masters. He is bound to hate one and love the other or give his loyalty to one and despise the other. You cannot serve God and the power of money at the same time.'"

In your prayer journal, identify in this portion of scripture a promise to receive or a command to obey.

Prayer:

Blessed is the name of the Lord, my God. He is mighty and glorious and worthy of all praise. I put my trust in him. I do not trust in wealth or riches, but I trust in the Lord, who has already given me freely all things that pertain to life and godliness. Father, help me to always recognize that money and wealth are tools to accomplish your will and establish your covenant. Help me to be a good steward of what you have given me. You said, a man's life does not consist of the things he possess, so help me to use the things I possess for your purpose. Help me to instantly obey your voice, to give at your direction any amount of any thing to anyone at anytime without hesitation so you can not only get to me what I have need of, but you can get through me what others need. I thank you for this work of grace working mightily in me today in Jesus' name, Amen.

Proclamation:

It is my joy to give. I give willingly and joyfully, because I have purposed in my heart to use the things the Lord has given me for his purpose and pleasure.

Memory Verse: 2 Timothy 2:15

"Study to show yourself approved unto God, a workman that needs not to be ashamed, rightly dividing the word of truth."

To every family member: "*I love you; you are blessed, and you are a blessing.*"
Don't forget the hugs.

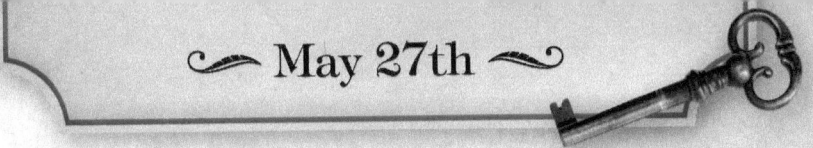

May 27th

Scripture: Ecclesiastes 11:4-6 (AMP)

He who observes the wind [and waits for all conditions to be favorable] will not sow, and he who regards the clouds will not reap. As you know not what is the way of the wind, or how the spirit comes to the bones in the womb of a pregnant woman, even so you know not the work of God, Who does all. In the morning sow your seed, and in the evening withhold not your hands, for you know not which shall prosper, whether this or that, or whether both alike will be good."

In your prayer journal, identify in this portion of scripture a promise to receive or a command to obey.

Prayer:

Father, your mercies endure forever. Your glory is above the heavens. There is no understanding of your might and power, for you are great and greatly to be praised. Help me to always keep my eyes on you instead of the circumstances. I ask you to keep me from presumption and procrastination. I know you have blessed me and gifted me uniquely for your purpose. I will not take lightly the assignment you have for me; therefore, I pray you will daily inspire me with vision and purpose to motivate me in the things you have ordained for me to walk in. Make me fruitful in everything I set my hand to and help me to succeed in every area so that my life may bring glory to you in Jesus' name, Amen.

Proclamation:

I will be busy doing the will of God today. I do not wait for all the conditions to be favorable before I step out in faith to do the things the Lord has put in my heart. I will not put off for tomorrow what I can accomplish today. I believe to see the glory of God in everything I do.

Memory Verse: 2 Timothy 2:15

"Study to show yourself approved unto God, a workman that needs not to be ashamed, rightly dividing the word of truth."

To every family member: *"I love you; you are blessed, and you are a blessing."*
Don't forget the hugs.

May 28th

Scripture: 1 Corinthians 12:6-11 (HCSB)

"And there are different activities, but the same God activates each gift in each person. A demonstration of the Spirit is given to each person to produce what is beneficial: to one is given a message of wisdom through the Spirit, to another, a message of knowledge by the same Spirit, to another, faith by the same Spirit, to another, gifts of healing by the one Spirit, to another, the performing of miracles, to another, prophecy, to another, distinguishing between spirits, to another, different kinds of languages, to another, interpretation of languages. But one and the same Spirit is active in all these, distributing to each person as He wills."

In your prayer journal, identify in this portion of scripture a promise to receive or a command to obey.

Prayer:

Heavenly Father, I thank you for the great plan of God being accomplished in the earth. You have given us your Holy Spirit, empowering us to do your will. I pray that every member of the Body of Christ will function in the gifts of the Holy Spirit. I know all of the gifts of the Spirit operate at the will of the Spirit and for the benefit of all who are present. I pray that every meeting of the Church will result in the demonstration of the spiritual gifts you have given. Bring forth those gifts, in our assemblies, that will meet the needs of those who are present. I pray the sick are healed, miraculous works are performed, and prophetic declarations are made. I pray for the moves of the Spirit to result in signs and wonders that will bring repentance to the lost and the power of God to those in need. I thank you for these things now in Jesus' name, Amen.

Proclamation:

Every time the church gathers together, the power of God is there. The Spirit of God is at work to demonstrate the goodness and love of God. The sick are healed, and the lost are saved, and Jesus is exalted.

Memory Verse: 2 Corinthians 10:3-5a

"For though we walk in the flesh, we do not war after the flesh; for the weapons of our warfare are not carnal, but mighty through God to the pulling down of strong holds, casting down imaginations and every high thing that exalts itself against the knowledge of God..."

To every family member: *"I love you; you are blessed, and you are a blessing."* Don't forget the hugs.

May 29th

Scripture: Romans 6:12-14 (KJV)

"Let not sin therefore reign in your mortal body, that ye should obey it in the lusts thereof. Neither yield ye your members as instruments of unrighteousness unto sin: but yield yourselves unto God, as those that are alive from the dead, and your members as instruments of righteousness unto God. For sin shall not have dominion over you: for ye are not under the law, but under grace."

In your prayer journal, identify in this portion of scripture a promise to receive or a command to obey.

Prayer:

God, my Father, you have given me victory over sin. You have delivered me from the power of sin, and you have made me righteous. My body is the temple of the Holy Spirit, and I ask you to help me escape every temptation to sin and deny the devil any access to my life. Father, help me to always yield the members of my physical body to the will of the Holy Spirit. I pray the Spirit of God will so fill my life that the words I speak and the things I do would bring glory and honor to you. Father, continuously fill me with the Spirit of God so I will be under the control of the Spirit and the deeds I do in my body will glorify you. I pray in Jesus' name, Amen.

Proclamation:

Sin does not have dominion over me. My old man died with Christ, and the life I now live, I live by the faith of the Son of God. I am not my own, but I have been bought with a price. It is reasonable for me to present my body as a living sacrifice to God for his will and purpose. I have been transformed by renewing my mind to the Word of God so I will always know his will and do his pleasure.

Memory Verse: 2 Corinthians 10:3-5a

"For though we walk in the flesh, we do not war after the flesh; for the weapons of our warfare are not carnal, but mighty through God to the pulling down of strong holds, casting down imaginations and every high thing that exalts itself against the knowledge of God..."

To every family member: *"I love you; you are blessed, and you are a blessing."* Don't forget the hugs.

May 30th

Scripture: Acts 1:8 (NRSV)

"'But you will receive power when the Holy Spirit has come upon you; and you will be my witnesses in Jerusalem, in all Judea and Samaria, and to the ends of the earth.'"

In your prayer journal, identify in this portion of scripture a promise to receive or a command to obey.

Prayer:

Heavenly Father, thank you for the Holy Spirit of God and the power of God that lives within me. You said I would receive miracle working power after the Holy Spirit comes upon me and this power would enable me to be an effective witness for Jesus in all the earth. You said the father's of this world give good gifts to their children and how much more you will give the Holy Spirit to those who ask you. I ask you now for the baptism in the Holy Spirit. Fill me with the Spirit of God and let the power of God rest upon me. You said to ask for this power and be continuously filled with the Spirit of God. Father, I ask you to give me now a fresh filling of the Holy Spirit and a renewed expectancy of the power of God working in me today. I receive it now in Jesus' name, Amen.

Proclamation:

I am filled with the Holy Spirit of God. The same Spirit that raised Jesus from the dead lives in me. He will bring healing to my physical body and give me power to declare the gospel of Jesus to the ends of the earth.

Memory Verse: 2 Corinthians 10:3-5a

"For though we walk in the flesh, we do not war after the flesh; for the weapons of our warfare are not carnal, but mighty through God to the pulling down of strong holds, casting down imaginations and every high thing that exalts itself against the knowledge of God…"

To every family member: "I love you; you are blessed, and you are a blessing."
Don't forget the hugs.

May 31st

Scripture: Isaiah 57:13b-15 (NKJV)

"'But he who puts his trust in Me shall possess the land, and shall inherit My holy mountain.' And one shall say, 'Heap it up! Heap it up! Prepare the way, take the stumbling block out of the way of My people.' For thus says the High and Lofty One who inhabits eternity, whose name is Holy: 'I dwell in the high and holy *place*, with him *who* has a contrite and humble spirit, to revive the spirit of the humble, and to revive the heart of the contrite ones.'"

In your prayer journal, identify in this portion of scripture a promise to receive or a command to obey.

Prayer:

My Father, you are high and holy. You are above all, and all praise and glory belong to you. Thank you for the promise of inheritance for those who put their trust in you. I pray all stumbling blocks and obstacles are removed from my way so nothing trips me up or causes me to fall. I humble myself before you today, for I know you will revive me and cause me to dwell in your presence. You resist the proud, but you give grace to the humble. I receive your marvelous grace that is working in me today, to strengthen me, so I am strong in you and in the power of your might. I give you thanks now in Jesus' name, Amen.

Proclamation:

I am an heir of God and a joint heir with Christ Jesus. He invites me to come boldly to the throne of his grace. I will ascend to the hill of the Lord and stand in his holy place with clean hands and a pure heart. I put my trust in the Lord, and he will strengthen my heart.

Memory Verse: 2 Corinthians 10:3-5a

"For though we walk in the flesh, we do not war after the flesh; for the weapons of our warfare are not carnal, but mighty through God to the pulling down of strong holds, casting down imaginations and every high thing that exalts itself against the knowledge of God..."

To every family member: *"I love you; you are blessed, and you are a blessing."*
Don't forget the hugs.

June 1st

Scripture: Proverbs 19:17 (NKJV)
"He who has pity on the poor lends to the Lord and He will pay back what he has given."

In your prayer journal, identify in this portion of scripture a promise to receive or a command to obey.

Prayer:

Father, I praise your wonderful name. I thank you for your greatness, which is far beyond what I could ever begin to imagine. There is nothing that escapes your notice. Whether it is a sparrow that falls to the ground or how many hairs are on my head, you know all things. You know and keep an accounting of everything good that is done. You are not unrighteous to forget the work and labor of love demonstrated by those who are called by your name who minister to those in need. You gave to the one who gives to the poor the promise of repayment from your hand. You said that what you will give back is a good measure that is pressed down, shaken together and running over of what was given. I pray today for opportunities to give to those to whom you would direct me, those who are calling upon you for help. Let me be the answer to someone's prayer today. I thank you that whatever I give to those in need will be restored to me with increase so I can grow strong to give more and more as you lead me by the Holy Spirit. I ask you for these things now in Jesus' name, Amen.

Proclamation:

I give freely and liberally to those in need. God makes me sensitive to the needs of others and supplies me with provision that meets my own need and gives me the ability to give to every good work.

Memory Verse: 2 Corinthians 10:3-5a

"For though we walk in the flesh, we do not war after the flesh; for the weapons of our warfare are not carnal, but mighty through God to the pulling down of strong holds, casting down imaginations and every high thing that exalts itself against the knowledge of God..."

To every family member: "I love you; you are blessed, and you are a blessing."
Don't forget the hugs.

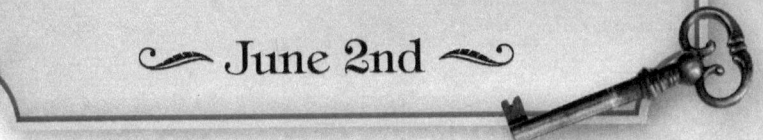

June 2nd

Scripture: John 16:33 (KJV)

"These things I have spoken unto you, that in me ye might have peace. In the world ye shall have tribulation: but be of good cheer; I have overcome the world."

In your prayer journal, identify in this portion of scripture a promise to receive or a command to obey.

Prayer:

Heavenly Father, you are above all. There is no might or power that can stand against you. Jesus destroyed the works of the devil, the god of this corrupt and wicked world's system. I thank you for giving me victory over the troubles of this world. You have given me your peace and victory to overcome the world with all of its chaos. I ask you to make me aware of your abiding presence with me. Reveal to me your provision in time of need, your wisdom in the midst of confusion, and your peace in times of trouble. I look to Jesus today who is the one who perfects my faith and causes me to triumph in every circumstance of life. I praise you, and I receive these things done this day in Jesus' name, Amen.

Proclamation:

I will not allow fear to occupy my thoughts, but I will think on those things that are good and pleasant and honest and just and pure. Peace rules in my thoughts. The reality of God's victory is mine. Troubles and tribulation may come against me, but the Lord always gives me a way of escape. My joy has no limits, and my victory is sure because, if God is for me, who can be against me?

Memory Verse: 2 Corinthians 10:3-5a

"For though we walk in the flesh, we do not war after the flesh; for the weapons of our warfare are not carnal, but mighty through God to the pulling down of strong holds, casting down imaginations and every high thing that exalts itself against the knowledge of God..."

To every family member: *"I love you; you are blessed, and you are a blessing."*
Don't forget the hugs.

June 3rd

Scripture: John 17:14-18 (NLV)

"'I have given Your Word to My followers. The world hated them because they do not belong to the world, even as I do not belong to the world. I do not ask You to take them out of the world. I ask You to keep them from the devil. My followers do not belong to the world just as I do not belong to the world. Make them holy for Yourself by the truth. Your Word is truth. As You sent Me into the world so I have sent them into the world also.'"

In your prayer journal, identify in this portion of scripture a promise to receive or a command to obey.

Prayer:

Father, thank you for saving me out of the world's system of fear and darkness, death and destruction. I do not belong to the world, but to the kingdom of God that is filled with righteousness, peace and joy. Even as Jesus prayed for me in the garden, I ask you to keep me from the works of the devil as he rules over this worldly system. May the Word of God work mightily in me today and cause your truth to be displayed through my life. Give me a fresh anointing of the Spirit of God to empower me and equip me to speak your Word with wisdom and demonstrate your love with power. Thank you for hearing me and causing these things to come to pass this day. In Jesus' name I pray, Amen.

Proclamation:

I am in this world, but I am not of this world. I have been delivered out of the kingdom of darkness, and I have been translated into the kingdom of God. I have been set-aside for God's holy purpose. His Word is truth, and it is God's truth that empowers me to go into all the world and declare God's love.

Memory Verse: 2 Corinthians 10:3-5a

"For though we walk in the flesh, we do not war after the flesh; for the weapons of our warfare are not carnal, but mighty through God to the pulling down of strong holds, casting down imaginations and every high thing that exalts itself against the knowledge of God..."

To every family member: "I love you; you are blessed, and you are a blessing."
Don't forget the hugs.

June 4th

Scripture: 2 Peter 1:5-8 (HCSB)

"For this very reason, make every effort to supplement your faith with goodness, goodness with knowledge, knowledge with self-control, self-control with endurance, endurance with godliness, godliness with brotherly affection and brotherly affection with love. For if these qualities are yours and are increasing, they will keep you from being useless or unfruitful in the knowledge of our Lord Jesus Christ."

In your prayer journal, identify in this portion of scripture a promise to receive or a command to obey.

Prayer:

My Father, I pray my life would be filled with the knowledge of your will. Help me to add to my life things that will promote fruitfulness and make me to know your will in all things. You have declared that, as I commit my works to you, my thoughts will be established according to your will and so my plans will succeed. Therefore, I choose this day to commit all of my works to you. According to your Word, I know that you are at work establishing my thoughts and my plans to accomplish and fulfill your purpose. Thank you for bringing this to pass this day in Jesus' name, Amen.

Proclamation:

I choose this day to fill my life with goodness to bless those I meet, knowledge to help instruct those who need direction, self-control to keep my flesh submitted to the will of God, endurance to persevere in times of difficulty, godliness to honor the Lord in all my ways, brotherly kindness to put the needs of others before my own and love to always accomplish the will of God. Therefore, I will walk in the revelation of the will of God in every circumstance of life, and I will be fruitful in every good work.

Memory Verse: Ephesians 1:3

"Blessed be the God and Father of our Lord Jesus Christ, who has blessed us with all spiritual blessings in heavenly places in Christ."

To every family member: *"I love you; you are blessed, and you are a blessing."*
Don't forget the hugs.

June 5th

Scripture: 2 Corinthians 8:9 (KJV)

"For ye know the grace of our Lord Jesus Christ, that, though he was rich, yet for your sakes he became poor, that ye through his poverty might be rich."

In your prayer journal, identify in this portion of scripture a promise to receive or a command to obey.

Prayer:

God my Father, I worship you this day and bless your holy name. You are worthy of all praise, for you have done great and glorious things for me. You have delivered me from darkness and have brought me into your kingdom of light. You have forgiven me of all sin and transgression and given me the gift of righteousness. You have delivered me from the curse that once filled my life because of the law of sin and death. You have granted me complete restoration of everything the devil ever stole from me. You are the restorer of my soul, and you cause me to dwell in paths of righteousness. Your goodness and mercy follows after me all the days of my life so I am richly blessed. I receive today the blessings of God Jesus provided for me when he took the judgment for my sin and gave me his righteousness. He carried my shame, my guilt, my sickness and disease and my poverty and failure so I can walk in success and prosperity. I give you praise for all these things that are coming to pass in my life today. In Jesus' name I pray, Amen.

Proclamation:

It is the blessing of the Lord that makes me rich and adds no sorrow to me. Jesus became poor with my poverty so that I can be rich with his prosperity. I am an heir of God and a joint heir with Christ Jesus.

Memory Verse: Ephesians 1:3

"Blessed be the God and Father of our Lord Jesus Christ, who has blessed us with all spiritual blessings in heavenly places in Christ."

To every family member: *"I love you; you are blessed, and you are a blessing."*
Don't forget the hugs.

June 6th

Scripture: 2 Peter 1:19-21 (NLT)

"Because of that experience, we have even greater confidence in the message proclaimed by the prophets. You must pay close attention to what they wrote, for their words are like a lamp shining in a dark place—until the Day dawns, and Christ the Morning Star shines in your hearts. Above all, you must realize that no prophecy in Scripture ever came from the prophet's own understanding or from human initiative. No, those prophets were moved by the Holy Spirit, and they spoke from God."

In your prayer journal, identify in this portion of scripture a promise to receive or a command to obey.

Prayer:

Father, I thank you for your precious Word to reveal to me the things of God. Your Word is a light that shines in the darkness of this world and leads to the Lord Jesus Christ. He is like the dawning of the day when the sun rises and dispels the darkness of the night. Your Word brings light into my life to cause me to see the way I should go and the things I should do. I ask you today for clarity. Give me eyes to see spiritual things and ears to hear your voice so my life will be built upon that sure foundation that cannot be destroyed by the storms of life. I know you spoke and your words brought into existence everything there is. Help me to speak your Word with faith and see the same power demonstrated to produce the things that will accomplish your will and bring forth your purpose. I thank you for your grace working in me today to hear your Word, receive your Word, believe your Word and speak your Word so I see your Word bring your kingdom to pass on the earth just as it is in heaven. In Jesus' name, Amen.

Proclamation:

I am not conformed to this world's ways, but my mind is transformed by the Word of God. God's light shines in my heart and gives me wisdom and direction for every decision I make.

Memory Verse: Ephesians 1:3

"Blessed be the God and Father of our Lord Jesus Christ, who has blessed us with all spiritual blessings in heavenly places in Christ."

To every family member: *"I love you; you are blessed, and you are a blessing."*
Don't forget the hugs.

June 7th

Scripture: Joshua 23:8-11 (NIV)

"But you are to hold fast to the Lord your God, as you have until now. 'The Lord has driven out before you great and powerful nations; to this day no one has been able to withstand you. One of you routs a thousand, because the Lord your God fights for you, just as he promised. So be very careful to love the Lord your God.'"

In your prayer journal, identify in this portion of scripture a promise to receive or a command to obey.

Prayer:

O Lord God, you are powerful and mighty. You overthrow nations and kingdoms to establish your purpose. You give victory to the righteous, and you bring down the wicked. I thank you today for the power of God that fills my life. You said that I would receive miracle-working power by the Holy Spirit. If one can chase a thousand and two can put ten thousand to flight, I know that with God nothing is impossible for me. Lord, you said that, if I abide in you and your Word abides in me, I can ask whatever I will, and it will be done for me. I ask you today for wisdom and revelation so I will not be deceived by the way things appear to be, but I will see clearly the real obstacles that are in my way. I stand against every wicked work of darkness that hinders the will of God being accomplished in my life and family. I command those wicked works to cease and go from me by the authority of the name of my Lord Jesus Christ. I thank you, Lord, that no one is able to withstand me because you are with me. I give you praise for these things in Jesus' name, Amen.

Proclamation:

I love the Lord with all my heart. He is my life. He is a very present help to me in times of trouble. He will lift me up on high and be my fortress and my high tower of refuge. I will call upon the Lord, and he will hear me and answer me and show me his salvation.

Memory Verse: Ephesians 1:3

"Blessed be the God and Father of our Lord Jesus Christ, who has blessed us with all spiritual blessings in heavenly places in Christ."

To every family member: *"I love you; you are blessed, and you are a blessing."*
Don't forget the hugs.

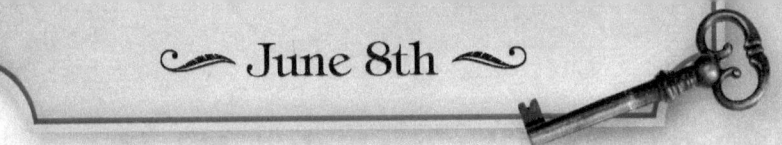

June 8th

Scripture: Psalms 145:8-13 (KJV)

"The Lord is gracious, and full of compassion; slow to anger, and of great mercy. The Lord is good to all: and his tender mercies are over all his works. All thy works shall praise thee, O Lord; and thy saints shall bless thee. They shall speak of the glory of thy kingdom, and talk of thy power; To make known to the sons of men his mighty acts, and the glorious majesty of his kingdom. Thy kingdom is an everlasting kingdom, and thy dominion endureth throughout all generations."

In your prayer journal, identify in this portion of scripture a promise to receive or a command to obey.

Prayer:

My Father, I thank you today for who you are. You are gracious and kind and good to all. Your tender mercies are poured out on me today. I praise you, and I want to declare your greatness by the words I speak and by the blessings of God that fill every aspect of my life so people will look at me and see your goodness. Help me to make known to all the mighty acts of God and the glorious majesty of your kingdom. I pray that I will declare to this generation and to the one to come your greatness and tell them of all the wonderful things you have done for me. Thank you for the ability you give me to bring glory to your great name. I pray in Jesus' name, Amen.

Proclamation:

The Lord my God is good. He is faithful to fulfill all he has spoken. God will give me his strength because I will wait upon him. He will lift me up above the turmoil and strife that come against me. He will set me on high because I know his name. I will call upon the Lord, and he will answer me, and he will show me great and mighty things. God does not withhold his power, his wisdom, his glory or his love from those who call upon him sincerely.

Memory Verse: Ephesians 1:3

"Blessed be the God and Father of our Lord Jesus Christ, who has blessed us with all spiritual blessings in heavenly places in Christ."

To every family member: *"I love you; you are blessed, and you are a blessing."*
Don't forget the hugs.

June 9th

Scripture: Matthew 9:36-38 (CEB)

"Now when Jesus saw the crowds, he had compassion for them because they were troubled and helpless, like sheep without a shepherd. Then he said to his disciples, 'The size of the harvest is bigger than you can imagine, but there are few workers. Therefore, plead with the Lord of the harvest to send out workers for his harvest.'"

In your prayer journal, identify in this portion of scripture a promise to receive or a command to obey.

Prayer:

Father, I see in your Word your great love for people. Jesus was moved with compassion and healed the sick or delivered the oppressed, bringing your kingdom to those in need. I pray, as Jesus said, for the great harvest, the people who are lost and without hope to be brought into your family and into your kingdom. Father, raise up many who will go this day into the harvest fields of this world and declare the good news of your salvation. I pray for an awakening of the people of God to see their calling as harvesters in your kingdom. Let the love of God move us to pray for the harvest and see the power of God at work within us showing the world your love. I know we can do nothing apart from you, but as I pray today, I believe that you are working a mighty work in me and in all who are called by your name to be effective and fervent in prayer for the harvest and empowered by the Spirit of God. We will see the multitudes delivered from the power of darkness and brought into the kingdom of your dear Son. In Jesus' name I pray, Amen.

Proclamation:

The power of God is within me to help me speak the good news of the gospel of Jesus Christ that will bring many into the kingdom of God.

Memory Verse: Ephesians 1:3

"Blessed be the God and Father of our Lord Jesus Christ, who has blessed us with all spiritual blessings in heavenly places in Christ."

To every family member: "I love you; you are blessed, and you are a blessing."
Don't forget the hugs.

June 10th

Scripture: Habakkuk 2:14 (KJV)
"For the earth shall be filled with the knowledge of the glory of the Lord, as the waters cover the sea."

In your prayer journal, identify in this portion of scripture a promise to receive or a command to obey.

Prayer:
My Father, I thank you for the promise of your Word declaring that all the earth shall be filled with the knowledge of your glory in the same way the waters cover the sea. Lord, when Moses asked to see your glory, you said you would cause all of your goodness to pass before him and then you would declare the name of the Lord. I come into agreement with your Word that you will fill this earth with the knowledge of your goodness and the name of the Lord will be declared over all the earth. The name of Jesus, as Savior and healer, deliverer and protector, supplier and provider will bring to all the people of the earth the knowledge of your goodness. I pray for all nations and people of all languages to know your glory, your name and your goodness. Lord, cover the earth with your glory and pour out your Spirit on all flesh that all nations would serve you and stand in awe of your greatness. I pray those who are called by your name will give demonstration to your love and declare your Word with all boldness. I give you thanks for bringing this to pass in Jesus' name. Amen.

Proclamation:
I declare that the Body of Christ is rising up all over the world to bring the gospel of our Lord Jesus Christ to every person and to make disciples of all nations, teaching them to observe all things the Lord said and did. This great army of believers will carry the Word of God and give demonstration to the love of God in every corner of the earth. Then the glory of the Lord will cover all the earth, and the name of the Lord will be glorified.

Memory Verse: Ephesians 1:3
"Blessed be the God and Father of our Lord Jesus Christ, who has blessed us with all spiritual blessings in heavenly places in Christ."

To every family member: *"I love you; you are blessed, and you are a blessing."*
Don't forget the hugs.

June 11th

Scripture: Zechariah 4:6 (NKJV)

"So he answered and said to me: 'This is the word of the Lord to Zerubbabel: "Not by might nor by power, but by My Spirit," Says the Lord of hosts.'"

In your prayer journal, identify in this portion of scripture a promise to receive or a command to obey.

Prayer:

Father, I know that apart from you I can do nothing. I am dependent on you and on the Spirit of God who lives in me to do and accomplish your will and to fulfill your purpose in my life. You said that the Holy Spirit would abide with me forever and he would receive the things of God and reveal them to me. I thank you for the working of the Spirit of God in my life today. I recognize the things I do that glorify you are not by my own wisdom or strength or ability but are the result of the Spirit of God working in me. You, Lord, are able to do exceeding, abundantly above everything I can think or imagine by the Spirit of God and his power that works in me today. Help me to hear your voice, to receive your Word and follow after your leading so that I might accomplish your will and bring glory to your name. In Jesus' name I pray, Amen.

Proclamation:

The same Spirit that raised Jesus from the dead lives in me. I am not alone nor do I rely on my own strength because what I do is not by my might nor by my power, but by the Spirit of God.

Memory Verse: Matthew 6:33

"But seek first the kingdom of God and his righteousness and all these things shall be added unto you."

To every family member: "I love you; you are blessed, and you are a blessing." Don't forget the hugs.

June 12th

Scripture: Matthew 6:19-21 (PHILLIPS)

"Don't pile up treasures on earth, where moth and rust can spoil them and thieves can break in and steal. But keep your treasure in Heaven where there is neither moth nor rust to spoil it and nobody can break in and steal. For wherever your treasure is, you may be certain that your heart will be there too!"

In your prayer journal, identify in this portion of scripture a promise to receive or a command to obey.

Prayer:

Lord, my God, I worship you this day. I praise your glorious name for you are worthy of all glory and honor. Because of your great love, I can come before your throne with all boldness, and I know you receive me and hear me and invite me into your presence. I want to thank you for freely giving me everything that pertains to life. You have promised to take care of my daily needs and clothe me with fine things, for if you take care of the birds of the air and the flowers of the field, how much more will you take care of me? I put my trust in you and my treasure in heavenly things, for there is not anything I will ever need that heaven cannot provide. I know I have a heavenly account where all my most valuable things are kept. They cannot be stolen or destroyed as earthly things can. You have given me access to all I will ever need when I pray and receive what you have supplied for me. In Jesus' name I thank you, Amen.

Proclamation:

My trust is not in earth-bound riches, but in the living God, who liberally gives me all things to enjoy. My treasures cannot be stolen and will never decay or be used up, for they are reserved in heaven for me to access whenever I need them.

Memory Verse: Matthew 6:33

"But seek first the kingdom of God and his righteousness and all these things shall be added unto you."

To every family member: "*I love you; you are blessed, and you are a blessing.*"
Don't forget the hugs.

June 13th

Scripture: Romans 15:13 (KJV)

"Now the God of hope fill you with all joy and peace in believing, that ye may abound in hope, through the power of the Holy Ghost."

In your prayer journal, identify in this portion of scripture a promise to receive or a command to obey.

Prayer:

My Heavenly Father, you are the God of hope. You fill my life with joyful anticipation. You are working in me to cause me to will and do your good pleasure. I know every work of God is working for my good to bring me into peace and cause me to abound in hope by the power of the Holy Spirit. You are my hope. Therefore, I am always expecting good things to happen. Father, I ask you to bring to pass those things I have been praying about and speaking to. Keep me from discouragement, for you said those who trust in you would never be disappointed. I thank you for the kingdom of God that is in me, your righteousness, peace and joy that comes by the Holy Spirit. I praise you for these things now in Jesus' name, Amen.

Proclamation:

I am filled with excitement and expectation of the goodness of God filling every aspect of my life. Every time the phone or doorbell rings or the mail arrives, I expect good news. My God is the God of hope, and he is faithful to fulfill his promises to me.

Memory Verse: Matthew 6:33

"But seek first the kingdom of God and his righteousness and all these things shall be added unto you."

To every family member: "I love you; you are blessed, and you are a blessing."
Don't forget the hugs.

June 14th

Scripture: 2 Corinthians 5:20-21 (NRSV)

"So we are ambassadors for Christ, since God is making his appeal through us; we entreat you on behalf of Christ, be reconciled to God. For our sake he made him to be sin who knew no sin, so that in him we might become the righteousness of God."

In your prayer journal, identify in this portion of scripture a promise to receive or a command to obey.

Prayer:

My Father, I am amazed at your love and goodness towards me. You brought me into your kingdom and delivered me from darkness and destruction by your grace. You have made me to be an ambassador for you to represent you to the people of the world. I pray you help me to represent you well. Jesus carried for me my sin and judgment and gave me in exchange his righteousness and love. Father, I humble myself before you today to commit this day to you and to fulfill the purpose you have for me. I ask you to establish my thoughts and direct me in all my ways so I am always at the right place at the right time with the right people to fulfill and accomplish your good pleasure. Fill me afresh with the Spirit of God and help me to be more aware of the kingdom of God within me than the circumstances that seem to surround me. I trust you today to help me to be fruitful and successful in every way that would bring glory to you. In Jesus' name I pray, Amen.

Proclamation:

The mighty hand of God rests upon me today to empower me with his strength, to establish my thoughts and to direct my paths. This day is a good day. It is the day the Lord has made, and I will rejoice and be glad in it.

Memory Verse: Matthew 6:33

"But seek first the kingdom of God and his righteousness and all these things shall be added unto you."

To every family member: "I love you; you are blessed, and you are a blessing." Don't forget the hugs.

June 15th

Scripture: Acts 3:19-21 (MSG)

"Now it's time to change your ways! Turn to face God so he can wipe away your sins, pour out showers of blessing to refresh you, and send you the Messiah he prepared for you, namely, Jesus. For the time being he must remain out of sight in heaven until everything is restored to order again just the way God, through the preaching of his holy prophets of old, said it would be."

In your prayer journal, identify in this portion of scripture a promise to receive or a command to obey.

Prayer:

Heavenly Father, I thank you for the blessings of heaven that are poured out on me today. You have wiped away all of my sin so I can stand before you without fear or guilt or shame. You are restoring to me everything I lost because of my sin and rebellion. You, Lord, are my redeemer, my Savior and the one who lifts me up out of difficult circumstances and makes me joyful in your presence. Keep me today from every evil work and make me sensitive to the leading of the Spirit of God. Thank you for restoring to me all things the devil stole from me and my family members, even from generations past. You are restoring the years that were lost, the finances stolen away and the broken relationships sabotaged by the wicked works of the enemy. Thank you, Lord, for restoring your purpose for this planet and all you created to glorify you. I praise you for bringing these things to pass in Jesus' name, Amen.

Proclamation:

I am walking today in the blessings of the Lord. He is pouring out more than I can receive and is bringing me once again into the place and purpose he originally designed for me.

Memory Verse: Matthew 6:33

"But seek first the kingdom of God and his righteousness and all these things shall be added unto you."

To every family member: *"I love you; you are blessed, and you are a blessing."*
Don't forget the hugs.

June 16th

Scripture: Psalms 37:23-24 (NLT)

"The Lord directs the steps of the godly. He delights in every detail of their lives. Though they stumble, they will never fall, for the Lord holds them by the hand."

In your prayer journal, identify in this portion of scripture a promise to receive or a command to obey.

Prayer:

Father, I want to bless your name and declare your goodness and glory. You are worthy to be praised, and your glory is above the heavens and earth. All creation declares your works, and all who know you delight in you and give you praise. Thank you for leading me today in the way that I should go. You are interested in every detail of my life. You are touched with how I feel, and you even know my thoughts and the secret things in my heart. Keep me today from all harm and every wicked scheme of the devil. Keep me from falling by holding me up with your mighty right hand. Preserve me in all my ways and fulfill the desires of my heart when I set my affections on you. Reveal to me the things I need to know and keep me from presumption. Help me to acknowledge you in everything I do so I will walk in your wisdom and make decisions that will glorify you and bring your blessings to me and those about me. I thank you for this good day, in Jesus' name, Amen.

Proclamation:

God loves me and cares about me. He is compassionate and kind. He is full of mercy, and his goodness fills my life. I am greatly blessed of the Lord today. I increase more and more in his love and the knowledge of his will. His Word is true, his promises are sure, and he is faithful to do all he has declared. Heaven and earth may pass away, but God's Word stands forever.

Memory Verse: Matthew 6:33

"But seek first the kingdom of God and his righteousness and all these things shall be added unto you."

To every family member: *"I love you; you are blessed, and you are a blessing."*
Don't forget the hugs.

June 17th

Scripture: Proverbs 18:10 (NKJV)
"The name of the Lord is a strong tower; the righteous run to it and are safe."

In your prayer journal, identify in this portion of scripture a promise to receive or a command to obey.

Prayer:

My Father, I praise your great and mighty name. As the towers of refuge in days of old protected those who ran into them, so your name is my high tower of refuge and my place of protection. It was by the name of the Lord Jesus and faith in that name that made the crippled man whole at the gate of the Temple. It was at the name of Jesus the slave girl was set free of an evil spirit. Our salvation is by no other name. Jesus has all authority in heaven and in earth, so I stand today before you and pray in the name of Jesus Christ my Lord. I thank you for my salvation, deliverance, preservation and safety. I receive your blessing and provision, your wisdom and grace to help me in every area of need. I declare these things now, in Jesus' name, Amen.

Proclamation:

The Lord is my shelter and strength, my refuge and my strong tower. I abide under the shadow of the Almighty, and he covers me with his presence. He lifts me up on high and has promised to answer me when I call upon him. Because I know his name, I put my trust in him, for the Lord will not forsake those who seek him.

Memory Verse: Matthew 6:33
"But seek first the kingdom of God and his righteousness and all these things shall be added unto you."

To every family member: *"I love you; you are blessed, and you are a blessing."*
Don't forget the hugs.

June 18th

Scripture: John 16:7-11 (NLT)

"Nevertheless I tell you the truth. It is to your advantage that I go away; for if I do not go away, the Helper will not come to you; but if I depart, I will send Him to you. And when He has come, He will convict the world of sin, and of righteousness, and of judgment: of sin, because they do not believe in Me; of righteousness, because I go to My Father and you see Me no more; of judgment, because the ruler of this world is judged."

In your prayer journal, identify in this portion of scripture a promise to receive or a command to obey.

Prayer:

Heavenly Father, I thank you for your wisdom and your ways. You have not left me alone, but you have sent the Spirit of God to abide with me forever. He has come to help me and to comfort me and to convince me that I am now the righteousness of God because of what Jesus did for me. Jesus defeated the devil bringing judgment on his wicked works and giving me the victory I could never gain on my own. I am righteous, forgiven and redeemed from the curse of sin. I have the Greater One living on the inside of me. No weapon formed against me can defeat me, and no enemy can rob me of this great salvation Jesus purchased for me. I pray I always walk in the reality of these spiritual things as the Spirit of God continues to convince me of this truth. I thank you for it now, in Jesus' name, Amen.

Proclamation:

The Spirit of the living God lives in me. He takes the things of God and reveals them to me. He bears witness to my spirit that I am a child of God. He convinces me of my righteousness before God and teaches me about things to come. God has judged the devil and declared him defeated. God has taken my judgment and declared me righteous. God is for me, so I cannot fail.

Memory Verse: John 14:16-17

"And I will pray the Father, and he shall give you another Comforter, that he may abide with you for ever; Even the Spirit of truth; whom the world cannot receive, because it sees him not, neither knows him; but you know him for he dwells with you, and shall be in you."

To every family member: "*I love you; you are blessed, and you are a blessing.*"
Don't forget the hugs.

June 19th

Scripture: Acts 10:38 (KJV)

"How God anointed Jesus of Nazareth with the Holy Ghost and with power: who went about doing good, and healing all that were oppressed of the devil; for God was with him."

In your prayer journal, identify in this portion of scripture a promise to receive or a command to obey.

Prayer:

My Father, you are great and greatly to be praised. You sent your Son Jesus to save us, deliver us, and redeem us from sin and all its results. When Jesus was anointed as the Christ (Anointed One) with the Holy Spirit, he defeated the devil in the wilderness; he healed the sick, and raised the dead and brought help and hope to the people by the power of the Spirit upon him. I thank you that the same Spirit that anointed Jesus with power is the same Spirit you have given to me. Jesus said that I would receive power after the Holy Spirit comes upon me to do the works of Jesus and bring the power of God to people in need. I pray I walk in the anointing you provide to declare your Word and perform your works. Help me to hear your voice and follow your leading by the Holy Spirit within me. In Jesus' name I pray, Amen.

Proclamation:

The Spirit of God has anointed me to do the works of God. It is not by my own energy or effort that brings the help of God to people in need, but it is the power of the Spirit of God. I am continuously being filled with the Spirit of God so I might do the things God would have me to do, accomplishing his purpose and fulfilling his will. In myself I can do nothing, but through Christ I can do all things.

Memory Verse: John 14:16-17

"And I will pray the Father, and he shall give you another Comforter, that he may abide with you for ever; Even the Spirit of truth; whom the world cannot receive, because it sees him not, neither knows him; but you know him for he dwells with you, and shall be in you."

To every family member: "I love you; you are blessed, and you are a blessing."
Don't forget the hugs.

June 20th

Scripture: Acts 16:25-26 (HCSB)

"About midnight Paul and Silas were praying and singing hymns to God, and the prisoners were listening to them. Suddenly there was such a violent earthquake that the foundations of the jail were shaken, and immediately all the doors were opened, and everyone's chains came loose."

In your prayer journal, identify in this portion of scripture a promise to receive or a command to obey.

Prayer:

God, my Father, I want to be a worshiper like Paul and Silas, to praise you with singing and pray with great faith so those in prison and chains are set free. I thank you that Jesus came to set the captives free, to heal the broken hearted and to open the prison doors to those who are bound. As he came to give us life and life more abundantly, I pray for the power of God to be released as I pray to bind the wicked works of darkness and to see those who are oppressed and bound set at liberty. Every knee must bow to the authority of Jesus' name; and in his name you said I can ask whatever I will and it shall be done. I call for the will of God to be done in my life, in my family and in my community. You are righteous in all your ways, so when I pray, I thank you that righteousness comes into every circumstance that is not right according to your will. I believe blind eyes will see, deaf ears will hear and those who are bound in fear and hopelessness are set free to walk in the health, liberty and hope you have for them. I ask these things to be done this day, in Jesus' name, Amen.

Proclamation:

The Spirit of the Lord is within me, and he has anointed me to pray and to call forth the will of God in the lives of those for whom I pray.

Memory Verse: John 14:16-17

"And I will pray the Father, and he shall give you another Comforter, that he may abide with you for ever; Even the Spirit of truth; whom the world cannot receive, because it sees him not, neither knows him; but you know him for he dwells with you, and shall be in you."

To every family member: *"I love you; you are blessed, and you are a blessing."*
Don't forget the hugs.

June 21st

Scripture: Isaiah 35:4-6 (HCSB)

"Say to the cowardly: 'Be strong; do not fear! Here is your God; vengeance is coming. God's retribution is coming; He will save you.' Then the eyes of the blind will be opened and the ears of the deaf unstopped. Then the lame will leap like a deer and the tongue of the mute will sing for joy for water will gush in the wilderness and streams in the desert"

In your prayer journal, identify in this portion of scripture a promise to receive or a command to obey.

Prayer:

My God, I praise you. I bless the name of my Lord Jesus Christ. Thank you for watching over me to keep and preserve me from all harm. You make me strong and keep me from all fear. You supply all I need and bless me with abundance. I will not fear, for you are with me. I will not be afraid because I know you love me. Even in times of trouble, you are there to rescue me and bring me through every difficulty into a place of peace. Lord, open the eyes of the blind and cause the deaf to hear. Make the lame to walk and bring forth a river of supply for those in need. Display your great goodness and tender mercies that all people in all places may hear and bow down to your great name. Be glorified this day, in Jesus' name, Amen.

Proclamation:

Jesus overcame the world and defeated the devil. He now rules with all power and authority to restore what was stolen, to heal what has been broken, to make right what was wrong and to restore all things.

Memory Verse: John 14:16-17

"And I will pray the Father, and he shall give you another Comforter, that he may abide with you for ever; Even the Spirit of truth; whom the world cannot receive, because it sees him not, neither knows him; but you know him for he dwells with you, and shall be in you."

To every family member: "I love you; you are blessed, and you are a blessing."
Don't forget the hugs.

～ June 22nd ～

Scripture: 1 Corinthians 15:51-54 (MSG)

"But let me tell you something wonderful, a mystery I'll probably never fully understand. We're not all going to die—but we are all going to be changed. You hear a blast to end all blasts from a trumpet, and in the time that you look up and blink your eyes—it's over. On signal from that trumpet from heaven, the dead will be up and out of their graves, beyond the reach of death, never to die again. At the same moment and in the same way, we'll all be changed. In the resurrection scheme of things, this has to happen: everything perishable taken off the shelves and replaced by the imperishable, this mortal replaced by the immortal. Then the saying will come true: Death swallowed by triumphant Life! Who got the last word, oh, Death? Oh, Death, who's afraid of you now?"

In your prayer journal, identify in this portion of scripture a promise to receive or a command to obey.

Prayer:

My Heavenly Father, your ways are wonderful, and I delight in all your promises. I believe Jesus arose from the dead and came out of the tomb to show his victory over death and the grave. I thank you for your promise of resurrection on the last day when Jesus returns. I believe the graves will be opened and the dead will rise never to die again. I believe all who are alive at that time will be changed and transformed from mortal to immortal and from imperfect to perfect in a moment of time. You will remove the wicked, but you will glorify the just and bring them into your presence forever. I bless your holy name and thank you for this promise of eternal victory. In Jesus' name I pray, Amen.

Proclamation:

Jesus died in our place and paid for our sin. He arose in victory over death and defeated the grave. I am free from the fear of death, for I have been delivered from the bondage of sin. In Jesus' name, I am free.

Memory Verse: John 14:16-17

"And I will pray the Father, and he shall give you another Comforter, that he may abide with you for ever; Even the Spirit of truth; whom the world cannot receive, because it sees him not, neither knows him; but you know him for he dwells with you, and shall be in you."

To every family member: "*I love you; you are blessed, and you are a blessing.*" Don't forget the hugs.

June 23rd

Scripture: 2 Chronicles 20:20-22 (GW)

"After he had advised the people, he appointed people to sing to the Lord and praise him for the beauty of his holiness. As they went in front of the troops, they sang, "Thank the Lord because his mercy endures forever!" As they started to sing praises, the Lord set ambushes against the Ammonites, Moabites, and the people of Mount Seir who had come into Judah. They were defeated."

In your prayer journal, identify in this portion of scripture a promise to receive or a command to obey.

Prayer:

Heavenly Father, you defend the righteous and defeat the wicked by your mighty power. You said that we were not to trust in ourselves but in you who are faithful to deliver us from every evil work. As Jehoshaphat put the singers in front of Israel's armies, I will first of all, before I do anything else, praise you. You are well able to deliver me and make me victorious over any enemy that would rise up against me. I know I do not war against people, but against spiritual wickedness. The weapons you have given me are mighty and will give me success over any advancing foe. I open my mouth to sing praises to you and you will cause my enemies to destroy each other. You will give me victory and bring me success over every evil work. I praise your wonderful name, and it's in Jesus' name I pray, Amen.

Proclamation:

When the enemy comes against me, the Lord raises up a wall of defense for me. When I worship and praise the Lord my God, my enemies are put to flight, and my foes run in terror, for if God is for me, who can be against me?

Memory Verse: John 14:16-17

"And I will pray the Father, and he shall give you another Comforter, that he may abide with you for ever; Even the Spirit of truth; whom the world cannot receive, because it sees him not, neither knows him; but you know him for he dwells with you, and shall be in you."

To every family member: "I love you; you are blessed, and you are a blessing." Don't forget the hugs.

June 24th

Scripture: Psalms 8:1-2 (NKJV)

"O Lord, our Lord, how excellent is Your name in all the earth, who have set Your glory above the heavens! Out of the mouth of babes and nursing infants you have ordained strength, because of Your enemies, that You may silence the enemy and the avenger."

In your prayer journal, identify in this portion of scripture a promise to receive or a command to obey.

Prayer:

Father, I want to sing your praise and bless your name. I want to lift up my voice above every other voice in praise to you. You will silence every enemy and cause the avenger to run away because your great power is seen when people of faith begin to praise you. Even infants and those with no strength of their own will see your delivering power when their mouths are open in praise. Your might and power are without measure, and your greatness is above all I could ever imagine. Thank you for hearing me when I pray and receiving my praise. Help me to know in times of crisis or in times of peace that you are always worthy of my praise. In Jesus' name I pray, Amen.

Proclamation:

The Lord my God hears my prayer. I open my mouth in praise to him, and every other voice becomes silent. My enemies run in fear because the Lord brings me help in my time of need. I will remember to praise the Lord in every situation, for he is my strength and a very present help in times of trouble.

Memory Verse: John 14:16-17

"And I will pray the Father, and he shall give you another Comforter, that he may abide with you for ever; Even the Spirit of truth; whom the world cannot receive, because it sees him not, neither knows him; but you know him for he dwells with you, and shall be in you."

To every family member: *"I love you; you are blessed, and you are a blessing."*
Don't forget the hugs.

Faith Family Minute

～ June 25th ～

Scripture: Matthew 7:9-12 (VOICE)

"Think of it this way: if your son asked you for bread, would you give him a stone? *Of course not*—you would give him a loaf of bread. If your son asked for a fish, would you give him a snake? *No, to be sure, you would give him a fish—the best fish you could find.* So if you, who are sinful, know how to give your children good gifts, how much more so does your Father in heaven, who is perfect, know how to give great gifts to His children! This is what our Scriptures come to teach: in everything, in every circumstance, do to others as you would have them do to you."

In your prayer journal, identify in this portion of scripture a promise to receive or a command to obey.

Prayer:

My Father, I am so glad that I have received the Spirit of God and can call you Abba (Daddy) Father. The Word of God declares that every good and perfect gift comes from you. You are the Father of lights and in you there is no darkness at all. Everything you give is good, and you have freely given to me all things that pertain to life. Thank you for your good gifts and the gift of the Holy Spirit who reveals to me the things of God. Show me, Father, the things of God. Show me the things to come and the things you would have me to know. As I have freely received from you, help me to freely give to others. May the gifts of God and the spiritual things you have deposited in me work through me to be a blessing to many. I ask these things in Jesus' name, Amen.

Proclamation:

I am filled with the Spirit of God. He gives me everything I could ever desire. His gifts work in me and through me to be a blessing to all I meet.

Memory Verse: Ephesians 2:8-9

"For by grace are you saved through faith; and that not of yourselves: it is the gift of God: not of works, lest any one should boast."

To every family member: *"I love you; you are blessed, and you are a blessing."*
Don't forget the hugs.

June 26th

Scripture: Ephesians 2:1-6 (RSV)

"And you he made alive, when you were dead through the trespasses and sins in which you once walked, following the course of this world, following the prince of the power of the air, the spirit that is now at work in the sons of disobedience. Among these we all once lived in the passions of our flesh, following the desires of body and mind, and so we were by nature children of wrath, like the rest of mankind. But God, who is rich in mercy, out of the great love with which he loved us, even when we were dead through our trespasses, made us alive together with Christ (by grace you have been saved), and raised us up with him, and made us sit with him in the heavenly places in Christ Jesus."

In your prayer journal, identify in this portion of scripture a promise to receive or a command to obey.

Prayer:

Father, you have delivered me from the power of darkness and have brought me into your glorious kingdom. I am free from the power of sin and the rebellious spirit of this world that once worked in me. When you raise Jesus (who died for me) from the dead, you also raised me up to be seated with Jesus in a place of victory. By your grace, I am to rule in life. By your authority, I am to bring everything into agreement with your Word. Thank you for the mighty name of Jesus by which I pray and call forth your will. Although I live in this world, I am a citizen of heaven. You said those who believe in Jesus as Lord have overcome this world. Thank you for making me victorious over the world and blessed with all spiritual blessing in Jesus Christ. It is in Jesus' name I pray, Amen.

Proclamation:

I am in the world, but not of the world. I have overcome the world because I believe that Jesus Christ is Lord.

Memory Verse: Ephesians 2:8-9

"For by grace are you saved through faith; and that not of yourselves: it is the gift of God: not of works, lest any one should boast."

To every family member: *"I love you; you are blessed, and you are a blessing."*
Don't forget the hugs.

June 27th

Scripture: 1 Peter 2:9-10 (NLT)

"But you are not like that, for you are a chosen people. You are royal priests, a holy nation, God's very own possession. As a result, you can show others the goodness of God, for he called you out of the darkness into his wonderful light. "Once you had no identity as a people; now you are God's people. Once you received no mercy; now you have received God's mercy."

In your prayer journal, identify in this portion of scripture a promise to receive or a command to obey.

Prayer:

Heavenly Father, you love me and made me your very own possession. You brought me into your family and called me by your name. You said I am a royal priest, a member of your holy nation. I have left the darkness and have entered into your light. Help me to show others your great goodness. Lord, I pray for those who are only identified with darkness, loss and misery. I ask you to send someone who can show them the way out of their darkness and sorrow. As you caused the light to shine out of darkness in creation, let the light of the glorious gospel of Christ Jesus shine on these to give them the light that brings them to the knowledge of Jesus and brings them out of their darkness into your light, your mercy and your family. I pray these things now, in Jesus' name, Amen.

Proclamation:

I am chosen by God as a priest of his royal family. I am a citizen of his holy nation. My identity is one who has received mercy, and I am known as one of the people of God.

Memory Verse: Ephesians 2:8-9

"For by grace are you saved through faith; and that not of yourselves: it is the gift of God: not of works, lest any one should boast."

To every family member: "I love you; you are blessed, and you are a blessing."
Don't forget the hugs.

June 28th

Scripture: Psalms 2:6-8 (NIV)

"The kings of the earth rise up and the rulers band together against the Lord and against his anointed, saying, 'Let us break their chains and throw off their shackles.' The One enthroned in heaven laughs; the Lord scoffs at them. He rebukes them in his anger and terrifies them in his wrath, saying, 'I have installed my king on Zion, my holy mountain.' I will proclaim the Lord's decree: He said to me, "You are my son; today I have become your father. Ask me and I will make the nations your inheritance, the ends of the earth your possession."

In your prayer journal, identify in this portion of scripture a promise to receive or a command to obey.

Prayer:

God, my Father, you are Almighty and all powerful. You have created all things and yet the kings of the earth and rulers of nations foolishly defy you. You laugh at their plans and rebuke them in their rebellion, but you have declared that Jesus, the King of kings, sits on the throne of your kingdom to rule the nations. Father, I ask you, according to your Word, for the nations. I pray for kings and presidents and rulers and prime ministers and all who hold positions of authority to bow before you and acknowledge Jesus as Lord over all the earth. I pray for godly men and women who will honor you and submit themselves to you to hold these positions as leaders of the nations. I pray that the wicked and ungodly who will not humble themselves before you will be removed and replaced by those who will honor you. I pray for the fulfillment of these things now, in Jesus' name, Amen.

Proclamation:

The day will come when such a mighty outpouring of the Spirit of God will cover all the earth, and all flesh will come and bow down before him.

Memory Verse: Ephesians 2:8-9

"For by grace are you saved through faith; and that not of yourselves: it is the gift of God: not of works, lest any one should boast."

To every family member: *"I love you; you are blessed, and you are a blessing."* Don't forget the hugs.

June 29th

Scripture: 1 Peter 3:8-12 (NASB)

"To sum up, all of you be harmonious, sympathetic, brotherly, kindhearted, and humble in spirit; not returning evil for evil or insult for insult, but giving a blessing instead; for you were called for the very purpose that you might inherit a blessing. For, 'The one who desires life, to love and see good days, must keep his tongue from evil and his lips from speaking deceit. He must turn away from evil and do good; he must seek peace and pursue it. For the eyes of the Lord are toward the righteous, and His ears attend to their prayer, but the face of the Lord is against those who do evil.'"

In your prayer journal, identify in this portion of scripture a promise to receive or a command to obey.

Prayer:

Lord, my God, I bless you this day. I thank you for goodness and mercies that are poured out on me today. You have purposed for me to inherit a blessing, and you tell me to bless others. I believe as I give it shall be given to me in abundance and whatever I sow will be what I reap. I choose to bless those who bless me and those who curse me and count me as an enemy. I will not insult those who would insult me, but I will bless them instead. Lord, your eyes are over the righteous, and you pay attention to their prayers, so I know you watch me and hear me as I seek to do what is right and good in your eyes. I ask you to help me keep my tongue from speaking anything except that which edifies and builds up those I meet today. I thank you for this work of God working in me and through me for your glory and for my blessing in Jesus' name, Amen.

Proclamation:

I will only speak words to encourage and build up those I meet today. I am blessed, and I will continue to speak blessings. People enjoy being around me because my words bring them hope and life.

Memory Verse: Ephesians 2:8-9

"For by grace are you saved through faith; and that not of yourselves: it is the gift of God: not of works, lest any one should boast."

To every family member: *"I love you; you are blessed, and you are a blessing."*
Don't forget the hugs.

June 30th

Scripture: Romans 4:3-8 (NCV)

"...because the Scripture says, 'Abraham believed God, and God accepted Abraham's faith, and that faith made him right with God.' When people work, their pay is not given as a gift, but as something earned. But people cannot do any work that will make them right with God. So they must trust in him, who makes even evil people right in his sight. Then God accepts their faith, and that makes them right with him. David said the same thing. He said that people are truly blessed when God, without paying attention to their deeds, makes people right with himself. 'Blessed are they whose sins are forgiven, whose wrongs are pardoned. Blessed is the person whom the Lord does not consider guilty.'"

In your prayer journal, identify in this portion of scripture a promise to receive or a command to obey.

Prayer:

Heavenly Father, I know your love for me is perfect and there is nothing I can do to earn your love or make myself right with you. I can only express my faith in the work of Jesus. He lived without sin so I could receive his gift to me of a perfect life. He took the judgment for my sin and carried it himself so I would not have to. He rose from the dead to give me eternal life without death. He is seated on the throne at the right hand of God, the Father, hearing my prayer and praying for me so I can rule as a king in life. I have done nothing to deserve it, but I am glad to receive everything Jesus did for me. I thank you for your blessings and forgiveness now, in Jesus' name, Amen.

Proclamation:

Jesus did all the work for me. I receive all the benefits without working. My faith is strong, and my life is full because of the love of God for me.

Memory Verse: Ephesians 2:8-9

"For by grace are you saved through faith; and that not of yourselves: it is the gift of God: not of works, lest any one should boast."

To every family member: *"I love you; you are blessed, and you are a blessing."* Don't forget the hugs.

July 1st

Scripture: Psalms 150 (KJV)

"Praise ye the Lord. Praise God in his sanctuary: praise him in the firmament of his power. Praise him for his mighty acts: praise him according to his excellent greatness. Praise him with the sound of the trumpet: praise him with the psaltery and harp. Praise him with the timbrel and dance: praise him with stringed instruments and organs. Praise him upon the loud cymbals: praise him upon the high sounding cymbals. Let every thing that hath breath praise the Lord. Praise ye the Lord."

In your prayer journal, identify in this portion of scripture a promise to receive or a command to obey.

Prayer:

Father, I desire to worship and praise your great name with my voice and with instruments of praise. You said to let every thing that has breath praise you. As long as I live I want to daily praise your name. Even inanimate objects as horns and stringed instruments are to give praise to you because you are great and worthy to be praised. All of creation gives praise to you. The mountains and the hills sing and the trees of the field clap their hands. The oceans roar and the heavens declare your greatness. Lord, your praise is to be continually in my mouth. I ask you to help me guard my mouth from complaining and my eyes from focusing on the things that are wrong instead of on your greatness, your power and the wonderful promises you have spoken over me. I thank you for these things now, in Jesus' name, Amen.

Proclamation:

All of God's creation speaks of his glory and power. I will join my voice with those in heaven and earth that are bringing praise to the Lord my God.

Memory Verse: Ephesians 2:8-9

"For by grace are you saved through faith; and that not of yourselves: it is the gift of God: not of works, lest any one should boast."

To every family member: *"I love you; you are blessed, and you are a blessing."*
Don't forget the hugs.

July 2nd

Scripture: 1 Thessalonians 1:2-7 (NASB)

"We give thanks to God always for all of you, making mention of *you* in our prayers; constantly bearing in mind your work of faith and labor of love and steadfastness of hope in our Lord Jesus Christ in the presence of our God and Father, knowing, brethren beloved by God, *His* choice of you; for our gospel did not come to you in word only, but also in power and in the Holy Spirit and with full conviction; just as you know what kind of men we proved to be among you for your sake. You also became imitators of us and of the Lord, having received the word in much tribulation with the joy of the Holy Spirit, so that you became an example to all the believers in Macedonia and in Achaia."

In your prayer journal, identify in this portion of scripture a promise to receive or a command to obey.

Prayer:

My Father, I pray I become the kind of person who works in faith, labors in love and is steadfast in hope so others might give thanks for my service to them and to you. I ask you to bless the works of my hands and make me fruitful in prayer and in demonstrating the love of God. I pray for more than just the ability to speak your Word, but also for the demonstration of your power as I pray and minister to others. I pray the Spirit of God will convince those who hear your Word and will touch them with your mighty power to bring healing to the sick, hope to the discouraged and salvation to the lost. I ask these things in Jesus' name, Amen.

Proclamation:

The Spirit of God abides within me, and the power of God is upon me to effectively speak God's Word and demonstrate his power and goodness to all.

Memory Verse: Joshua 1:9

"Have not I commanded you? Be strong and of a good courage, be not afraid, neither be dismayed, for the Lord your God is with you wherever you go."

To every family member: *"I love you; you are blessed, and you are a blessing."*
Don't forget the hugs.

July 3rd

Scripture: Hebrews 10:19-22 (GNT)

"We have, then, my friends, complete freedom to go into the Most Holy Place by means of the death of Jesus. He opened for us a new way, a living way, through the curtain—that is, through his own body. We have a great priest in charge of the house of God. So let us come near to God with a sincere heart and a sure faith, with hearts that have been purified from a guilty conscience and with bodies washed with clean water."

In your prayer journal, identify in this portion of scripture a promise to receive or a command to obey.

Prayer:

My Heavenly Father, thank you for granting me access to the very throne of God. Because Jesus died for me, the veil that separated me from God was torn apart. The sin barrier that kept me from entering God's holy presence was removed, and Jesus made a way for me to enter your presence without guilt or shame or fear. I come boldly to your throne of grace as you have commanded me, and I receive your grace and mercy to help me every time I have a need. Just as clean water washes my body, so the blood of Jesus washes my conscience from guilt. I approach you with confidence, knowing you accept me and hear me. I ask you to open my ears to hear your voice so I am ever increasing in faith. Help me to recognize your will and pray boldly by calling forth the things you want to do and accomplish in the lives of those for whom I pray. Thank you for hearing me now. In Jesus' name I pray, Amen.

Proclamation:

Jesus is the way into the holy presence of God. He made the way for me and qualified me to stand in the presence of God without fear. I pray the will of God and by faith I call into being those things that are according to his will so God is glorified and his will accomplished.

Memory Verse: Joshua 1:9

"Have not I commanded you? Be strong and of a good courage, be not afraid, neither be dismayed, for the Lord your God is with you wherever you go."

To every family member: "*I love you; you are blessed, and you are a blessing.*" Don't forget the hugs.

July 4th

Scripture: 1 Corinthians 10:1-5, 11 (MSG)

"Remember our history, friends, and be warned. All our ancestors were led by the providential Cloud and taken miraculously through the Sea. They went through the waters, in a baptism like ours, as Moses led them from enslaving death to salvation life. They all ate and drank identical food and drink, meals provided daily by God. They drank from the Rock, God's fountain for them that stayed with them wherever they were. And the Rock was Christ. But just experiencing God's wonder and grace didn't seem to mean much—most of them were defeated by temptation during the hard times in the desert, and God was not pleased.

These are all warning markers—danger!—in our history books, written down so that we don't repeat their mistakes."

In your prayer journal, identify in this portion of scripture a promise to receive or a command to obey.

Prayer:

Father, I am glad you have given me as a promise-land an inheritance in your kingdom. Keep me from temptation and unbelief so I do not fail to live in the place of your blessings as many did in Moses's day. Those who ate and drank from your miraculous provision eventually died in the desert without enjoying the land you had promised them. They saw your miracles and still refused to enter the land because they were afraid of the enemies and saw themselves as too weak and too few to win the victory. Help me to never consider the enemy as too strong or the opposition too great so I look at myself instead of trusting you. You are my help and strength. Jesus already defeated my enemy, and the Spirit of God gives me power to receive all you have given me. I thank you for your victory in Jesus' name, Amen.

Proclamation:

There is no enemy too strong or need too great for God to handle.

Memory Verse: Joshua 1:9

"Have not I commanded you? Be strong and of a good courage, be not afraid, neither be dismayed, for the Lord your God is with you wherever you go."

To every family member: *"I love you; you are blessed, and you are a blessing."* Don't forget the hugs.

July 5th

Scripture: 1 Corinthians 10:13 (PHILLIPS)

"No temptation has come your way that is too hard for flesh and blood to bear. But God can be trusted not to allow you to suffer any temptation beyond your powers of endurance. He will see to it that every temptation has a way out, so that it will never be impossible for you to bear it."

In your prayer journal, identify in this portion of scripture a promise to receive or a command to obey.

Prayer:

Lord, my God, I bless you. I worship your holy name, for you are faithful. You watch over me to protect and keep me from every wicked work of the enemy. You are able to keep me from temptation. You said if I humble myself before you, drawing close to you, and resist the devil he will flee from me. Therefore, I ask you to keep me from entering into temptation when it comes. Help me recognize it for what it is and show me the way out to avoid its trap. Thank you for leading me in righteous paths today. I will walk in the place of blessing and reign over all the devices of the enemy. I declare these things now, in Jesus' name, Amen.

Proclamation:

I will give the devil no place in my life. I will not yield to temptations of the flesh, but I will bring my body under subjection to the will of God and will cast down every exalted thought that is contrary to the Word of God. Sin does not have dominion over me because Jesus has redeemed me, forgiven me, empowered me and given to me the shield of faith, the sword of the Spirit and all the armor of God to quench every fiery arrow and overcome every wicked spirit in the heavens or on the earth. I am more than a conqueror.

Memory Verse: Joshua 1:9

"Have not I commanded you? Be strong and of a good courage, be not afraid, neither be dismayed, for the Lord your God is with you wherever you go."

To every family member: *"I love you; you are blessed, and you are a blessing."*
Don't forget the hugs.

July 6th

Scripture: 2 Chronicles 7:14 (KJV)

"If my people, which are called by my name, shall humble themselves, and pray, and seek my face, and turn from their wicked ways; then will I hear from heaven, and will forgive their sin, and will heal their land."

In your prayer journal, identify in this portion of scripture a promise to receive or a command to obey.

Prayer:

Heavenly Father, you are faithful to watch over your Word to perform it in our lives. If you said it, you will do it, and if you spoke it, you will bring it to pass. I purpose to humble myself before you today. I will seek your face. I will seek your presence, and I will turn away from any wicked way, any way of doing things I know is displeasing to you. You have promised to hear my prayer and to forgive and heal this land. Our land desperately needs your healing. Our people are divided, and many of our leaders are corrupt. I ask you to stir the hearts of all those who are called by your name and who live in this nation. I pray for the repentance of your people and the healing of our nation. Bring us again into a place of unity and agreement with one another and in alignment with you. Uncover and expose any corruption in the leaders or systems operating in this land that are displeasing to you. Root out and remove the wicked and ungodly and lift up the righteous to govern this land in righteousness and with justice. Father, I ask you to heal what is broken in our nation that we once again may be one nation under God. I thank you for hearing and answering this prayer now in Jesus' name, Amen.

Proclamation:

God will uncover and expose what is hidden and unrighteous. He will scatter the proud and promote the righteous who will accomplish his will.

Memory Verse: Joshua 1:9

"Have not I commanded you? Be strong and of a good courage, be not afraid, neither be dismayed, for the Lord your God is with you wherever you go."

To every family member: "*I love you; you are blessed, and you are a blessing.*"
Don't forget the hugs.

July 7th

Scripture: Proverbs 8:33-36 (NASB)

"Heed instruction and be wise, and do not neglect it. Blessed is the man who listens to me, watching daily at my gates, waiting at my doorposts. For he who finds me finds life and obtains favor from the Lord. But he who sins against me injures himself; all those who hate me love death."

In your prayer journal, identify in this portion of scripture a promise to receive or a command to obey.

Prayer:

God, my Father, I pray for your wisdom to fill my life. Your Word declares that the man who seeks wisdom as if it were a hidden treasure will find favor and blessings from the Lord. You said if I ask for wisdom you will give it to me liberally. I believe I receive your wisdom working in me today. I ask you to open my ears and my eyes to hear and see things the way they are and not just as they appear to be. Your wisdom will bring me knowledge and understanding. You said wisdom has riches and honor and brings me better things than silver and gold. I thank you for your wisdom now in Jesus' name, Amen.

Proclamation:

Wisdom is to be desired above all else. All the things that may be desired are not to be compared to it. The wisdom of God brings me favor and counsel, riches and honor. I will walk in the wisdom of God today.

Memory Verse: Joshua 1:9

"Have not I commanded you? Be strong and of a good courage, be not afraid, neither be dismayed, for the Lord your God is with you wherever you go."

To every family member: "I love you; you are blessed, and you are a blessing." Don't forget the hugs.

July 8th

Scripture: Jeremiah 33:1-3 (NLV)

"While Jeremiah was still shut up in the open space of the prison, the Word of the Lord came to him a second time, saying, 'This is what the Lord says Who made the earth. The Lord made it to last. The Lord is His name. "Call to Me, and I will answer you. And I will show you great and wonderful things which you do not know."'"

In your prayer journal, identify in this portion of scripture a promise to receive or a command to obey.

Prayer:

My Heavenly Father, you know all things. The earth is yours and all that is in it. You know the secret treasures hidden in darkness. You know when I sit down and when I rise up, and you even know my thoughts while they are still a long way off. There is nothing you don't know. You said to call upon you and you would answer me and show me great and mighty things that I do not know. I call on you today to show me what I need to know. Give me knowledge, wisdom and understanding. Help me to understand the times and seasons I am living in. You, Lord are not the author of confusion but of peace; therefore, I commit my works to you today, and I believe you will cause my thoughts to be aligned with your will so my plans will be established and succeed. I receive these things now, in Jesus' name, Amen

Proclamation:

God knows the end from the beginning. He knows everything, and he is able to cause me to know and understand his plans and how to perform them.

Memory Verse: Joshua 1:9

"Have not I commanded you? Be strong and of a good courage, be not afraid, neither be dismayed, for the Lord your God is with you wherever you go."

To every family member: "I love you; you are blessed, and you are a blessing." Don't forget the hugs.

July 9th

Scripture: 1 Corinthians 15:21-26 (NKJV)

"For since by man *came* death, by Man also *came* the resurrection of the dead. For as in Adam all die, even so in Christ all shall be made alive. But each one in his own order: Christ the firstfruits, afterward those *who* are Christ's at His coming. Then *comes* the end, when He delivers the kingdom to God the Father, when He puts an end to all rule and all authority and power. For He must reign till He has put all enemies under His feet. The last enemy *that* will be destroyed *is* death."

In your prayer journal, identify in this portion of scripture a promise to receive or a command to obey.

Prayer:

Father, I thank you today for the promise of the resurrection. Just as Jesus was raised from the dead, so you will raise me up from death. As Jesus was victorious over death, I am also victorious. I pray, as long as I am in this mortal body, I will live in health and strength. You said you would satisfy me with long life; therefore, I believe I will live as long as I want to in order to fulfill my assignment and ministry here. I thank you that I don't have to fear death because Jesus has already given me eternal life. I have this promise: when my body has fulfilled its purpose and lost its usefulness, it will cease to function, but my spirit and soul will come to you. When Jesus returns, death will be destroyed, and at the resurrection, this mortal flesh will receive immortality. I praise you for bringing to pass this wonderful promise, in Jesus' name, Amen.

Proclamation:

I will live forever. As far reaching as Adam's sin was to bring death into this world and on every person, so much greater is the redemptive work of Christ to give me life now and forever.

Memory Verse: 2 Timothy 3:16-17

"All scripture is given by inspiration of God, and is profitable for doctrine, for reproof, for correction, for instruction in righteousness; that the man of God may be perfect, thoroughly furnished unto all good works."

To every family member: *"I love you; you are blessed, and you are a blessing."*
Don't forget the hugs.

July 10th

Scripture: 2 Chronicles 32:7-8 (KJV)

"Be strong and courageous, be not afraid nor dismayed for the king of Assyria, nor for all the multitude that is with him: for there be more with us than with him: With him is an arm of flesh; but with us is the Lord our God to help us, and to fight our battles. And the people rested themselves upon the words of Hezekiah king of Judah."

In your prayer journal, identify in this portion of scripture a promise to receive or a command to obey.

Prayer:

My Heavenly Father, I praise you. You are faithful to watch over me and keep me from every enemy. Help me to be strong and courageous today, putting my faith in you. Just as king Hezekiah encouraged the people of Judah to see that though they were greatly outnumbered by the armies of the enemy, the certainty of victory belonged to them. The enemy king only had physical strength but they had the power of God. Help me to see that whatever may come against me has no power to defeat me because you are with me. Keep me from looking at the things that appear to be impossible and instead to put my focus on you. In Jesus' name I pray, Amen.

Proclamation:

I am strong and courageous because I know God is with me. I do not just look at the things that are seen, but I focus on the things that are not seen, those invisible things of God, who always brings me victory.

Memory Verse: 2 Timothy 3:16-17

"All scripture is given by inspiration of God, and is profitable for doctrine, for reproof, for correction, for instruction in righteousness; that the man of God may be perfect, thoroughly furnished unto all good works."

To every family member: *"I love you; you are blessed, and you are a blessing."*
Don't forget the hugs.

July 11th

Scripture: Isaiah 41:10-13 (GW)

"Don't be afraid, because I am with you. Don't be intimidated; I am your God. I will strengthen you. I will help you. I will support you with my victorious right hand. Everyone who is angry with you will be ashamed and disgraced. Those who oppose you will be reduced to nothing and disappear. You will search for your enemies, but you will not find them. Those who are at war with you will be reduced to nothing and no longer exist. I, the Lord your God, hold your right hand and say to you, 'Don't be afraid; I will help you.'"

In your prayer journal, identify in this portion of scripture a promise to receive or a command to obey.

Prayer:

Father, you have given me such wonderful promises. Over and over again you tell me to not be afraid but to trust you. I take hold of your Word today and declare what you have promised. You will help me today. You will support me with your victorious right hand. Those who oppose me wrongfully will be ashamed and disgraced, reduced to nothing and will disappear. You will hold my hand and give me victory because you are with me. I thank you for this promise and for the power of God that is at work on my behalf this day. In Jesus' name I pray, Amen.

Proclamation:

The strong, victorious hand of the Lord my God, is with me. He will fight for me. He will destroy my enemies and bring me victory. I will not be afraid.

Memory Verse: 2 Timothy 3:16-17

"All scripture is given by inspiration of God, and is profitable for doctrine, for reproof, for correction, for instruction in righteousness; that the man of God may be perfect, thoroughly furnished unto all good works."

To every family member: *"I love you; you are blessed, and you are a blessing."*
Don't forget the hugs.

July 12th

Scripture: Mark 1:40-42 (AMP)

"And a leper came to Him, begging Him on his knees and saying to Him, If You are willing, You are able to make me clean. And being moved with pity *and* sympathy, Jesus reached out His hand and touched him, and said to him, I am willing; be made clean! And at once the leprosy [completely] left him and he was made clean [by being healed]."

In your prayer journal, identify in this portion of scripture a promise to receive or a command to obey.

Prayer:

Heavenly Father, I thank you for your great power, for there is no one like you. You can do all things. There is nothing too hard for you. You have created all things, and by your power, all creation is sustained, but most of all, I thank you for your great love. As Jesus was moved with compassion and healed the leper, he is also moved with compassion for me. As your Word declares, Jesus is touched with the feelings of my infirmities. He knows my sorrows and pains; he is aware of my struggles and is willing to help me in every way. Lord, just as the leper came to you for help, I come to you today to find your help for my needs. I receive your healing for my body, your peace for my mind and abundant provision for my every need. I thank you for your great love for me, and because you love me, I can pray with confidence and by faith receive all things. In Jesus' name I pray, Amen.

Proclamation:

I walk today in the revelation of God's love for me. He who gave his own Son for me will also freely give me all things that pertain to life.

Memory Verse: 2 Timothy 3:16-17

"All scripture is given by inspiration of God, and is profitable for doctrine, for reproof, for correction, for instruction in righteousness; that the man of God may be perfect, thoroughly furnished unto all good works."

To every family member: *"I love you; you are blessed, and you are a blessing."*
Don't forget the hugs.

July 13th

Scripture: Romans 5:17 (NKJV)

"For if by the one man's offense death reigned through the one, much more those who receive abundance of grace and of the gift of righteousness will reign in life through the One, Jesus Christ."

In your prayer journal, identify in this portion of scripture a promise to receive or a command to obey.

Prayer:

Heavenly Father, you are worthy of all praise and honor and glory. All might and strength belong to you. You sent Jesus so I could reign in life. In the beginning, you created man to rule and have dominion and authority. When man failed, Jesus came and restored man to God's original purpose. Because of Adam's sin I died, but because of Jesus, I have been delivered from the power of sin and death. Because of your grace, I now have righteousness, and reign in life. You have given me authority in the name of Jesus and power by the Holy Spirit to declare on this earth your will as it is in heaven. Help me to walk in your authority and power with wisdom and confidence, always doing your will. I pray in Jesus' name, Amen.

Proclamation:

I have received the gift of righteousness. Jesus took my sin and unrighteousness and gave me his righteousness, so I will rule and reign in life.

Memory Verse: 2 Timothy 3:16-17

"All scripture is given by inspiration of God, and is profitable for doctrine, for reproof, for correction, for instruction in righteousness; that the man of God may be perfect, thoroughly furnished unto all good works."

To every family member: "I love you; you are blessed, and you are a blessing."
Don't forget the hugs.

July 14th

Scripture: Galatians 5:6 (MSG)

"For in Christ, neither our most conscientious religion nor disregard of religion amounts to anything. What matters is something far more interior: faith expressed in love."

In your prayer journal, identify in this portion of scripture a promise to receive or a command to obey.

Prayer:

Heavenly Father, your Word declares that you are gracious and kind, full of compassion and tender mercies. Your very character is love. There is no wickedness or evil in you. You will always do what is right and good, and as a Father you love me with a perfect love. I thank you that I do not have to perform some difficult religious ritual or walk in sorrow and self-abhorrence to please you. I just need to honor you, by putting my faith in you, trusting you and believing that your purpose and desire for me is only good. Jesus did away with all religious observances by giving his life for me, fulfilling all the works necessary to please you. My faith is not in what I can do to gain your approval, but my faith is in what Jesus did for me. I thank you today for faith. You have given me a measure of faith so powerful it can remove mountains and bring forgiveness, healing and life to me and to those I pray for. This faith only works by love, so help me to live out of the love of God in my heart so my faith would be great and you would be pleased. In Jesus' name I pray, Amen.

Proclamation:

I don't please God by religious works; I please him by faith that works by love.

Memory Verse: 2 Timothy 3:16-17

"All scripture is given by inspiration of God, and is profitable for doctrine, for reproof, for correction, for instruction in righteousness; that the man of God may be perfect, thoroughly furnished unto all good works."

To every family member: *"I love you; you are blessed, and you are a blessing."*
Don't forget the hugs.

July 15th

Scripture: Daniel 7:13-14 (KJV)

"I saw in the night visions, and, behold, one like the Son of man came with the clouds of heaven, and came to the Ancient of days, and they brought him near before him. And there was given him dominion, and glory, and a kingdom, that all people, nations, and languages, should serve him: his dominion is an everlasting dominion, which shall not pass away, and his kingdom that which shall not be destroyed."

In your prayer journal, identify in this portion of scripture a promise to receive or a command to obey.

Prayer:

Heavenly Father, your kingdom is everlasting and your dominion is forever. When Jesus ascended from the Mount of Olives, he was carried by a cloud of angels who brought him to you, the Ancient of days. He was seated on the throne of your glory and forever reigns at your right hand. I thank you for your faithfulness in raising Christ from the dead. Because he is there, ever living to make intercession for me, I know I can approach your throne with boldness and confidence. Help me to understand the work Jesus accomplished for me so I will never attempt to receive from you anything based on my own works or goodness. My faith is in what Jesus did for me. I thank you for hearing me and helping me receive everything you have freely given me. In Jesus' name I pray, Amen.

Proclamation:

I have been delivered out of the kingdom of darkness, and I have been translated into the kingdom of God. Righteousness, peace and joy are mine. I can ask whatever I will, and it shall be done for me by my Father in heaven. Jesus has all authority in heaven and earth. He rules over all and has given authority to his family to stand in his name and declare the will of God in the earth until every knee bows and every tongue confesses that Jesus Christ is Lord.

Memory Verse: 2 Timothy 3:16-17

"All scripture is given by inspiration of God, and is profitable for doctrine, for reproof, for correction, for instruction in righteousness; that the man of God may be perfect, thoroughly furnished unto all good works."

To every family member: "I love you; you are blessed, and you are a blessing." Don't forget the hugs.

July 16th

Scripture: Mark 6:4-6 (RSV)

"And Jesus said to them, 'A prophet is not without honor, except in his own country, and among his own kin, and in his own house.' And he could do no mighty work there, except that he laid his hands upon a few sick people and healed them. And he marveled because of their unbelief."

In your prayer journal, identify in this portion of scripture a promise to receive or a command to obey.

Prayer:

My Father, I pray I will be able to receive everything Jesus has done for me. I do not want to be like those who could not receive because of their unbelief. Help me to know your will so I will not be deceived. Help me to know your grace so I will not try to earn, by my own efforts, answered prayer or miraculous works. Help me to recognize your voice so I will not be distracted by the many voices in the world. Help me to persevere when opposition comes against your Word so your promises will not be robbed from me. Help me to be rooted and grounded in your love so I will never question your willingness to answer me or your faithfulness to fulfill your promises to me. I thank you for these things now in Jesus' name, Amen.

Proclamation:

I have ears to hear the voice of God. I will not be distracted by negative reports that would bring fear into my life. My heart is fixed trusting in the Lord. My heart is established I will not fear. I will proclaim the name of the Lord and by his name I will receive all his promises. I am blessed beyond measure. I am full of faith, and I can hear God's voice. I obey his Word, and the blessings of God abound in my life as I follow after him with all my heart.

Memory Verse: Philippians 1:6

"Being confident of this very thing, that he which has begun a good work in you will perform it until the day of Jesus Christ."

To every family member: *"I love you; you are blessed, and you are a blessing."*
Don't forget the hugs.

July 17th

Scripture: 1 Corinthians 12:12-20 (RSV)

"For just as the body is one and has many members, and all the members of the body, though many, are one body, so it is with Christ. For by one Spirit we were all baptized into one body—Jews or Greeks, slaves or free—and all were made to drink of one Spirit. For the body does not consist of one member but of many. If the foot should say, "Because I am not a hand, I do not belong to the body," that would not make it any less a part of the body. And if the ear should say, "Because I am not an eye, I do not belong to the body," that would not make it any less a part of the body. If the whole body were an eye, where would be the hearing? If the whole body were an ear, where would be the sense of smell? But as it is, God arranged the organs in the body, each one of them, as he chose. If all were a single organ, where would the body be? As it is, there are many parts, yet one body."

In your prayer journal, identify in this portion of scripture a promise to receive or a command to obey.

Prayer:

My Heavenly Father, you have designed the Body of Christ to fit perfectly together and function together for the purpose of accomplishing your will. As Jesus is the head of the body and each member of the body shares together in the life of Christ; help us to have the same care for one another as we would for the members of our own body. Father, help us serve together in our unique positions and functions according to your purpose because you have fitted us together to be one. Just as Jesus is the head of the body, may we all be submitted to the will of Jesus working in unity to fulfill his will. Help us to recognize one another as valuable members of the body of Christ. I pray in Jesus' name, Amen.

Proclamation:

The Body of Christ is made up of many members. I will help those around me to fulfill their purpose as they help me to fulfill mine.

Memory Verse: Philippians 1:6

"Being confident of this very thing, that he which has begun a good work in you will perform it until the day of Jesus Christ."

To every family member: "I love you; you are blessed, and you are a blessing."
Don't forget the hugs.

July 18th

Scripture: Mark 3:31-35 (AMP)

"Then His mother and His brothers came and, standing outside, they sent word to Him, calling [for] Him. And a crowd was sitting around Him, and they said to Him, Your mother and Your brothers *and Your sisters* are outside asking for You. And He replied, Who are My mother and My brothers? And looking around on those who sat in a circle about Him, He said, See! Here are My mother and My brothers; For whoever does the things God wills is My brother and sister and mother!"

In your prayer journal, identify in this portion of scripture a promise to receive or a command to obey.

Prayer:

God, my Father, I am so glad I can call you Abba (Daddy) Father. You have birthed me into your family by the incorruptible seed of the Word of God. Your Word abides forever. It cannot fail or be corrupted. It will produce the fruit of the life it contains. I have been born into your family and have been given your name. All who have been born-again of the Spirit of God are my brothers and sisters. We share together the inheritance of God as children of God, heirs and joint heirs with Christ Jesus. I pray your love would abound in us as your children and we would bear the kind of fruit that would reveal your life to the world. In Jesus' name I pray, Amen.

Proclamation:

God is my Father, and Jesus is my elder brother. All who believe in him are my brothers and sisters, for we have been born into the family of God by the seed of God's incorruptible Word.

Memory Verse: Philippians 1:6

"Being confident of this very thing, that he which has begun a good work in you will perform it until the day of Jesus Christ."

To every family member: *"I love you; you are blessed, and you are a blessing."*
Don't forget the hugs.

July 19th

Scripture: Proverbs 26:20-22 (NIV)

"Without wood a fire goes out; without a gossip a quarrel dies down. As charcoal to embers and as wood to fire, so is a quarrelsome person for kindling strife. The words of a gossip are like choice morsels; they go down to the inmost parts."

In your prayer journal, identify in this portion of scripture a promise to receive or a command to obey.

Prayer:

Father, I pray for the wisdom of God to fill my life so I know how to speak words that bring an end to strife and quarreling. Keep me from speaking words of gossip or saying things that do not build up to strengthen and encourage those who hear me. I know my words are powerful and can be filled with life or death. I ask you to always help me choose life and speak life into every situation. I desire for your Word to transform my thinking and my speaking to always glorify you. I thank you Lord that I am a new creation, created in your image and after your likeness, and because I am, I speak words of life and blessing that will bless others and bring your blessings into my life. I thank you for these things now. In Jesus' name I pray, Amen.

Proclamation:

My words are filled with either life or death. There is power in my mouth to speak blessing or cursing into my life and into the lives of others. I purpose today to fill my mouth with words of life that will bring forth blessings to all who hear me.

Memory Verse: Philippians 1:6

"Being confident of this very thing, that he which has begun a good work in you will perform it until the day of Jesus Christ."

To every family member: *"I love you; you are blessed, and you are a blessing."*
Don't forget the hugs.

July 20th

Scripture: 1 Timothy 4:12-15 (NIV)

"Don't let anyone look down on you because you are young, but set an example for the believers in speech, in conduct, in love, in faith and in purity. Until I come, devote yourself to the public reading of Scripture, to preaching and to teaching. Do not neglect your gift, which was given you through prophecy when the body of elders laid their hands on you. Be diligent in these matters; give yourself wholly to them, so that everyone may see your progress."

In your prayer journal, identify in this portion of scripture a promise to receive or a command to obey.

Prayer:

My Father, I believe you are at work in me today. Help me to be an example to others by speaking words of life and walking in love and faith and purity. Thank you for the Holy Spirit who lives in me and empowers me to fulfill your will by the ability you have given me. You did not create me to fail but to accomplish your good pleasure. Help me to be diligent to hear and to do the Word of God. Help me to be fruitful and prosper in the things you have called me to do so others see what I do and hear what I say and glorify my Father in heaven. I ask these things in Jesus' wonderful name, Amen.

Proclamation:

God has given me his Word, his Spirit and gifted me with spiritual endowments to live an abundant life, filled with joy and blessings so all who see me will glorify my Father in heaven.

Memory Verse: Philippians 1:6

"Being confident of this very thing, that he which has begun a good work in you will perform it until the day of Jesus Christ."

To every family member: "I love you; you are blessed, and you are a blessing." Don't forget the hugs.

July 21st

Scripture: Revelation 7:9-12 (HCSB)

"After this I looked, and there was a vast multitude from every nation, tribe, people, and language, which no one could number, standing before the throne and before the Lamb. They were robed in white with palm branches in their hands. And they cried out in a loud voice: Salvation belongs to our God, who is seated on the throne and to the Lamb! All the angels stood around the throne, the elders, and the four living creatures, and they fell facedown before the throne and worshiped God, saying: Amen! Blessing and glory and wisdom and thanksgiving and honor and power and strength be to our God forever and ever. Amen."

In your prayer journal, identify in this portion of scripture a promise to receive or a command to obey.

Prayer:

Heavenly Father, you are worthy of all praise. Jesus has redeemed us and chosen all people of all nations to worship and praise him for this great salvation. I thank you, Lord, for you have washed us from our sin and given us your righteousness. I will declare with the angels of heaven and all the redeemed from every nation blessings and glory and wisdom and thanksgiving and honor and power and strength be to our God forever and ever, Amen.

Proclamation:

Jesus is Lord over all the earth. All creation gives him praise. He is the Lamb of God, the Savior of all mankind and has redeemed our lives from destruction and filled us with his loving kindness and tender mercies.

Memory Verse: Philippians 1:6

"Being confident of this very thing, that he which has begun a good work in you will perform it until the day of Jesus Christ."

To every family member: *"I love you; you are blessed, and you are a blessing."*
Don't forget the hugs.

July 22nd

Scripture: 1 Thessalonians 2:13 (NKJV)

"For this reason we also thank God without ceasing, because when you received the word of God which you heard from us, you welcomed it not as the word of men, but as it is in truth, the word of God, which also effectively works in you who believe."

In your prayer journal, identify in this portion of scripture a promise to receive or a command to obey.

Prayer:

My Father, I thank you for your precious Word. Your Word is not just that which is written down as a record of what you have said, but your Word is the personification of You, who created all things. Your Word became flesh, and men beheld the glory of the living Word of God made into the person of the Lord Jesus Christ. I believe your Word is not the word of men, but the eternal Word of the everlasting God. I ask you, Father, to help me hear by your Word the voice of God. Your Word brings me faith that causes your Word to work in me effectively. Father, strengthen my faith as I hear your Word so I might please you in everything I do. Make me fruitful in every good work and cause me to give demonstration to the power and glory of your Word so people might know you and be born-again of the incorruptible seed of the living Word of God. I thank you for these things in Jesus' name, Amen.

Proclamation:

The Word of God works mightily in me because I believe the Word of God. Jesus said man shall not live by bread alone but by every Word that proceeds out of the mouth of God. I treasure the Word of God more than my daily bread. I honor the Word of God and give God's Word first place in my life.

Memory Verse: Philippians 1:6

"Being confident of this very thing, that he which has begun a good work in you will perform it until the day of Jesus Christ."

To every family member: *"I love you; you are blessed, and you are a blessing."*
Don't forget the hugs.

July 23rd

Scripture: 2 Thessalonians 1:11-12 (NLT)

"So we keep on praying for you, asking our God to enable you to live a life worthy of his call. May he give you the power to accomplish all the good things your faith prompts you to do. Then the name of our Lord Jesus will be honored because of the way you live, and you will be honored along with him. This is all made possible because of the grace of our God and Lord, Jesus Christ."

In your prayer journal, identify in this portion of scripture a promise to receive or a command to obey.

Prayer:

My Heavenly Father, just as Paul prayed for the believers in Thessalonica, I pray for myself and for all those I know who have a heart after you. I pray you enable us to live worthy of your calling and you give us the power to accomplish all the good things the Spirit of God prompts us to do. I pray the name of the Lord Jesus will be honored by the way we live and we will be honored as we glorify you. I thank you for the grace of God that works mightily in us who believe. You Lord are able to do exceeding, abundantly above all we could ever ask or think according to the power of God that is working in us. I receive these things now in Jesus' name, Amen.

Proclamation:

I walk worthy of the calling of the Lord to magnify him and to accomplish his will by the power of the Holy Spirit. God has not left me to live life by my own strength or by my own wisdom. He has not left me alone but has sent the Holy Spirit to live in me and to reveal to me the things the Lord has done for me and wants me to know and to do. I am fruitful in every good work, and I am able to do all the Lord wants me to do by his grace.

Memory Verse: Luke 10:19

"Behold, I give unto you power to tread on serpents and scorpions and over all the power of the enemy and nothing shall by any means hurt you."

To every family member: "I love you; you are blessed, and you are a blessing."
Don't forget the hugs.

July 24th

Scripture: Titus 3:4-7 (MSG)

"But when God, our kind and loving Savior God, stepped in, he saved us from all that. It was all his doing; we had nothing to do with it. He gave us a good bath, and we came out of it new people, washed inside and out by the Holy Spirit. Our Savior Jesus poured out new life so generously. God's gift has restored our relationship with him and given us back our lives. And there's more life to come—an eternity of life! You can count on this."

In your prayer journal, identify in this portion of scripture a promise to receive or a command to obey.

Prayer:

Father, you have saved us from the judgment our sin required. You redeemed us from destruction and washed and cleansed us of all iniquity. You delivered us from the works of darkness and brought us into the kingdom of your dear Son. We were helpless and unable to free ourselves from our sin or break away from the stronghold of the wicked one who deceived us and held us in captivity. I thank you Lord for your great love and kindness towards us when you nailed our sin to the cross of Christ and restored us to a right relationship with God. Thank you that Jesus came to give us life and to give us life more abundantly. In Jesus' name I pray, Amen

Proclamation:

I was imprisoned with unforgiveness and blinded to the truth by the evil works of darkness, but God in his love and mercy forgave me and delivered me. He removed my sin and cleansed me from all wrong. God brought me into his kingdom and gave me an inheritance in his family.

Memory Verse: Luke 10:19

"Behold, I give unto you power to tread on serpents and scorpions and over all the power of the enemy and nothing shall by any means hurt you."

To every family member: "I love you; you are blessed, and you are a blessing."
Don't forget the hugs.

July 25th

Scripture: 1 Thessalonians 5:14-18 (NKJV)

"Now we exhort you, brethren, warn those who are unruly, comfort the fainthearted, uphold the weak, be patient with all. See that no one renders evil for evil to anyone, but always pursue what is good both for yourselves and for all. Rejoice always, pray without ceasing, in everything give thanks; for this is the will of God in Christ Jesus for you."

In your prayer journal, identify in this portion of scripture a promise to receive or a command to obey.

Prayer:

Father, I bless your wonderful name. You are worthy of all praise. I pray for your grace to work in me so I could encourage those who need hope and comfort today. Help me to pursue what is good and right in your eyes. Keep me from every evil work and help me to walk in the revelation of what you have done for me so I am always filled with thanksgiving and praise to you. Lord, it is my desire to acknowledge you in everything I do. I know you live in me and my life is in you. I purpose to include you in my thoughts, my conversations and all I do so I am in a constant place of praying and hearing your voice and giving you thanks. I thank you for bringing these things to pass in my life today. In Jesus' name I pray, Amen.

Proclamation:

It is God's will for me to continually praise him and give thanks for everything he does for me. As I acknowledge the Lord in everything, I am reminding myself of his abiding presence, and I will never be afraid or discouraged.

Memory Verse: Luke 10:19

"Behold, I give unto you power to tread on serpents and scorpions and over all the power of the enemy and nothing shall by any means hurt you."

To every family member: *"I love you; you are blessed, and you are a blessing."*
Don't forget the hugs.

July 26th

Scripture: Romans 5:1-2 (PHILLIPS)

"Since then it is by faith that we are justified, let us grasp the fact that we have peace with God through our Lord Jesus Christ. Through him we have confidently entered into this new relationship of grace, and here we take our stand, in happy certainty of the glorious things he has for us in the future."

In your prayer journal, identify in this portion of scripture a promise to receive or a command to obey.

Prayer:

My Heavenly Father, I thank you for your great love for me. You made me righteous and gave me peace. I have access to you, to receive your grace for my every need. You have accepted me into your family and given to me every good and perfect gift. You forgive me, cleanse me, protect me and bless me. Your thoughts about me are more than I can number and you rejoice over me with singing. You have richly blessed me. Thank you for all these things you have done for me. I did not deserve them or earn them, but I receive them today because you accomplished all this for me by the Lord Jesus Christ. I love you. In Jesus' name, Amen.

Proclamation:

Jesus opened for me the door into the presence of God. He was the only one who could, for he has the keys to the kingdom of Heaven. He clothed me in robes of righteousness and washed me with the water of the Word of God, making me acceptable and welcomed in his family.

Memory Verse: Luke 10:19

"Behold, I give unto you power to tread on serpents and scorpions and over all the power of the enemy and nothing shall by any means hurt you."

To every family member: *"I love you; you are blessed, and you are a blessing."*
Don't forget the hugs.

July 27th

Scripture: Mark 4:30-32 (PHILLIPS)

"Then he continued, 'What can we say the kingdom of God is like? How shall we put it in a parable? It is like a tiny grain of mustard-seed which, when it is sown, is smaller than any seed that is ever sown. But after it is sown in the earth, it grows up and becomes bigger than any other plant. It shoots out great branches so that birds can come and nest in its shelter.'"

In your prayer journal, identify in this portion of scripture a promise to receive or a command to obey.

Prayer:

Lord, I thank you today for your kingdom. You delivered me from the kingdom of darkness, and you have translated me into the kingdom of your dear Son, Jesus. I know it is your good pleasure to give me the kingdom of God, which is righteousness, peace and joy in the Holy Spirit. When Jesus came, he brought with him the kingdom of God, and when he died, the seed of the kingdom was planted in the earth. Father, thank you that from the day of Christ's resurrection until today the kingdom of God is growing and filling all the earth with your glory. I pray my life gives demonstration of your kingdom within me. I pray for the power of your kingdom to be seen as I pray for the sick and hopeless and as I share the good news of your love today. Help me, strengthen me and equip me with everything I need to glorify your great name and see the glory of the Lord cover all the earth. In Jesus' name, Amen.

Proclamation:

The kingdom of God is within me. God brought me into his kingdom and put his kingdom inside of me. I am an ambassador of the kingdom of God to do his business and to proclaim his glory.

Memory Verse: Luke 10:19

"Behold, I give unto you power to tread on serpents and scorpions and over all the power of the enemy and nothing shall by any means hurt you."

To every family member: *"I love you; you are blessed, and you are a blessing."*
Don't forget the hugs.

July 28th

Scripture: Isaiah 58:6-8 (NLT)

"No, this is the kind of fasting I want: free those who are wrongly imprisoned; lighten the burden of those who work for you. Let the oppressed go free and remove the chains that bind people. Share your food with the hungry and give shelter to the homeless. Give clothes to those who need them and do not hide from relatives who need your help. Then your salvation will come like the dawn and your wounds will quickly heal. Your godliness will lead you forward and the glory of the Lord will protect you from behind."

In your prayer journal, identify in this portion of scripture a promise to receive or a command to obey.

Prayer:

My Father, thank you for your promises for those who fast according to your good pleasure. It is not what I deny myself that pleases you as much as what I give to those in need. Help me today to recognize the needs of others. Make me to be tenderhearted and sensitive to those who need my help today. I purpose in my heart to obey you in these things. I know your salvation will show up for me as sure as the sun rises in the morning. My health will be restored, and you will lead me by the Spirit of God in every good path as the glory of the Lord protects me from every evil work. Thank you for these things now in Jesus' name, Amen.

Proclamation:

I will honor God today by choosing the kind of fast that truly pleases him. I purpose to help those who are burdened and oppressed, in captivity or in need of daily provisions. I watch out for my own family by praying and calling forth the will of God into their lives. I will walk in God's salvation that brings me health, direction and protection today. In Jesus' name, Amen.

Memory Verse: Luke 10:19

"Behold, I give unto you power to tread on serpents and scorpions and over all the power of the enemy and nothing shall by any means hurt you."

To every family member: *"I love you; you are blessed, and you are a blessing."* Don't forget the hugs.

July 29th

Scripture: Numbers 23:19 (NKJV)

"God is not a man, that He should lie, nor a son of man, that He should repent. Has He said, and will He not do? Or has He spoken, and will He not make it good?"

In your prayer journal, identify in this portion of scripture a promise to receive or a command to obey.

Prayer:

Heavenly Father, I desire to worship you and bless your holy name. I thank you for your faithfulness and your promises that are sure and certain for all who receive them. Your truth endures forever, and you will watch over your Word to perform it. You will not lie, for your Word is truth. If you said it, you will bring it to pass, for Lord, you are faithful. You said whatever I ask in faith, believing, I will receive, and whatever I ask in Jesus' name, you will do. Father, help me to declare your Word with boldness and to ask for those things that accomplish your will and glorify your name. I ask for revelation that comes by the Spirit of God so I will understand how to pray and what to do to please you and bring forth your purpose. In Jesus' name, Amen.

Proclamation:

God is faithful to perform his Word. If he said it, I can stand on it as a sure and immovable foundation. It will surely come to pass.

Memory Verse: Luke 10:19

"Behold, I give unto you power to tread on serpents and scorpions and over all the power of the enemy and nothing shall by any means hurt you."

To every family member: *"I love you; you are blessed, and you are a blessing."*
Don't forget the hugs.

July 30th

Scripture: Colossians 3:15-17 (KJV)

"And let the peace of God rule in your hearts, to the which also ye are called in one body; and be ye thankful. Let the word of Christ dwell in you richly in all wisdom; teaching and admonishing one another in psalms and hymns and spiritual songs, singing with grace in your hearts to the Lord. And whatsoever ye do in word or deed, do all in the name of the Lord Jesus, giving thanks to God and the Father by him."

In your prayer journal, identify in this portion of scripture a promise to receive or a command to obey.

Prayer:

Father, I praise you today with all my heart. I thank you for your peace that rules in my life. I am thankful that, out of all the people in the world, you have revealed your love to me. I want your Word to live richly in me. I treasure and value your Word above everything else. You said if I lack wisdom to ask and you would give wisdom to me liberally. I ask you for wisdom to teach and encourage others. I rejoice in the things of God. My heart is filled with singing and joy because of your grace. I pray that, whatever I do or say, I do in the name of the Lord Jesus and bring glory to you. I thank you for working mightily in me this day. In Jesus' name, Amen.

Proclamation:

The peace of God rules in my heart today. I refuse to allow my peace to be disrupted or my joy to be stolen. I am thankful to God. I sing and give praise to him by psalms, hymns and spiritual songs because my heart is filled with the grace of God. Everything I do or say is in the authority of the name of the Lord Jesus. I am greatly blessed.

Memory Verse: Ephesians 3:20

"Now unto him that is able to do exceeding abundantly above all that we ask or think, according to the power that works in us."

To every family member: *"I love you; you are blessed, and you are a blessing."*
Don't forget the hugs.

July 31st

Scripture: John 16:23-24 (NASB)

"In that day you will not question Me about anything. Truly, truly, I say to you, if you ask the Father for anything in My name, He will give it to you. Until now you have asked for nothing in My name; ask and you will receive, so that your joy may be made full."

In your prayer journal, identify in this portion of scripture a promise to receive or a command to obey.

Prayer:

My Father, you are great and greatly to be praised. You are amazing in glory and strength and power, and your love is beyond understanding. I thank you today for your Word and the promise of answered prayer. As Jesus instructed us, I pray to you in his name. I pray you fill me with the knowledge of your will. I pray that I will not be deceived by the way things appear but instead I will see them as they really are. I pray for the gifts of the Holy Spirit to work mightily in me today. Lord, I do not attempt to do things in my own wisdom or strength, but do them in yours. Father, fill me afresh with the Spirit of God, equipping and preparing me for every good work that pleases you. In Jesus' name I pray, Amen.

Proclamation:

Jesus said I could ask the Father for anything in his name and he would do it so my joy would be full. I can pray with confidence, knowing that whatever I ask I will receive.

Memory Verse: Ephesians 3:20

"Now unto him that is able to do exceeding abundantly above all that we ask or think, according to the power that works in us."

To every family member: *"I love you; you are blessed, and you are a blessing."*
Don't forget the hugs.

August 1st

Scripture: Isaiah 12:2-5 (NCV)

"God is the one who saves me; I will trust him and not be afraid. The Lord, the Lord gives me strength and makes me sing. He has saved me. You will receive your salvation with joy as you would draw water from a well. At that time you will say, praise the Lord and worship him. Tell everyone what he has done and how great he is. Sing praise to the Lord, because he has done great things. Let all the world know what he has done."

In your prayer journal, identify in this portion of scripture a promise to receive or a command to obey.

Prayer:

My Father, I will not be afraid, for you are with me. I will trust you, for you give me strength. You have saved me from my enemies and filled me with joy. As one draws water from a well, so I draw joy from the wells of salvation you have placed within me. Within me is the river of life, the Spirit of God, and everywhere this river flows, it brings life to everything it touches. I pray for the opportunities you bring me today to declare the wonderful things the Lord has done for me. Help me to make known the wonderful works of God so all the world will know what you have done for them. In Jesus' name, Amen.

Proclamation:

God is at work in me today. He will strengthen me and help me to walk in faith and victory. I will boldly declare the good works of God and tell of his great love and abundant mercies. I do not trust in man or in my own abilities, for apart from God I can do nothing, but living in me is the Spirit of Almighty God. The same Spirit that raised Christ from the dead dwells in me. He will help me. He will empower me with the desire to do and achieve his good pleasure.

Memory Verse: Ephesians 3:20

"Now unto him that is able to do exceeding abundantly above all that we ask or think, according to the power that works in us."

To every family member: *"I love you; you are blessed, and you are a blessing."*
Don't forget the hugs.

August 2nd

Scripture: 2 Chronicles 14:11-12 (KJV)

"And Asa cried unto the Lord his God, and said, Lord, it is nothing with thee to help, whether with many, or with them that have no power: help us, O Lord our God; for we rest on thee, and in thy name we go against this multitude. O Lord, thou art our God; let no man prevail against thee. So the Lord smote the Ethiopians before Asa, and before Judah; and the Ethiopians fled."

In your prayer journal, identify in this portion of scripture a promise to receive or a command to obey.

Prayer:

My Heavenly Father, just as King Asa called upon you and you heard his voice and answered his prayer, I thank you for hearing and answering me today. Apart from you, I have no might or power, but my faith is in you. You have promised to be with me and to give me wisdom to make wise and godly choices that will be a blessing to me and bring glory and honor to you. Even if I am surrounded by impossible circumstances, you are more than enough to put me over and give me victory. I will stand still and see your salvation. In Jesus' name, Amen.

Proclamation:

I am strong in the Lord and in the power of his might. The Spirit of the Lord abides with me, and the strong hand of God is on my side. He will bring me victory over every enemy and will cause me to walk in the land of my inheritance. I will tread upon all the power of the enemy, and nothing by any means shall hurt me. The Lord, my God blesses the works of my hands, and he establishes all my ways. I will walk in the blessings of the Lord because I know his name. His name is Jesus, and at the mention of his name, every knee bows and every tongue confesses that Jesus is Lord.

Memory Verse: Ephesians 3:20

"Now unto him that is able to do exceeding abundantly above all that we ask or think, according to the power that works in us."

To every family member: "I love you; you are blessed, and you are a blessing."
Don't forget the hugs.

August 3rd

Scripture: John 15:7-8 (NKJV)

"If you abide in Me, and My words abide in you, you will ask what you desire, and it shall be done for you. By this My Father is glorified, that you bear much fruit; so you will be My disciples."

In your prayer journal, identify in this portion of scripture a promise to receive or a command to obey.

Prayer:

Father, your Word declares your desire for me to pray and to receive the answers to my prayers. My answered prayers bring glory to you. Father, I choose to abide in you, to acknowledge your presence and to seek your wisdom and counsel for every decision I make. Lord, I desire to include you in every conversation I have and acknowledge your presence everywhere I go. I want to live in you and hear your Word, your voice speaking to me. I ask you to continuously fill me with your Spirit so I will accomplish your will and please you with every word I speak and in everything I do. I ask these things in Jesus' name, Amen.

Proclamation:

The anointing of God is upon me, and the Spirit of God is within me. The Word of God abides with me, and the voice of God speaks to me. I will acknowledge the presence of the Lord and include him in my daily work to hear his voice and pray his will so my prayers will be answered and the will of God fulfilled.

Memory Verse: Ephesians 3:20

"Now unto him that is able to do exceeding abundantly above all that we ask or think, according to the power that works in us."

To every family member: *"I love you; you are blessed, and you are a blessing."*
Don't forget the hugs.

August 4th

Scripture: John 16:13-15 (HCSB)

"When the Spirit of truth comes, He will guide you into all the truth. For He will not speak on His own, but He will speak whatever He hears. He will also declare to you what is to come. He will glorify Me, because He will take from what is Mine and declare it to you. Everything the Father has is Mine. This is why I told you that He takes from what is Mine and will declare it to you."

In your prayer journal, identify in this portion of scripture a promise to receive or a command to obey.

Prayer:

My Father, I thank you for the Holy Spirit of God. He is my Comforter and my Helper in every time of need. I pray today that the Spirit of God will reveal to me the things of God. I pray he will show me things to come and cause me to know the things you have freely given to me. Because he is the Spirit of truth, I pray I will walk according to the truth. Father, keep me from deception and the lies of my enemy. Cause me to see clearly those things that are of you and recognize those things that are not. Open my ears to hear your voice and to walk in your ways. I pray in Jesus' name, Amen.

Proclamation:

I have not received the spirit of this world but the Spirit of God so I can know the things God has given to me. I hear the voice of God who leads me and teaches me and reveals to me who he is and what he has done for me.

Memory Verse: Ephesians 3:20

"Now unto him that is able to do exceeding abundantly above all that we ask or think, according to the power that works in us."

To every family member: "I love you; you are blessed, and you are a blessing."
Don't forget the hugs.

August 5th

Scripture: Proverbs 24:3-4 (NASB)

"By wisdom a house is built, and by understanding it is established; and by knowledge the rooms are filled with all precious and pleasant riches."

In your prayer journal, identify in this portion of scripture a promise to receive or a command to obey.

Prayer:

My Heavenly Father, you are mighty in power, and you have all wisdom and understanding. You know all things. Your Word declares that you know when I sit down and when I stand up, the number of hairs on my head and even my thoughts long before I think them. You said if I need wisdom I can ask you for it and you will give it to me liberally. I ask you today for wisdom, knowledge and understanding so my house, my life and my family will be established on that sure immovable foundation of the Lordship of Jesus Christ. I receive the wisdom of God to prosper in everything I do. You bless the works of my hands and the meditation of my heart. Help me to be firmly rooted and grounded in the love of God so my life will bring honor and praise to you and I will be fruitful in every good work. I pray in Jesus' name, Amen.

Proclamation:

I have the Spirit of God within. He teaches me and guides me into all truth. He takes the things of God and reveals them to me. I am anointed to achieve all of God's purpose for me and his pleasure for my life.

Memory Verse: Ephesians 3:20

"Now unto him that is able to do exceeding abundantly above all that we ask or think, according to the power that works in us."

To every family member: *"I love you; you are blessed, and you are a blessing."* Don't forget the hugs.

August 6th

Scripture: Isaiah 46:9-10 (KJV)

"Remember the former things of old: for I am God, and there is none else; I am God, and there is none like me, Declaring the end from the beginning, and from ancient times the things that are not yet done, saying, My counsel shall stand, and I will do all my pleasure."

In your prayer journal, identify in this portion of scripture a promise to receive or a command to obey.

Prayer:

My Father, I worship and bless your holy name. You are great and worthy of praise. There is none like you; you alone are to be worshipped. You know all things. You know how things will turn out before they even begin because your counsel will stand and you will bring to pass that which is your good pleasure. I thank you today for your faithfulness. I put my trust in you, for you are able to keep me from evil and to protect me from the devices of the enemy and to cause me to triumph in every circumstance of life. Help me to focus on the fulfilled promises in your Word and not be sidetracked by the opposition trying to distract me. Though mountains rise up in opposition to your will, I can speak to them in your name and demand them to move out of the way. Thank you for your grace that is working mightily in me today, equipping me and empowering me to see your will accomplished in this world even as it is done in heaven. In Jesus' name I pray, Amen.

Proclamation:

I will boldly declare the Word of the Lord today. He has called me and anointed me to speak his Word and to declare his name. I call on the name of the Lord Jesus Christ and declare him Lord over my life and all I do this day. God grants me favor and wisdom to perform his will and bring glory to his name.

Memory Verse: John 15:7

"If you abide in me, and my words abide in you, you shall ask what you will and it shall be done unto you."

To every family member: *"I love you; you are blessed, and you are a blessing."*
Don't forget the hugs.

August 7th

Scripture: 2 Peter 3:9 (VOICE)

"Now the Lord is not slow about enacting His promise—slow is how some people want to characterize it—no, He is not slow but patient and merciful to you, not wanting anyone to be destroyed, but wanting everyone to turn away from following his own path and to turn toward God's."

In your prayer journal, identify in this portion of scripture a promise to receive or a command to obey.

Prayer:

Heavenly Father, I want to thank you for your love and goodness that you have shown me today. Out of all the people in the world, you have touched my life with your love by bringing to me the gospel of the Lord Jesus Christ. You loved me and paid the price for my forgiveness and so much more. You have given me your righteousness and brought me into your family. I pray that your will be fulfilled in the earth. You are not willing for anyone to be destroyed, but instead desire all to repent and turn to you so they might receive your life. I know Jesus will return at the end of this age and there will be rewards for the righteous and judgment for the wicked. Father, you purposely delay your judgment on the wicked, desiring their repentance and salvation because of your great love for them. Help me to walk with the same love and compassion you have for those who have not yet turned to you. I thank you in Jesus' name, Amen.

Proclamation:

God is not in a hurry to fulfill his promise of judgment on the wicked because he is not willing for them to perish. God does not take delight in judgment, but in forgiveness. His delight is when the wicked repent and humbly turn to him so he can forgive their sinfulness and bless them as his own children.

Memory Verse: John 15:7

"If you abide in me, and my words abide in you, you shall ask what you will and it shall be done unto you."

To every family member: "I love you; you are blessed, and you are a blessing." Don't forget the hugs.

August 8th

Scripture: 1 John 2:7-11 (PHILLIPS)

"I am not really writing to tell you of any new command, brothers of mine. It is the old, original command which you had at the beginning; it is the old message which you have heard before. And yet as I give it to you again I know that it is true—in your life as it was in his. For the darkness is beginning to lift and the true light is now shining in the world. Anyone who claims to be "in the light" and hates his brother is, in fact, still in complete darkness. The man who loves his brother lives and moves in the light, and has no reason to stumble. But the man who hates his brother is shut off from the light and gropes his way in the dark without seeing where he is going. To move in the dark is to move blindfold."

In your prayer journal, identify in this portion of scripture a promise to receive or a command to obey.

Prayer:

God, my Father, I know the love of God has been shed-abroad in my heart by the Holy Spirit. You have placed your love within me and your love is the very light of life. Your light reveals the love of God. You have commanded us to love one another just as you love us. I pray for your grace to work in me so I always choose to walk in love. Father, help me to love and bless even those who count themselves my enemies. I do not want to be blinded by the darkness that hate brings, but I want to walk in the light as you are in the light. The Word of God declares that in you is light and in you there is no darkness at all. Help me to see people as you do and respond to them with the love of God so you can turn them from darkness to light and from the power of Satan to God. I thank you for bringing these things to pass this day, in Jesus' name, Amen.

Proclamation:

The light, the revelation of God's love is shining bright. It shines in the darkness and the darkness must flee. It shines in the hearts of those who have been blinded by hate and hurt and turns them to the love of God.

Memory Verse: John 15:7

"If you abide in me, and my words abide in you, you shall ask what you will and it shall be done unto you."

To every family member: "I love you; you are blessed, and you are a blessing." Don't forget the hugs.

August 9th

Scripture: 2 Thessalonians 2:13-15 (NLT)

"As for us, we can't help but thank God for you, dear brothers and sisters loved by the Lord. We are always thankful that God chose you to be among the first to experience salvation—a salvation that came through the Spirit who makes you holy and through your belief in the truth. He called you to salvation when we told you the Good News; now you can share in the glory of our Lord Jesus Christ. With all these things in mind, dear brothers and sisters, stand firm and keep a strong grip on the teaching we passed on to you both in person and by letter."

In your prayer journal, identify in this portion of scripture a promise to receive or a command to obey.

Prayer:

My Father, thank you for this great salvation. You have delivered me from the power of death. You have redeemed me and brought me into your kingdom. You have washed me from my sin and given me your righteousness. I am beloved and cherished in your eyes because your mercy is great towards me. Father, I pray for understanding and insight into your Word. Help me to stand firm on the sure foundation of your Word. Your Word is truth, and you will watch over and perform it in my life. Help me to receive your Word as the Spirit of God reveals it to me, and help me to take hold of the promises of God not allowing them to slip away from me. I will treasure your Word more than silver or gold because I know your Word will build me up and give me an inheritance with all who are in your kingdom. I thank you for these things in Jesus' name, Amen.

Proclamation:

I have experienced the salvation of God. The Word of God and the Spirit of God are working in me to make me strong in the Lord and in the power of his might to heal me and bless me and equip me, making me useful for God's kingdom.

Memory Verse: John 15:7

"If you abide in me, and my words abide in you, you shall ask what you will and it shall be done unto you."

To every family member: *"I love you; you are blessed, and you are a blessing."*
Don't forget the hugs.

August 10th

Scripture: 1 Thessalonians 5:16-23 (KJV)

"Rejoice evermore. Pray without ceasing. In every thing give thanks: for this is the will of God in Christ Jesus concerning you. Quench not the Spirit. Despise not prophesyings. Prove all things; hold fast that which is good. Abstain from all appearance of evil. And the very God of peace sanctify you wholly; and I pray God your whole spirit and soul and body be preserved blameless unto the coming of our Lord Jesus Christ."

In your prayer journal, identify in this portion of scripture a promise to receive or a command to obey.

Prayer:

My God and Father of my Lord Jesus Christ, I rejoice in you and give you thanks, for this is the will of God for me to always rejoice in you and be thankful to you for all the wonderful things you have done for me. Help me to recognize what is of the Spirit of God and what is not. I will honor your Word and by your Word judge every prophetic utterance. I will take to heart what I know is from you. You will confirm to me the things that are of God, and I will hold fast to them. Thank you for sanctifying me completely spirit, soul and body. I know it is not by my works that I am preserved blameless, but by your grace. Father, I pray you will always make me aware of your abiding presence with me, and I will acknowledge you in everything I do. In Jesus' name, Amen.

Proclamation:

I will rejoice in the Lord and pray continually for this is his will for me. I do not quench the Spirit of God or ignore his leading. I listen for his word, and I hold fast to his promises, for he sanctifies me and makes me blameless all my days.

Memory Verse: John 15:7

"If you abide in me, and my words abide in you, you shall ask what you will and it shall be done unto you."

To every family member: "*I love you; you are blessed, and you are a blessing.*"
Don't forget the hugs.

August 11th

Scripture: Zechariah 14:8-9 (KJV)

"And it shall be in that day, that living waters shall go out from Jerusalem; half of them toward the former sea, and half of them toward the hinder sea: in summer and in winter shall it be. And the Lord shall be king over all the earth: in that day shall there be one Lord, and his name one."

In your prayer journal, identify in this portion of scripture a promise to receive or a command to obey.

Prayer:

Heavenly Father, thank you for your promise of living water. I know this water is not of earthly origin, but it is the Spirit of God. Jesus said, if I thirst after you, I shall be filled and out of my inner most being will flow rivers of living water. You have made me a precious stone, a building block with others to create the city of New Jerusalem. From this spiritual city, the living waters will flow. Lord help me to keep my well from being filled up with the dirt and obstructions of this world that hinder the flow of this living water. Fill me afresh today with the Spirit of God and touch all those I meet with the life of your Spirit that flows freely from me. In Jesus' name I pray, Amen.

Proclamation:

I hunger and thirst after God, and he fills me with his Spirit. His abundant life flows from me like a river, and it gives life to everyone it touches. It heals the broken and brings hope to those who are distressed. This river is the river of God. It is a river of life that brings life by the power of the Holy Spirit.

Memory Verse: John 15:7

"If you abide in me, and my words abide in you, you shall ask what you will and it shall be done unto you."

To every family member: *"I love you; you are blessed, and you are a blessing."*
Don't forget the hugs.

August 12th

Scripture: Revelation 1:5-6 (NLV)

"May you have loving-favor and peace from Jesus Christ Who is faithful in telling the truth. Jesus Christ is the first to be raised from the dead. He is the head over all the kings of the earth. He is the One Who loves us and has set us free from our sins by His blood. Christ has made us a holy nation of religious leaders who can go to His God and Father. He is the One to receive honor and power forever! Let it be so."

In your prayer journal, identify in this portion of scripture a promise to receive or a command to obey.

Prayer:

My Heavenly Father, thank you for your great love for me. I thank you for giving me access into your presence through my Lord Jesus Christ. He is above all. He is the one with all power and authority to rule over the nations and the kings of the earth who bow before him. When Jesus defeated death, he gave me victory over death. I will live forever, and death no longer has any power over me. Jesus has made me a citizen of the kingdom of God, and he gave me authority to enter before your throne to worship, to pray and to rejoice in your wonderful presence without fear or condemnation. I stand before you this day and declare your will over my life, my family, my business and my ministry. I call forth the will of God to be done on the earth even as it is done in heaven. I thank you that today I walk in the kingdom of righteousness, peace and joy in the Holy Spirit, everywhere I go and in every thing I do. In Jesus' name I pray, Amen.

Proclamation:

I am a citizen of heaven, and Jesus gave me the authority to enter the holiest place of God's presence with boldness and with joy. I am to declare the will of God to be done on earth and to pray the Word of God before the Father who answers my prayer to glorify his name and causes my joy to overflow.

Memory Verse: John 15:7

"If you abide in me, and my words abide in you, you shall ask what you will and it shall be done unto you."

To every family member: "I love you; you are blessed, and you are a blessing."
Don't forget the hugs.

August 13th

Scripture: 1 John 5:13-15 (NKJV)

"These things I have written to you who believe in the name of the Son of God, that you may know that you have eternal life and that you may *continue* to believe in the name of the Son of God. Now this is the confidence that we have in Him, that if we ask anything according to His will, He hears us. And if we know that He hears us, whatever we ask, we know that we have the petitions that we have asked of Him."

In your prayer journal, identify in this portion of scripture a promise to receive or a command to obey.

Prayer:

Heavenly Father, I believe Jesus Christ is the Son of God, and because I do, I have eternal life. As I pray, I am filled with faith, knowing that you hear me. Because you hear me, I am confident that what I have asked of you, you will bring to pass. Thank you for hearing me. Father, you know what I need even before I ask. You said, if I seek the kingdom of God above everything else, all the things I have need of will be supplied. Lord, you have a custom of giving people what they ask. You gave king Hezekiah fifteen more years. You told David, if what you had given him was not enough, all he needed to do was to ask and you would give him his heart's desire. You give more than is needed and supply me with exceedingly abundantly more than I can ask or imagine. Help me to ask and to receive because it is your good pleasure to give me every good thing. In Jesus' name I pray, Amen.

Proclamation:

My God supplies all my needs according to his riches in glory through Jesus Christ my Lord. Whatever I desire, I can pray for and receive with confidence, for if God hears me, I have what I ask, and when I pray in the name of Jesus, he always hears me.

Memory Verse: James 1:13

"Let no man say when he is tempted, I am tempted of God; for God cannot be tempted with evil, neither tempts he any man."

To every family member: "I love you; you are blessed, and you are a blessing." Don't forget the hugs.

August 14th

Scripture: Psalms 91:1-2 (KJV)

"He that dwelleth in the secret place of the most High shall abide under the shadow of the Almighty. I will say of the Lord, He is my refuge and my fortress: my God; in him will I trust."

In your prayer journal, identify in this portion of scripture a promise to receive or a command to obey.

Prayer:

God and Father of my Lord Jesus Christ, I desire to be close to you and to live with a constant awareness of your presence with me. If I know you are with me, I know nothing can stand against me. You are my refuge and strength. You are a shield for me, and you are a fortress of safety to preserve my life and protect me from every wicked work of the enemy. I will confess your Word over my life and over those for whom I pray. You Lord will lift me up above the chaos of the world and comfort me and speak peace to me. You will answer me and deliver me and satisfy me with long life and show me your salvation. I thank you for this mighty work of God working in my life today, in Jesus' name, Amen.

Proclamation:

The Lord God, the creator of all things will help me with everything I do today. He will reveal to me his loving kindness and tender mercies. He will answer me and empower me to do all his pleasure and see his will done on earth as it is in heaven.

Memory Verse: James 1:13

"Let no man say when he is tempted, I am tempted of God; for God cannot be tempted with evil, neither tempts he any man."

To every family member: "I love you; you are blessed, and you are a blessing."
Don't forget the hugs.

August 15th

Scripture: Joshua 2:8-11 (NKJV)

"Now before they lay down, she came up to them on the roof, and said to the men: "I know that the Lord has given you the land, that the terror of you has fallen on us, and that all the inhabitants of the land are fainthearted because of you. For we have heard how the Lord dried up the water of the Red Sea for you when you came out of Egypt, and what you did to the two kings of the Amorites who *were* on the other side of the Jordan, Sihon and Og, whom you utterly destroyed. And as soon as we heard *these things*, our hearts melted; neither did there remain any more courage in anyone because of you, for the Lord your God, He *is* God in heaven above and on earth beneath."

In your prayer journal, identify in this portion of scripture a promise to receive or a command to obey.

Prayer:

My Father, I pray the fear of the Lord would be upon all the people of every nation. Not a dread or terrifying fear, but a godly fear that would cause all to honor you and be in awe of your power and greatness. I pray for all who are called by your name to walk with the anointing of your Spirit and in the authority of your name speak your Word to show all that Jesus is Lord of all. Help me to represent you well. As an ambassador of your kingdom help me to express the love of God and to function in the power of God so people's faith will not be in words and ideas alone, but in the power and demonstration of the Holy Spirit. Father show yourself mighty and strong through your Church so all will see the image and likeness of God through those you have changed by your mercy and grace. I believe this good work of God that you started in me will be accomplished and others will know this godly fear and run to you. In Jesus' name I pray, Amen.

Proclamation:

Our God is awesome. He is the Creator of all things, and he loves his creation.

Memory Verse: James 1:13

"Let no man say when he is tempted, I am tempted of God; for God cannot be tempted with evil, neither tempts he any man."

To every family member: *"I love you; you are blessed, and you are a blessing."* Don't forget the hugs.

August 16th

Scripture: Mark 4:24-29 (NASB)

"And He was saying to them, 'Take care what you listen to. By your standard of measure it will be measured to you; and more will be given you besides. For whoever has, to him *more* shall be given; and whoever does not have, even what he has shall be taken away from him.' And He was saying, 'The kingdom of God is like a man who casts seed upon the soil; and he goes to bed at night and gets up by day, and the seed sprouts and grows—how, he himself does not know. The soil produces crops by itself; first the blade, then the head, then the mature grain in the head. But when the crop permits, he immediately puts in the sickle, because the harvest has come.'"

In your prayer journal, identify in this portion of scripture a promise to receive or a command to obey.

Prayer:

Father, thank you for allowing me to hear your Word. I will measure carefully the value of your Word as greater than any other. I will treasure your Word and not allow it to be stolen from me. I will meditate on it day and night because I know it will produce good fruit in my life. Help me to hear and to revere the Word of God. It is more valuable than gold, and its fruit is better than the finest treasures of the world. Your Word will produce, in my life, faith to believe. It will edify me and strengthen me. Your Word will give me an inheritance that cannot be stolen from me. Father, give me the treasures that only your Word can give me. May my heart bring forth a harvest of fruit that will produce glory to you. I pray in Jesus' name, Amen.

Proclamation:

The gospel, the Word of God, is the power of God unto salvation for everyone who believes. I believe the Word of God.

Memory Verse: James 1:13

"Let no man say when he is tempted, I am tempted of God; for God cannot be tempted with evil, neither tempts he any man."

To every family member: "*I love you; you are blessed, and you are a blessing.*"
Don't forget the hugs.

August 17th

Scripture: Exodus 33:9-11 (KJV)

"And it came to pass, as Moses entered into the tabernacle, the cloudy pillar descended, and stood at the door of the tabernacle, and the Lord talked with Moses. And all the people saw the cloudy pillar stand at the tabernacle door: and all the people rose up and worshipped, every man in his tent door. And the Lord spake unto Moses face to face, as a man speaketh unto his friend. And he turned again into the camp: but his servant Joshua, the son of Nun, a young man, departed not out of the tabernacle."

In your prayer journal, identify in this portion of scripture a promise to receive or a command to obey.

Prayer:

My Heavenly Father, give me a heart to know you as Joshua did. He chose to stay in your presence instead of returning to the camp. As you raised Joshua up and put your anointing upon him to accomplish your will, I ask you to anoint me with your Spirit and give me wisdom to accomplish your purpose for me. I ask you to anoint me with fresh oil from heaven today and restore my soul. Bring me times of refreshing that come from your presence and cause the joy of your salvation to fill me to overflowing. You Father are able to do exceeding abundantly above all I could ever ask or think according to the power of God that is working inside of me. Thank you for that power of the Holy Spirit who lives in me and works through me in Jesus' name, Amen.

Proclamation:

I will follow after the Lord with all of my heart. I will listen to hear his voice, and I will be quick to obey his Word.

Memory Verse: James 1:13

"Let no man say when he is tempted, I am tempted of God; for God cannot be tempted with evil, neither tempts he any man."

To every family member: "I love you; you are blessed, and you are a blessing." Don't forget the hugs.

August 18th

Scripture: Mark 5:27-30 (KJV)

"When she had heard of Jesus, came in the press behind, and touched his garment. For she said, If I may touch but his clothes, I shall be whole. And straightway the fountain of her blood was dried up; and she felt in her body that she was healed of that plague. And Jesus, immediately knowing in himself that virtue had gone out of him, turned him about in the press, and said, Who touched my clothes?"

In your prayer journal, identify in this portion of scripture a promise to receive or a command to obey.

Prayer:

Praise the name of the Lord my God, for he is worthy of all praise. Lord, my God, just as this woman accessed the power of God by her faith, help me to walk in the same kind of miracle receiving faith. She believed in her heart and confessed with her mouth that she would be made whole the moment she touched Jesus' clothes and she was. Father, you said whatever I desire, when I pray, to believe I receive it and I shall have it. You said, if I abide in you and your Word abides in me, I can ask what I will and it shall be done. I look in your Word to find your will, and I have the help of the Spirit of God to pray. I believe I will receive today the things I desire in Jesus' name, Amen.

Proclamation:

Without faith it is impossible to please God, but when I trust him, I bring him joy. The Word of God teaches me to ask without limits and receive more than I ask for.

Memory Verse: James 1:13

"Let no man say when he is tempted, I am tempted of God; for God cannot be tempted with evil, neither tempts he any man."

To every family member: *"I love you; you are blessed, and you are a blessing."*
Don't forget the hugs.

August 19th

Scripture: John 3:34-36 (MSG)

"'The One that God sent speaks God's words. And don't think he rations out the Spirit in bits and pieces. The Father loves the Son extravagantly. He turned everything over to him so he could give it away—a lavish distribution of gifts.

That is why whoever accepts and trusts the Son gets in on everything, life complete and forever! And that is also why the person who avoids and distrusts the Son is in the dark and doesn't see life. All he experiences of God is darkness, and an angry darkness at that.'"

In your prayer journal, identify in this portion of scripture a promise to receive or a command to obey.

Prayer:

My Father, I thank you for complete and eternal life that is mine because I believe and receive your Son, the Lord Jesus. You anointed him with the Spirit of God and by the power of the Holy Spirit he freely gave me gifts of salvation and healing, life and peace. Every good thing is mine because of my Lord Jesus Christ. I pray you help me understand and receive as mine everything Jesus did for me. You said that the Spirit of God would take the things of God and reveal them to me. I believe the Spirit of God reveals to me today more and more of what Jesus did for me. I pray now in Jesus' name, Amen.

Proclamation:

Jesus said everything the Father has is his and that the Spirit of God would take what belongs to him and reveal it to me. Jesus has freely given me all things that pertain to life. He has given me life and life more abundantly. He does not withhold any good thing from me, for he loves me and empowers me to receive, as a first-born son, an inheritance that is filled with joy and blessings. I am an heir of God and a joint-heir with Jesus. I am in the world, but I am not of the world. I operate in the kingdom of God that lives within me. I will forever be thankful and bless the Lord for all the wonderful things he has done for me.

Memory Verse: James 1:13

"Let no man say when he is tempted, I am tempted of God; for God cannot be tempted with evil, neither tempts he any man."

To every family member: *"I love you; you are blessed, and you are a blessing."*
Don't forget the hugs.

August 20th

Scripture: Zephaniah 3:17 (NKJV)

"'The Lord your God in your midst, The Mighty One, will save; He will rejoice over you with gladness, He will quiet *you* with His love, He will rejoice over you with singing.'"

In your prayer journal, identify in this portion of scripture a promise to receive or a command to obey.

Prayer:

Heavenly Father, your love and mercy are greater than words could describe. Over and over in scripture, you tell me how much you love me. You desire for me to know you and trust you in everything. Your promises to me are easy to receive because they are given guaranteed by your great love. Father, I want to always walk with the revelation of your great love for me. If I know you love me, I will always trust you. If I know you love me I know you will always save me. You are not far away but live in me and rejoice over me with joy and gladness. I am grateful for your amazing love. I thank you for it in Jesus' name, Amen.

Proclamation:

My God is mighty. He will save me. He will deliver me and bring me into a good place filled with his presence and abundant in his blessings. I am greatly blessed of the Lord this day.

Memory Verse: 2 Corinthians 9:6-7

"But this I say, He that sows sparingly shall reap also sparingly and he which sows bountifully shall reap also bountifully. Every man according as he purposes in his heart, so let him give, not grudgingly or of necessity for God loves a cheerful giver."

To every family member: *"I love you; you are blessed, and you are a blessing."*
Don't forget the hugs.

August 21st

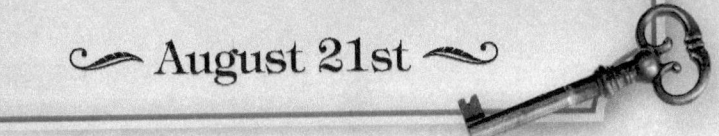

Scripture: 2 Corinthians 5:17-19 (PHILLIPS)

"For if a man is in Christ he becomes a new person altogether—the past is finished and gone, everything has become fresh and new. All this is God's doing, for he has reconciled us to himself through Jesus Christ; and he has made us agents of the reconciliation. God was in Christ personally reconciling the world to himself—not counting their sins against them—and has commissioned us with the message of reconciliation."

In your prayer journal, identify in this portion of scripture a promise to receive or a command to obey.

Prayer:

God my Father, you are glorious in majesty and great in mercy. You are worthy of praise. You have redeemed my life from destruction and crowned me with your loving-kindness and tender mercies. I rejoice in you this day. I thank you for making me brand new, for changing me from who I was into a brand new person when you brought me into your family. You do not remember my past against me, for Jesus removed from me all sin and iniquity. I pray, as a representative of your kingdom, I would walk before you, every day of my life, with a conscious awareness of your abiding presence. Help me to represent you well to all I meet. Help me to be an agent of reconciliation. Give me a fresh anointing of the Spirit of God and establish my thoughts so I will hear you clearly and follow your direction. I thank you for these things now. In Jesus' name I pray, Amen.

Proclamation:

I am yielded to the Spirit of God today. He will lead me to say and to do what is good and right according to his will. I will walk as a citizen of heaven to gain the attention of everyone so they may see God's goodness and life.

Memory Verse: 2 Corinthians 9:6-7

"But this I say, He that sows sparingly shall reap also sparingly and he which sows bountifully shall reap also bountifully. Every man according as he purposes in his heart, so let him give, not grudgingly or of necessity for God loves a cheerful giver."

To every family member: "I love you; you are blessed, and you are a blessing." Don't forget the hugs.

August 22nd

Scripture: 1 Corinthians 3:9-11 (HCSB)

"For we are God's coworkers. You are God's field, God's building. According to God's grace that was given to me, I have laid a foundation as a skilled master builder, and another builds on it. But each one must be careful how he builds on it. For no one can lay any other foundation than what has been laid down. That foundation is Jesus Christ."

In your prayer journal, identify in this portion of scripture a promise to receive or a command to obey.

Prayer:

Heavenly Father, thank you for not leaving me to just do the best I can, but you have given me all the help I need. Like a building, you gave me a solid and immovable foundation that will support me in every circumstance of life. Jesus, the living Word of God is my sure and certain foundation. I ask you to help me to build my life on this rock of revelation by hearing and obeying your Word. You, Father are working with me so I become be a skillful master builder who depends on your wisdom and strength to get the job done. Help me to be a foundation layer in the lives of others so their house, their lives are able to come through the storms without damage. I thank you for your grace that helps me to do and accomplish your will in Jesus' name, Amen.

Proclamation:

God is working in me and with me to empower me to do his will and be fruitful and productive in the kingdom of God. It pleases God to use me today. When I depend on him, he works through me, blessing the work of my hands and the words of my mouth.

Memory Verse: 2 Corinthians 9:6-7

"But this I say, He that sows sparingly shall reap also sparingly and he which sows bountifully shall reap also bountifully. Every man according as he purposes in his heart, so let him give, not grudgingly or of necessity for God loves a cheerful giver."

To every family member: *"I love you; you are blessed, and you are a blessing."*
Don't forget the hugs.

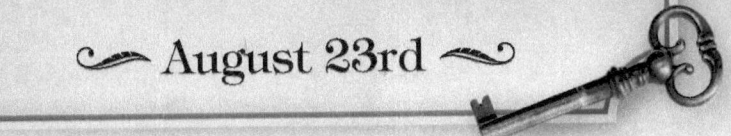

August 23rd

Scripture: 1 Corinthians 3:12-15 (HCSB)

"If anyone builds on that foundation with gold, silver, costly stones, wood, hay, or straw, each one's work will become obvious, for the day will disclose it, because it will be revealed by fire; the fire will test the quality of each one's work. If anyone's work that he has built survives, he will receive a reward. If anyone's work is burned up, it will be lost, but he will be saved; yet it will be like an escape through fire."

In your prayer journal, identify in this portion of scripture a promise to receive or a command to obey.

Prayer:

Father, I stand before you today in the name of my Lord Jesus Christ. I thank you for free access into your presence, to stand before you and bring my requests. I ask you to help me build into my life and the lives of others with things that will last long past my lifetime here. Help me to build with those things that are eternal, incorruptible and have everlasting value. I pray my time, my money and the things I give my attention to will all work towards this purpose of building that which will last forever. I know the wood, hay and straw represent things that have no real lasting value. They are temporary, and when they are gone, they leave little behind. I pray the things I do will be as silver, gold and precious stones that will last and will become for me the joy of my reward and the satisfaction of your purpose. I pray in Jesus' name, Amen.

Proclamation:

I purpose that my time, my money and my attention will be given to people and purposes that will produce lasting fruit and bring glory to God.

Memory Verse: 2 Corinthians 9:6-7

"But this I say, He that sows sparingly shall reap also sparingly and he which sows bountifully shall reap also bountifully. Every man according as he purposes in his heart, so let him give, not grudgingly or of necessity for God loves a cheerful giver."

To every family member: "I love you; you are blessed, and you are a blessing." Don't forget the hugs.

August 24th

Scripture: Isaiah 61:1-3 (VOICE)

"The Spirit of the Lord, the Eternal, is on me. *The Lord has appointed me for a special purpose.* He has anointed me to bring good news to the poor. He has sent me to repair broken hearts, and to declare to those who are held captive and bound in prison, 'Be free from your imprisonment!' *He has sent me* to announce the year *of jubilee, the season* of the Eternal's favor: *for our enemies* it will be a day of God's wrath; for those who mourn it will be *a time of* comfort. As for those who grieve over Zion, *God has sent me* to give them a *beautiful* crown in exchange for ashes, to anoint them with gladness instead of sorrow, to wrap them in *victory, joy, and* praise instead of depression and sadness. People will call them *magnificent, like great towering* trees standing for what is right. They stand to the glory of the Eternal who planted them."

In your prayer journal, identify in this portion of scripture a promise to receive or a command to obey.

Prayer:

Heavenly Father, you anointed Jesus with the Holy Spirit and power who went everywhere healing the sick, delivering the oppressed and declaring liberty to the prisoner. He declared the day of the Lord's favor, the jubilee had come. You also sent the Spirit of God to anoint me and all who are called by your name to continue to do the same works Jesus did by the power of the same Holy Spirit. I pray now for those I know who need their broken hearts repaired. I pray for those who are imprisoned by bitterness and unforgiveness. I ask you Lord to bring them beauty for ashes, the oil of joy for their sorrow and raise them up as a strong and fruitful tree that will glorify you. I take authority over all the wicked works of the enemy, and I bind him and declare these loosed and made free in Jesus' name, Amen.

Proclamation:

The same Spirit that raised Christ from the dead lives in me.

Memory Verse: 2 Corinthians 9:6-7

"But this I say, He that sows sparingly shall reap also sparingly and he which sows bountifully shall reap also bountifully. Every man according as he purposes in his heart, so let him give, not grudgingly or of necessity for God loves a cheerful giver."

To every family member: "I love you; you are blessed, and you are a blessing."
Don't forget the hugs.

August 25th

Scripture: Isaiah 61:4 (AMP)
"And they shall rebuild the ancient ruins; they shall raise up the former desolations and renew the ruined cities, the devastations of many generations."

In your prayer journal, identify in this portion of scripture a promise to receive or a command to obey.

Prayer:
Father, those you have saved, healed, delivered and set free of bondages and sorrows are the same ones you have commissioned to rebuild what has been ruined and to raise up what was wasted and destroyed. I pray for your church, that mighty army of God that has experienced your great salvation to rise up and build what the devil destroyed and establish your kingdom for the generations to come. You have given us the command to go into all the world and to declare the gospel to all. You have anointed us and supplied us with all we need to see the glory of the Lord fill all the earth even as the waters cover the sea. I pray we enlarge the spiritual place where we live in your presence and inherit the surrounding nations, even the uttermost parts of the earth to be reclaimed for your glory and kingdom. I pray we are not distracted from your assignment or discouraged by opposition, but we continue in faith and the love and power of God to accomplish your will and bring forth your purpose. I pray in Jesus' name, Amen.

Proclamation:
With the same comfort I have received, I comfort others. The victory God has given me enables me to come along side those in need and see them made whole, and together we are building with God an everlasting kingdom.

Memory Verse: 2 Corinthians 9:6-7
"But this I say, He that sows sparingly shall reap also sparingly and he which sows bountifully shall reap also bountifully. Every man according as he purposes in his heart, so let him give, not grudgingly or of necessity for God loves a cheerful giver."

To every family member: *"I love you; you are blessed, and you are a blessing."*
Don't forget the hugs.

August 26th

Scripture: Psalms 27:4 (KJV)

"One thing have I desired of the Lord, that will I seek after; that I may dwell in the house of the Lord all the days of my life, to behold the beauty of the Lord, and to enquire in his temple."

In your prayer journal, identify in this portion of scripture a promise to receive or a command to obey.

Prayer:

God, my Father, I worship you, I adore you, I thank you for this great salvation you have given to me. Your presence is more important to me than anything else. For in your presence I find the fullness of joy and the peace that surpasses all understanding. In your presence is unspeakable joy and the fullness of life is with you. Father, you said if I hunger and thirst after you I will be filled. I hunger and thirst to experience your presence, and because I do, I thank you for filling me afresh with the Spirit of God. By faith I enter into your holy presence to access your grace that will supply me with all I need and more than I can imagine. Father, you are good. You are gracious and full of compassion. I will be satisfied in your presence, so fill me with the knowledge of your will I pray in Jesus' name, Amen.

Proclamation:

I will not be sidetracked or distracted by things of no value, but instead I will follow after the Lord with all of my heart. The eyes of the Lord search the earth to find someone whose heart is perfect and upright before him. I desire to be that someone and to bring pleasure to God because my delight is in him. There is no better place to be than in the presence of God, the Creator of the ends of the earth and to know that this Almighty God delights in me because he loves me.

Memory Verse: 2 Corinthians 9:6-7

"But this I say, He that sows sparingly shall reap also sparingly and he which sows bountifully shall reap also bountifully. Every man according as he purposes in his heart, so let him give, not grudgingly or of necessity for God loves a cheerful giver."

To every family member: "I love you; you are blessed, and you are a blessing."
Don't forget the hugs.

August 27th

Scripture: Romans 14:13-17 (HCSB)

"Therefore, let us no longer criticize one another. Instead decide never to put a stumbling block or pitfall in your brother's way. (I know and am persuaded by the Lord Jesus that nothing is unclean in itself. Still, to someone who considers a thing to be unclean, to that one it is unclean. For if your brother is hurt by what you eat, you are no longer walking according to love. Do not destroy that one Christ died for by what you eat. Therefore, do not let your good be slandered, for the kingdom of God is not eating and drinking, but righteousness, peace, and joy in the Holy Spirit."

In your prayer journal, identify in this portion of scripture a promise to receive or a command to obey.

Prayer:

Father, thank you for the Spirit of God who lives in me and empowers me to walk in love and makes me sensitive to the needs of others. Make me aware of any activity I might participate in that would bring offence or cause someone else to stumble in his or her Christian walk. I desire to honor you in everything I do. Whether I eat or drink or whatever I do, help me do all things for the honor and glory of God. Also, I pray you will help me not to be critical or condemning of others. You said love covers a multitude of sins. Lord, you are the righteous judge because you look on the heart and all I can see is what is on the outside. Father, I receive your grace to help me do what I need to do, and I pray for others who need your help to do and say those things that please you. It is in Jesus' wonderful name I pray, Amen.

Proclamation:

I choose to walk in the love of God today towards everyone I meet or even think about. I will make right decisions that will glorify God and will encourage others to follow the Lord with all their heart.

Memory Verse: Ephesians 4:31-32

"Let all bitterness and wrath and anger and clamor and evil speaking be put away from you with all malice. And be kind one to another, tenderhearted, forgiving one another, even as God for Christ's sake has forgiven you."

To every family member: "I love you; you are blessed, and you are a blessing."
Don't forget the hugs.

August 28th

Scripture: Ephesians 4:11-15 (NLT)

"Now these are the gifts Christ gave to the church: the apostles, the prophets, the evangelists, and the pastors and teachers. Their responsibility is to equip God's people to do his work and build up the church, the body of Christ. This will continue until we all come to such unity in our faith and knowledge of God's Son that we will be mature in the Lord, measuring up to the full and complete standard of Christ. Then we will no longer be immature like children. We won't be tossed and blown about by every wind of new teaching. We will not be influenced when people try to trick us with lies so clever they sound like the truth. Instead, we will speak the truth in love, growing in every way more and more like Christ, who is the head of his body, the church."

In your prayer journal, identify in this portion of scripture a promise to receive or a command to obey.

Prayer:

My Heavenly Father, I worship you and give you praise for the gifts you have given to your Church so we can all grow in the knowledge of God and come to a place of unity and agreement. I pray every believer will honor the gifts you have given and receive instruction and demonstration through these men and women of God that give a true example of spiritual maturity. Keep us from false teaching that would corrupt those who hear it and help us recognize what is of God and what is not. Help us to speak the truth in love so Christ, the head of this spiritual body, is glorified. I pray in Jesus' name, Amen.

Proclamation:

I honor the gifts God has given to strengthen and equip the Church. I will pray for these leaders and receive from them what God would have me receive so I can give to others.

Memory Verse: Ephesians 4:31-32

"Let all bitterness and wrath and anger and clamor and evil speaking be put away from you with all malice. And be kind one to another, tenderhearted, forgiving one another, even as God for Christ's sake has forgiven you."

To every family member: "I love you; you are blessed, and you are a blessing."
Don't forget the hugs.

August 29th

Scripture: Romans 12:19-21 (PHILLIPS)

"Never take vengeance into your own hands, my dear friends: stand back and let God punish if he will. For it is written: 'Vengeance is mine. I will repay'. ... these are God's words: 'Therefore if your enemy hungers, feed him; if he thirsts, give him a drink; for in so doing you will heap coals of fire on his head'. Don't allow yourself to be overpowered with evil. Take the offensive—overpower evil by good!"

In your prayer journal, identify in this portion of scripture a promise to receive or a command to obey.

Prayer:

My Heavenly Father, you are the righteous judge, and you are able to defend me and rescue me in every circumstance of life. You are my shield and fortress, my high tower of refuge and strength. My trust is in you, for you are always with me. Help me to honor your Word by blessing my enemies and doing good to those who consider themselves to be an adversary. You, Lord will restore to me what others have unjustly taken. You will preserve me from every wicked device of the enemy. Thank you for protecting me and making me to be victorious and to overpower evil with good. In Jesus' name I pray, Amen.

Proclamation:

I will not be afraid of threats from the enemy. I do not have time to consider things others have done to offend me. I will trust the Lord to take care of me.

Memory Verse: Ephesians 4:31-32

"Let all bitterness and wrath and anger and clamor and evil speaking be put away from you with all malice. And be kind one to another, tenderhearted, forgiving one another, even as God for Christ's sake has forgiven you."

To every family member: *"I love you; you are blessed, and you are a blessing."* Don't forget the hugs.

Faith Family Minute

August 30th

Scripture: Jeremiah 32:27 (KJV)
"Behold, I am the Lord, the God of all flesh: is there any thing too hard for me?"

In your prayer journal, identify in this portion of scripture a promise to receive or a command to obey.

Prayer:

My Father, I know you have created all things. You made the world and everything in it. You created the universe and spoke the stars into existence. I am amazed at your power and wisdom. Most of all, I am amazed at your love for me. Forgive me for the times I have doubted you or thought you were ignoring me. You who know the end from the beginning and call things that do not exist into existence, you are able to do all things. Nothing is too difficult for you. Because Jesus perfectly expressed your love for people when he healed the sick and gave sight to the blind and even raised the dead, I know your love is the same for me and you will do for me what you did for others in need. Lord, you are my healer and my provider. You will comfort me and bring me peace so I can say of the Lord," He is my help; nothing is too difficult for him." I receive now strength for my body, wisdom for my mind and provision that meets all of my needs and causes me to increase more and more, day by day. Father, thank you for these things now in Jesus' name, Amen.

Proclamation:

The Lord my God is mighty to save. There is no searching of his understanding, and his might and power have no limits. God will take care of me.

Memory Verse: Ephesians 4:31-32
"Let all bitterness and wrath and anger and clamor and evil speaking be put away from you with all malice. And be kind one to another, tenderhearted, forgiving one another, even as God for Christ's sake has forgiven you."

To every family member: "I love you; you are blessed, and you are a blessing."
Don't forget the hugs.

August 31st

Scripture: John 14:15-18 (NKJV)

"If you love Me, keep My commandments. And I will pray the Father, and He will give you another Helper, that He may abide with you forever— the Spirit of truth, whom the world cannot receive, because it neither sees Him nor knows Him; but you know Him, for He dwells with you and will be in you. I will not leave you orphans; I will come to you."

In your prayer journal, identify in this portion of scripture a promise to receive or a command to obey.

Prayer:

My Father, I thank you today for the Spirit of God who lives in me. He is my helper. I am not as an orphan without help because the Spirit of God has created in me a brand new person that never existed before he entered my life. The Spirit of God has given me new life, spiritual life, so I can receive all the wonderful things the Lord has freely given me. The Spirit of God lives in me and speaks to me to give me direction and reveal to me the things of God. I acknowledge the work of the Spirit of God to help me become the person you created me to be. Father, make me aware of the abiding presence of the Holy Spirit and help me to always request his leading and direction for every decision I make. Give me ears to hear what the Spirit of God would say to me today. I pray in Jesus' name, Amen.

Proclamation:

God lives in me in the person of the Holy Spirit. All power and might, all wisdom and understanding dwell inside of me, in him. I do not need to try and get God's attention or hope he hears my prayer because the Spirit of God will never leave me or forsake me.

Memory Verse: Ephesians 4:31-32

"Let all bitterness and wrath and anger and clamor and evil speaking be put away from you with all malice. And be kind one to another, tenderhearted, forgiving one another, even as God for Christ's sake has forgiven you."

To every family member: "I love you; you are blessed, and you are a blessing." Don't forget the hugs.

September 1st

Scripture: Ephesians 5:1-4 (MSG)

"Watch what God does, and then you do it, like children who learn proper behavior from their parents. Mostly what God does is love you. Keep company with him and learn a life of love. Observe how Christ loved us. His love was not cautious but extravagant. He didn't love in order to get something from us but to give everything of himself to us. Love like that. Don't allow love to turn into lust, setting off a downhill slide into sexual promiscuity, filthy practices, or bullying greed. Though some tongues just love the taste of gossip, those who follow Jesus have better uses for language than that. Don't talk dirty or silly. That kind of talk doesn't fit our style. Thanksgiving is our dialect."

In your prayer journal, identify in this portion of scripture a promise to receive or a command to obey.

Prayer:

My Father, I desire to follow you in all my ways. I want to please you by doing and saying those things that express your goodness and love to those who see me or hear my words. Jesus said he always did those things that please you and the works Jesus did, I am to do also. Father help me to follow his example and love people because you do and not for some ulterior purpose. I ask you to keep me from selfishness and pride. Put a guard over my mouth so I only speak words that encourage and strengthen those who hear me. I thank you for hearing me and fulfilling these things in my life. I pray in Jesus' name, Amen.

Proclamation:

God is at work inside of me, filling me with his love so I can genuinely love people as he does. My words are full of life, and the things I speak please God and build up those who hear me.

Memory Verse: Ephesians 4:31-32

"Let all bitterness and wrath and anger and clamor and evil speaking be put away from you with all malice. And be kind one to another, tenderhearted, forgiving one another, even as God for Christ's sake has forgiven you."

To every family member: "*I love you; you are blessed, and you are a blessing.*"
Don't forget the hugs.

September 2nd

Scripture: John 3:16-18 (AMP)

"For God so greatly loved and dearly prized the world that He [even] gave up His only begotten (unique) Son, so that whoever believes in (trusts in, clings to, relies on) Him shall not perish (come to destruction, be lost) but have eternal (everlasting) life. For God did not send the Son into the world in order to judge (to reject, to condemn, to pass sentence on) the world, but that the world might find salvation and be made safe and sound through Him. He who believes in Him [who clings to, trusts in, relies on Him] is not judged [he who trusts in Him never comes up for judgment; for him there is no rejection, no condemnation—he incurs no damnation]; but he who does not believe (cleave to, rely on, trust in Him) is judged already [he has already been convicted and has already received his sentence] because he has not believed in and trusted in the name of the only begotten Son of God. [He is condemned for refusing to let his trust rest in Christ's name.]"

In your prayer journal, identify in this portion of scripture a promise to receive or a command to obey.

Prayer:

God, my Father, your love is greater than I could ever imagine. You sent your Son Jesus to live a life totally free of sin, which he did, and because he was perfect, he was the only one who could give his life as a ransom for me. Jesus took the judgment for my sin so he could justly give me his righteousness even though I didn't earn it or deserve it. Father, my trust is in you and in Jesus my Savior. I will never stand in judgment or be rejected for my sin because you exchanged my sin for the righteousness of Christ Jesus. I am forever grateful. It is in Jesus' name I pray, Amen.

Proclamation:

I have the righteousness of Christ. I have received it as a gift from God, my Father. I am forgiven, not because of what I have done or what I failed to do but because of what Jesus did for me.

Memory Verse: Ephesians 4:31-32

"Let all bitterness and wrath and anger and clamor and evil speaking be put away from you with all malice. And be kind one to another, tenderhearted, forgiving one another, even as God for Christ's sake has forgiven you."

To every family member: "I love you; you are blessed, and you are a blessing." Don't forget the hugs.

September 3rd

Scripture: Colossians 1:9-13 (NIV)

"For this reason, since the day we heard about you, we have not stopped praying for you. We continually ask God to fill you with the knowledge of his will through all the wisdom and understanding that the Spirit gives, so that you may live a life worthy of the Lord and please him in every way: bearing fruit in every good work, growing in the knowledge of God, being strengthened with all power according to his glorious might so that you may have great endurance and patience, and giving joyful thanks to the Father, who has qualified you to share in the inheritance of his holy people in the kingdom of light. For he has rescued us from the dominion of darkness and brought us into the kingdom of the Son he loves."

In your prayer journal, identify in this portion of scripture a promise to receive or a command to obey.

Prayer:

God, my Father, as Paul prayed for the Church, I pray for myself. I ask you to fill me with the knowledge of your will so I live a life worthy of you, pleasing you in every way. Help me to be fruitful in every good work and continue to grow in the knowledge of you and be strengthened with all power. Help me to have great endurance and always be filled with thanksgiving, for you have qualified me to share in the inheritance of your people and live in your kingdom. Thank you, Lord, for rescuing me from the dominion of darkness and for bringing me into the kingdom of your dear Son. I praise you for these things working in me today in Jesus' name, Amen.

Proclamation:

God is at work in me helping me to be willing and obedient to hear and to do all of his good pleasure.

Memory Verse: Hebrews 11:6

"But without faith it is impossible to please him: for he that comes to God must believe that he is and he is a rewarder of them that diligently seek him."

To every family member: "I love you; you are blessed, and you are a blessing."
Don't forget the hugs.

September 4th

Scripture: James 1:5-8 (NRSV)

"If any of you is lacking in wisdom, ask God, who gives to all generously and ungrudgingly, and it will be given you. But ask in faith, never doubting, for the one who doubts is like a wave of the sea, driven and tossed by the wind; for the doubter, being double-minded and unstable in every way, must not expect to receive anything from the Lord."

In your prayer journal, identify in this portion of scripture a promise to receive or a command to obey.

Prayer:

Heavenly Father, you are the source of all true wisdom and understanding. I thank you for the promise of your Word that says I can ask you for wisdom and you will give it to me abundantly. I believe you release into my life the wisdom I need to make good decisions and discern what is righteous and good in your eyes. Give me wisdom and direction to know what is your will and what is not. I receive this wisdom now. I am confident that you will make my way plain and establish my thoughts to line up with your will so I will always do those things that will please you and will be a blessing to me and to those I know. In Jesus' name, Amen.

Proclamation:

I have the wisdom of God at work in me. God has promised to give me wisdom when I ask in faith. I have asked, and I believe God is able to give me wisdom to handle every situation in a way that pleases him.

Memory Verse: Hebrews 11:6

"But without faith it is impossible to please him: for he that comes to God must believe that he is and he is a rewarder of them that diligently seek him."

To every family member: *"I love you; you are blessed, and you are a blessing."*
Don't forget the hugs.

September 5th

Scripture: 1 Timothy 6:10-12 (NKJV)

"For the love of money is a root of all kinds of evil, for which some have strayed from the faith in their greediness, and pierced themselves through with many sorrows. But you, O man of God, flee these things and pursue righteousness, godliness, faith, love, patience, gentleness. Fight the good fight of faith, lay hold on eternal life, to which you were also called and have confessed the good confession in the presence of many witnesses."

In your prayer journal, identify in this portion of scripture a promise to receive or a command to obey.

Prayer:

My God, I thank you for the abundance you have given me. There is nothing I need you have not generously provided. Your blessings in my life cause me to prosper and increase from day to day. Father, I ask you to keep me from the love of money. I know money is good and it is a blessing of God, but as you warn me in your Word, greed brings many sorrows. I will fight the good fight of faith to guard my heart from the love of money and trust you to supply all my needs according to your riches in glory through my Lord Jesus Christ. I know you can give me more than what I can ask for or even imagine, so I will pursue righteousness, godliness, faith, love, patience and gentleness as I declare my faith in you. In Jesus' name I pray, Amen.

Proclamation:

God is my source. He is my provider. He will bless me and prosper me. I will never be in want or lack of any good thing. I am not greedy, and I do not set my heart on money. I set my heart on the things of God and receive from his hand all I need.

Memory Verse: Hebrews 11:6

"But without faith it is impossible to please him: for he that comes to God must believe that he is and he is a rewarder of them that diligently seek him."

To every family member: *"I love you; you are blessed, and you are a blessing."*
Don't forget the hugs.

September 6th

Scripture: Ephesians 5:25-30 (KJV)

"Husbands, love your wives, even as Christ also loved the church, and gave himself for it; That he might sanctify and cleanse it with the washing of water by the word, That he might present it to himself a glorious church, not having spot, or wrinkle, or any such thing; but that it should be holy and without blemish. So ought men to love their wives as their own bodies. He that loveth his wife loveth himself. For no man ever yet hated his own flesh; but nourisheth and cherisheth it, even as the Lord the church: For we are members of his body, of his flesh, and of his bones."

In your prayer journal, identify in this portion of scripture a promise to receive or a command to obey.

Prayer:

My Heavenly Father, thank you for loving me. You have joined me to yourself, even making me a member of your very own body. As marriage depicts the union of a husband to a wife, so you have made me to be joined to you. As two people become one in marriage, you have made me to become one with you. This mysterious union is greater than I can imagine. You, the everlasting God, the Creator of the universe, who are Almighty and all powerful, have sanctified and cleansed me by washing me with the Word of God. The Word of salvation you brought to me tells me that Jesus carried away my sin and cleansed me of everything that would separate me from you. You gave me faith to believe this wonderful work of God's love and then gave me your life bringing me into union with you. I thank you that I am joined to you as much as my body is joined to me. You are glorious and worthy of all praise. In Jesus' name, Amen.

Proclamation:

I have been joined to the Lord as part of his body, his flesh and his bones.

Memory Verse: Hebrews 11:6

"But without faith it is impossible to please him: for he that comes to God must believe that he is and he is a rewarder of them that diligently seek him."

To every family member: "*I love you; you are blessed, and you are a blessing.*"
Don't forget the hugs.

Faith Family Minute | 251

September 7th

Scripture: Isaiah 53:4-6 (NLT)

"Yet it was our weaknesses he carried; it was our sorrow that weighed him down. And we thought his troubles were a punishment from God, a punishment for his own sins! But he was pierced for our rebellion, crushed for our sins. He was beaten so we could be whole. He was whipped so we could be healed. All of us, like sheep, have strayed away. We have left God's paths to follow our own. Yet the Lord laid on him the sins of us all."

In your prayer journal, identify in this portion of scripture a promise to receive or a command to obey.

Prayer:

God, my Father, I worship you and praise your holy name. You have seen me in my weakness and rebellion and instead of condemning me you redeemed me. You laid on Jesus the punishment for my sin. He came to take upon himself the curse my sin produced and freed me from guilt and shame. I thank you today for Jesus my Savior and Deliverer who rescued me from bondage I could never have freed myself from. Jesus said, "He whom the Son sets free is free indeed." I declare today that Jesus has set me free. Sin does not have dominion over me because Jesus exchanged his life for my death, his wholeness for my brokenness, and took my deserved judgment to forgive and restore me to a position with God that is without guilt or shame. I am filled with awe for your great love for me, and I humble myself before you and ask you to show me your will and ways that I might please you and honor you for all the wonderful things you have done for me. It is in Jesus' name I pray, Amen.

Proclamation:

I am no longer under the bondage of sin, for Jesus set me free, and I am free indeed.

Memory Verse: Hebrews 11:6

"But without faith it is impossible to please him: for he that comes to God must believe that he is and he is a rewarder of them that diligently seek him."

To every family member: "I love you; you are blessed, and you are a blessing."
Don't forget the hugs.

September 8th

Scripture: 2 Peter 1:2-4 (HCSB)

"May grace and peace be multiplied to you through the knowledge of God and of Jesus our Lord. His divine power has given us everything required for life and godliness through the knowledge of Him who called us by His own glory and goodness. By these He has given us very great and precious promises, so that through them you may share in the divine nature, escaping the corruption that is in the world because of evil desires."

In your prayer journal, identify in this portion of scripture a promise to receive or a command to obey.

Prayer:

Father, you are the giver of every good thing. I thank you for the knowledge you have given me concerning your great and precious promises that bring me life and life more abundantly. You have shared with me your divine nature by making me a brand new creation, created in your image and after your likeness. Father, you keep me from the corruption of this world and evil desires so I might serve you with clean hands and a pure heart. Fill me afresh with the knowledge of your will. Help me to see clearly the promises you have freely given me so I always walk in your abundant blessings. Father, help me to be fruitful in every good work, bringing glory to your name. I pray in the name of Jesus, Amen.

Proclamation:

God has given me his life. Everything I will ever need to enjoy life and godliness is already mine. I will walk in the knowledge of God today by hearing his voice and receiving his Word as I spend time with him in the secret place of prayer and praise.

Memory Verse: Hebrews 11:6

"But without faith it is impossible to please him: for he that comes to God must believe that he is and he is a rewarder of them that diligently seek him."

To every family member: "I love you; you are blessed, and you are a blessing."
Don't forget the hugs.

September 9th

Scripture: James 5:14-16 (KJV)

"Is any sick among you? Let him call for the elders of the church; and let them pray over him, anointing him with oil in the name of the Lord: And the prayer of faith shall save the sick, and the Lord shall raise him up; and if he have committed sins, they shall be forgiven him. Confess your faults one to another, and pray one for another, that ye may be healed. The effectual fervent prayer of a righteous man availeth much."

In your prayer journal, identify in this portion of scripture a promise to receive or a command to obey.

Prayer:

Heavenly Father, you have blessed me with health and delivered me from sickness and disease. Thank you for helping me receive everything Jesus paid for. I know that in this world there are many challenges to my health. While I am in this world, my body has not yet experienced your promise of resurrection and immortality, but you have given me the Holy Spirit to live in me and make alive my mortal body. You said the prayer of faith would save the sick, and you would raise them up. Thank you, Lord, for raising me up when I am sick and empowering me to pray for others who are in need of healing. I believe your Word that the prayer of faith is powerful and effective. You have made me righteous and given me faith. Therefore, I can pray and see the effective, powerful working of your Word as I pray for those in need. I praise you for these things now in Jesus' name, Amen.

Proclamation:

My prayers exercise great force and accomplish the will of God as I pray for the sick.

Memory Verse: Hebrews 11:6

"But without faith it is impossible to please him: for he that comes to God must believe that he is and he is a rewarder of them that diligently seek him."

To every family member: "I love you; you are blessed, and you are a blessing."
Don't forget the hugs.

September 10th

Scripture: Acts 2:37-39 (KJV)

"Now when they heard this, they were pricked in their heart, and said unto Peter and to the rest of the apostles, Men and brethren, what shall we do? Then Peter said unto them, Repent, and be baptized every one of you in the name of Jesus Christ for the remission of sins, and ye shall receive the gift of the Holy Ghost. For the promise is unto you, and to your children, and to all that are afar off, even as many as the Lord our God shall call."

In your prayer journal, identify in this portion of scripture a promise to receive or a command to obey.

Prayer:

Heavenly Father, you gave the Holy Spirit to the 120 in the upper room on the Day of Pentecost. Peter preached of the promised gift of the Holy Spirit to those listening to him and he gave the same promise to those who would live years from that time and to all you would call. I thank you today for the gift of the Holy Spirit of God, the Comforter who lives in me, changes me and helps me to walk in the ways of God. It is through the power of the Holy Spirit that I can do the things that Jesus did. Lord, thank you for the baptism in the Spirit that empowers me to function in the gifts of the Spirit and live with a constant revelation of your abiding presence. I pray for every believer to be baptized with the same baptism they received on the Day of Pentecost so their witness of your great salvation is powerful and the knowledge of your will fills all the earth. I pray in Jesus' name, Amen.

Proclamation:

Jesus said those who believe would receive the gift of the Holy Spirit and they would be witnesses for him in all the world. I am an effective witness of the gospel of Christ because he empowers me by the Holy Spirit today.

Memory Verse: Galatians 3:13-14

"Christ has redeemed us from the curse of the law, being made a curse for us, for it is written, cursed is every one that hangs on a tree; that the blessing of Abraham might come on the Gentiles through Jesus Christ; that we might receive the promise of the Spirit through faith."

To every family member: *"I love you; you are blessed, and you are a blessing."*
Don't forget the hugs.

September 11th

Scripture: Galatians 5:5-6 (VOICE)

"We, on the other hand, continue to live through the Spirit's power and wait confidently in the hope that things will be put right through faith. Here's the thing: in Jesus the Anointed whether you are circumcised or not makes no difference. What makes a difference is faith energized by love."

In your prayer journal, identify in this portion of scripture a promise to receive or a command to obey.

Prayer:

My Father, you know all things, and there is no searching of your understanding. You have made a way for the power of the Holy Spirit to make right everything that is not right. Father you made eyes to see and legs to work and families to live in peace and enjoy your blessings. When these things fail to function, you make them right by the power of the Holy Spirit. You have given to me an assignment, with every other believer, to boldly declare the gospel of Christ and the kingdom of God that brings righteousness, peace and joy to those who receive it. You said, as I have freely received, I am to freely give and pray for those in need to see your will of righteousness working in them. Because faith works by love, I ask you to fill me with your love. I want to walk in love, first for you and then for people so what I do is really you working through me to bring to people what they need. I pray for this mighty work of God to work in me and through me today. In Jesus' name, Amen.

Proclamation:

Faith releases the power of God when the motivation comes from love. I will walk in the love of God today. I believe as God's love in me reaches out to those in need, faith will release the power of God to meet their needs.

Memory Verse: Galatians 3:13-14

"Christ has redeemed us from the curse of the law, being made a curse for us, for it is written, cursed is every one that hangs on a tree; that the blessing of Abraham might come on the Gentiles through Jesus Christ; that we might receive the promise of the Spirit through faith."

To every family member: *"I love you; you are blessed, and you are a blessing."*
Don't forget the hugs.

September 12th

Scripture: Acts 17:10-12 (NCV)

"That same night the believers sent Paul and Silas to Berea where they went to the synagogue. These people were more willing to listen than the people in Thessalonica. The Bereans were eager to hear what Paul and Silas said and studied the Scriptures every day to find out if these things were true. So, many of them believed, as well as many important Greek women and men."

In your prayer journal, identify in this portion of scripture a promise to receive or a command to obey.

Prayer:

My Father, the Word of God is powerful to bring salvation and to turn the hearts of people from darkness to light and from the power of Satan to God. Your Word will make strong those who hear it. It will give to them the inheritance of your kingdom when they believe. Help me to be like the Bereans, who studied the scriptures to find out if what they heard was true. Lord, you have warned us of false teachers and demonic deceptions that would try to enter your church and deceive the hearts of your people. I pray for all who have put their faith in you to search your Word and judge what they hear by the standard of your Word. Keep us from deception and give us revelation of your Word that declares your will. Thank you for the anointing that abides in us to teach us the things of God and to bear witness to the truth. I pray deception will be exposed and truth will be exalted. In Jesus' name, Amen.

Proclamation:

I will study the scriptures and listen for the Lord's instruction. He is well able to speak to me and make his will known.

Memory Verse: Galatians 3:13-14

"Christ has redeemed us from the curse of the law, being made a curse for us, for it is written, cursed is every one that hangs on a tree; that the blessing of Abraham might come on the Gentiles through Jesus Christ; that we might receive the promise of the Spirit through faith."

To every family member: *"I love you; you are blessed, and you are a blessing."*
Don't forget the hugs.

September 13th

Scripture: Deuteronomy 28:11-13 (AMP)

"And the Lord shall make you have a surplus of prosperity, through the fruit of your body, of your livestock, and of your ground, in the land which the Lord swore to your fathers to give you. The Lord shall open to you His good treasury, the heavens, to give the rain of your land in its season and to bless all the work of your hands; and you shall lend to many nations, but you shall not borrow. And the Lord shall make you the head, and not the tail; and you shall be above only, and you shall not be beneath, if you heed the commandments of the Lord your God which I command you this day and are watchful to do them."

In your prayer journal, identify in this portion of scripture a promise to receive or a command to obey.

Prayer:

Heavenly Father, your will is to bless us and increase us and cause us to prosper in everything we do. You promised Israel victory over their enemies and success in every realm of life if they would hear and obey your commandments. When they obeyed they flourished and when they rebelled they lost all they had gained. You gave them a sacrifice of lambs and goats when they failed to obey your words. You promised them a day a Savior would come to be the final sacrifice and bring your blessing to all the world. I know it is not about my obedience that will gain your approval and blessing, but faith in Jesus who obeyed completely your every command and gained for me your blessings for now and forever. I praise you for these things in Jesus' name, Amen.

Proclamation:

It is not by righteous works I have done, but by God's mercy and grace he has saved me and given me life and blessings.

Memory Verse: Galatians 3:13-14

"Christ has redeemed us from the curse of the law, being made a curse for us, for it is written, cursed is every one that hangs on a tree; that the blessing of Abraham might come on the Gentiles through Jesus Christ; that we might receive the promise of the Spirit through faith."

To every family member: *"I love you; you are blessed, and you are a blessing."*
Don't forget the hugs.

September 14th

Scripture: Isaiah 40:9-11 (NLT)

"O Zion, messenger of good news, shout from the mountaintops! Shout it louder, O Jerusalem. Shout, and do not be afraid. Tell the towns of Judah, "Your God is coming!" Yes, the Sovereign Lord is coming in power. He will rule with a powerful arm. See, he brings his reward with him as he comes. He will feed his flock like a shepherd. He will carry the lambs in his arms, holding them close to his heart. He will gently lead the mother sheep with their young."

In your prayer journal, identify in this portion of scripture a promise to receive or a command to obey.

Prayer:

Lord, my God, you are the Good Shepherd; we are your people and the sheep of your pasture. You lead us. You feed us. You protect us, and you love us, holding us close to your heart. We thank you now for your tender mercies and the gentle ways you deal with us. Thank you for your mighty power and strength and dominion that none can challenge. The reward of the Lord is his presence and it is more to be desired than riches or treasure. Your grace Lord is poured out upon us, and your faithfulness is beyond compare. I worship and adore your holy name. I thank you for this great salvation you have so freely given me. In Jesus' name, I give you praise, Amen.

Proclamation:

The Lord is my Shepherd; I will not be in want or need of any good thing.

Memory Verse: Galatians 3:13-14

"Christ has redeemed us from the curse of the law, being made a curse for us, for it is written, cursed is every one that hangs on a tree; that the blessing of Abraham might come on the Gentiles through Jesus Christ; that we might receive the promise of the Spirit through faith."

To every family member: *"I love you; you are blessed, and you are a blessing."*
Don't forget the hugs.

September 15th

Scripture: Hebrews 12:27-29 (AMP)

"Now this expression, Yet once more, indicates the final removal and transformation of all [that can be] shaken—that is, of that which has been created—in order that what cannot be shaken may remain and continue. Let us therefore, receiving a kingdom that is firm and stable and cannot be shaken, offer to God pleasing service and acceptable worship, with modesty and pious care and godly fear and awe; For our God [is indeed] a consuming fire."

In your prayer journal, identify in this portion of scripture a promise to receive or a command to obey.

Prayer:

Father, you have declared that you will shake everything that can be shaken so what cannot be shaken will remain. Everything that is built upon your Word and the revelation that Jesus is Lord is sure and unshakable. Nothing else will last. I desire to come to you every day and hear your voice and obey your Word so my life would be built upon that immovable foundation. Father, give me ears to hear what the Spirit of God would speak to me today. Help me to recognize your voice and be quick to do what you would show me to do. Keep me from presumption, from doing things that are only temporary and of no value. Help me not to hesitate when I hear your voice, but by faith boldly declare your Word and your will. I thank you for bringing to pass these things now in Jesus' name, Amen.

Proclamation:

My life is built upon the immovable, unshakable and eternal foundation of the Word of God. What God has said he will certainly do. He is faithful to fulfill his Word and bring to pass all he has promised.

Memory Verse: Galatians 3:13-14

"Christ has redeemed us from the curse of the law, being made a curse for us, for it is written, cursed is every one that hangs on a tree; that the blessing of Abraham might come on the Gentiles through Jesus Christ; that we might receive the promise of the Spirit through faith."

To every family member: "I love you; you are blessed, and you are a blessing."
Don't forget the hugs.

September 16th

Scripture: 1 Samuel 16:7 (KJV)

"But the Lord said unto Samuel, Look not on his countenance, or on the height of his stature; because I have refused him: for the Lord seeth not as man seeth; for man looketh on the outward appearance, but the Lord looketh on the heart."

In your prayer journal, identify in this portion of scripture a promise to receive or a command to obey.

Prayer:

Heavenly Father, you see and know all things. There is nothing that is hidden from you. I pray you keep me from presumption and help me to see people and circumstances as you do. I pray for your wisdom and spiritual understanding to help me judge every situation rightly so I can make wise and godly decisions that will produce your desired outcome. Help me look at the things that are not seen with natural eyes in order to see the things that only you can reveal to me. I receive these things now in Jesus' name and thank you for them, Amen.

Proclamation:

I walk by faith and not by sight. I do not judge according to the appearance of things, but the Spirit of the Lord leads me and brings me insight and revelation to see and know the will of God in every situation of life.

Memory Verse: Galatians 3:13-14

"Christ has redeemed us from the curse of the law, being made a curse for us, for it is written, cursed is every one that hangs on a tree; that the blessing of Abraham might come on the Gentiles through Jesus Christ; that we might receive the promise of the Spirit through faith."

To every family member: *"I love you; you are blessed, and you are a blessing."*
Don't forget the hugs.

September 17th

Scripture: Matthew 4:23-24 (HSCB)

"Jesus was going all over Galilee, teaching in their synagogues, preaching the good news of the kingdom, and healing every disease and sickness among the people. Then the news about Him spread throughout Syria. So they brought to Him all those who were afflicted, those suffering from various diseases and intense pains, the demon-possessed, the epileptics, and the paralytics. And He healed them."

In your prayer journal, identify in this portion of scripture a promise to receive or a command to obey.

Prayer:

My Father, I know Jesus always performed your will. He said without you he could do nothing and that he came to do, "not [his] own will but the will of [him] who sent [him]." Father, it is plain to me that it is your will for the good news of the kingdom to be preached everywhere and for all who are sick and diseased or tormented by the devil and those who are paralytics or epileptics to be healed. You have shown me in your Word to pray for your kingdom to come and your will to be done on earth just as it is done in heaven. So this day, I pray that the knowledge of your kingdom would be known and the power of God would be seen to heal and deliver and set free all who are sick and oppressed. As Jesus declared the coming of your kingdom when he preached your Word and healed the sick, I pray I would see the same powerful workings of God in my life as I carry the Word of your salvation and love to all you send me to this day. In Jesus' name I pray, Amen.

Proclamation:

The Word of God is living and powerful and sharper than any two edged sword. The Word of God is the sword of the Spirit, and when I pray the Word of God, I am declaring his will and establishing his purpose.

Memory Verse: Isaiah 53:4-5

"Surely he has borne our griefs, and carried our sorrows: yet we did esteem him stricken, smitten of God, and afflicted. But he was wounded for our transgressions, he was bruised for our iniquities: the chastisement of our peace was upon him; and with his stripes we are healed."

To every family member: "I love you; you are blessed, and you are a blessing."
Don't forget the hugs.

September 18th

Scripture: Psalms 119:129-130 (AMP)

"Your testimonies are wonderful [far exceeding anything conceived by man]; therefore my [penitent] self keeps them [hearing, receiving, loving, and obeying them]. The entrance and unfolding of Your words give light; their unfolding gives understanding (discernment and comprehension) to the simple."

In your prayer journal, identify in this portion of scripture a promise to receive or a command to obey.

Prayer:

Father, your Word is to be desired more than gold or any treasure, for your Word brings me life. It gives me understanding, and as I follow your Word, I prosper and have good success in everything I do. Your Word reveals to me the knowledge of your will and teaches me to prosper. You make me fruitful in every good work, and I live with a constant awareness of your abiding presence. Thank you for your Word that leads me and causes me to triumph every day of my life. I am grateful for your eternal Word and your faithfulness to perform your Word in my life. In Jesus' name I pray, Amen.

Proclamation:

The Word of God gives me light to follow the pathway God has set before me. When I walk in the light of his Word, I walk in the place of my inheritance and his goodness and mercy follows me every day of my life.

Memory Verse: Isaiah 53:4-5

"Surely he has borne our griefs, and carried our sorrows: yet we did esteem him stricken, smitten of God, and afflicted. But he was wounded for our transgressions, he was bruised for our iniquities: the chastisement of our peace was upon him; and with his stripes we are healed."

To every family member: "I love you; you are blessed, and you are a blessing." Don't forget the hugs.

September 19th

Scripture: 2 Corinthians 3:5-6 (HSCB)

"It is not that we are competent in ourselves to consider anything as coming from ourselves, but our competence is from God. He has made us competent to be ministers of a new covenant, not of the letter, but of the Spirit. For the letter kills, but the Spirit produces life."

In your prayer journal, identify in this portion of scripture a promise to receive or a command to obey.

Prayer:

Heavenly Father, You are my help in times of trouble, and you are my strength and life. All I have has come from you. Without you, I can do nothing, but in the anointing I have received from you, I can do all things. You have qualified me to accomplish all your will and purpose for my life. I am not on my own, for you are with me. I ask you Lord to make me an able minister of the gospel. Help me to follow the leading of the Holy Spirit so life is the result of everything I do or say. I pray in Jesus' name, Amen.

Proclamation:

Every good thing I have has come from God. Every good and perfect gift comes to me from God and strengthens me to follow the Spirit of God and produce the fruit of life to the glory of God.

Memory Verse: Isaiah 53:4-5

"Surely he has borne our griefs, and carried our sorrows: yet we did esteem him stricken, smitten of God, and afflicted. But he was wounded for our transgressions, he was bruised for our iniquities: the chastisement of our peace was upon him; and with his stripes we are healed."

To every family member: "I love you; you are blessed, and you are a blessing."
Don't forget the hugs.

September 20th

Scripture: Luke 10:38-42 (PHILLIPS)

"As they continued their journey, Jesus came to a village and a woman called Martha welcomed him to her house. She had a sister by the name of Mary who settled down at the Lord's feet and was listening to what he said. But Martha was very worried about her elaborate preparations and she burst in, saying, 'Lord, don't you mind that my sister has left me to do everything by myself? Tell her to get up and help me!' But the Lord answered her, 'Martha, my dear, you are worried and bothered about providing so many things. Only a few things are really needed, perhaps only one. Mary has chosen the best part and you must not tear it away from her!'"

In your prayer journal, identify in this portion of scripture a promise to receive or a command to obey.

Prayer:

Father, it is my desire to hear what you have to say to me. Help me not to be distracted by all the things I feel like I must do. Help me not to be so consumed with the deadlines and schedules and demands of others so I allow my time with you to be robbed from me. Help me to always choose the best instead of the loudest and remind me that you have the words of life. Father, you can multiply my time and give me in just a minute the plan or direction I need to save me hours. I believe you will prosper my time and give me wisdom and favor as I daily seek you first above all else. I praise you for these things now in Jesus' name, Amen.

Proclamation:

My God is able to do exceedingly, abundantly above all I could ever ask or think. He prospers my time and gives me wisdom to accomplish everything I need to do with skillful excellence. With God's help, I can accomplish in minutes things it takes others days because I seek after him and listen to receive his instructions for my day.

Memory Verse: Isaiah 53:4-5

"Surely he has borne our griefs, and carried our sorrows: yet we did esteem him stricken, smitten of God, and afflicted. But he was wounded for our transgressions, he was bruised for our iniquities: the chastisement of our peace was upon him, and with his stripes we are healed."

To every family member: *"I love you; you are blessed, and you are a blessing."*
Don't forget the hugs.

September 21st

Scripture: Malachi 3:10 (NKJV)

"'Bring all the tithes into the storehouse, that there may be food in My house, and try Me now in this,' says the Lord of hosts, 'If I will not open for you the windows of heaven and pour out for you such blessing that there will not be room enough to receive it.'"

In your prayer journal, identify in this portion of scripture a promise to receive or a command to obey.

Prayer:

My Father, I thank you for the promises of your Word. I desire to honor you with all my substance and with the first fruits of all I receive. Lord, I bring to you my tithe. I know everything I have has come from you. You are my provider and the supplier of all my needs. I know the windows of heaven are open over me. I know the blessings of the Lord are poured out in great measure, so I have abundance of all good things. Thank you, Lord, for your faithfulness to supply all I need this day and cause me to increase more and more so I can give to every good work in Jesus' name, Amen.

Proclamation:

I am full and complete not lacking any good thing. I honor the Lord with my tithe and all I have, and the Lord pours on me his blessings. The windows of heaven are open over me, and I am walking in daily increase. I have more today than I had yesterday, and tomorrow I will have even more because my God is the God of increase. He gives me power to obtain wealth so I can help to establish his covenant on the earth and see his will accomplished.

Memory Verse: Isaiah 53:4-5

"Surely he has borne our griefs, and carried our sorrows: yet we did esteem him stricken, smitten of God, and afflicted. But he was wounded for our transgressions, he was bruised for our iniquities: the chastisement of our peace was upon him; and with his stripes we are healed."

To every family member: "I love you; you are blessed, and you are a blessing."
Don't forget the hugs.

September 22nd

Scripture: 2 Corinthians 2:14 (MSG)

"In the Messiah, in Christ, God leads us from place to place in one perpetual victory parade. Through us, he brings knowledge of Christ. Everywhere we go, people breathe in the exquisite fragrance. Because of Christ, we give off a sweet scent rising to God, which is recognized by those on the way of salvation."

In your prayer journal, identify in this portion of scripture a promise to receive or a command to obey.

Prayer:

Heavenly Father, thank you for changing my life. You have brought me out of darkness and despair into a place of great victory. You lead me day by day and from victory to victory as I hear your voice and follow the Spirit of God. I pray I carry the fragrance of your presence everywhere I go. May I leave people with the realization of your presence and love so they have a tangible understanding of who you are. Help me to attract those I encounter today with the sweet fragrance that only you can give. I ask these things in Jesus' name, Amen.

Proclamation:

God is light, and in him there is no darkness. He is the source of everything that is good and pleasant. His presence brings joy, and every sense of man is touched with the beauty, fragrance, taste and sound of his glorious being. I am greatly blessed of the Lord today in all my ways. The more I learn about him, the more I am overwhelmed with the wonder of who he is.

Memory Verse: Isaiah 53:4-5

"Surely he has borne our griefs, and carried our sorrows: yet we did esteem him stricken, smitten of God, and afflicted. But he was wounded for our transgressions, he was bruised for our iniquities: the chastisement of our peace was upon him; and with his stripes we are healed."

To every family member: *"I love you; you are blessed, and you are a blessing."*
Don't forget the hugs.

September 23rd

Scripture: Joshua 14:10-12 (AMP)

"And now, behold, the Lord has kept me alive, as He said, these forty-five years since the Lord spoke this word to Moses, while the Israelites wandered in the wilderness; and now, behold, I am this day eighty-five years old. Yet I am as strong today as I was the day Moses sent me; as my strength was then, so is my strength now for war and to go out and to come in. So now give me this hill country of which the Lord spoke that day. For you heard then how the [giantlike] Anakim were there and that the cities were great and fortified; if the Lord will be with me, I shall drive them out just as the Lord said."

In your prayer journal, identify in this portion of scripture a promise to receive or a command to obey.

Prayer:

Lord, you are able to keep me and strengthen me. You can redeem the years and renew my youth. Just as Caleb declared your sustaining power in his life to give him, at eighty-five years of age, the same strength and vitality he had at forty I thank you for renewing my strength. You said those who wait upon the Lord will renew their strength and you would bring times of refreshing from your presence. You are ageless and timeless for in your presence there is eternal life. No death, no decay, nothing to diminish or lessen is found in you, only strength and life. Thank you today for filling me with you. In Jesus' name I pray, Amen.

Proclamation:

The Lord redeems the time and restores my strength so I can do everything that would please him and bring glory to his name.

Memory Verse: Isaiah 53:4-5

"Surely he has borne our griefs, and carried our sorrows: yet we did esteem him stricken, smitten of God, and afflicted. But he was wounded for our transgressions, he was bruised for our iniquities: the chastisement of our peace was upon him; and with his stripes we are healed."

To every family member: "I love you; you are blessed, and you are a blessing."
Don't forget the hugs.

September 24th

Scripture: Mark 4:38-41 (KJV)

"And he was in the hinder part of the ship, asleep on a pillow: and they awake him, and say unto him, Master, carest thou not that we perish? And he arose, and rebuked the wind, and said unto the sea, Peace, be still. And the wind ceased, and there was a great calm. And he said unto them, Why are ye so fearful? How is it that ye have no faith? And they feared exceedingly, and said one to another, What manner of man is this, that even the wind and the sea obey him?"

In your prayer journal, identify in this portion of scripture a promise to receive or a command to obey.

Prayer:

God, my Father, I know you can do anything, for there is nothing impossible with you. You made me in your image and after your likeness and given me dominion in this world. Help me to walk in faith and not in fear. The disciples were first frightened by the storm, and then they were frightened by the power Jesus showed when he stilled the storm and calmed the sea. I pray I am free of fear that can't please you and choose faith for the seemingly impossible that does please you. Help me to be strong in the you and in the power of your might, trusting you in times of trouble and believing for the power of the Spirit to calm the storms I face. I ask these things in Jesus' name, Amen.

Proclamation:

I received power when the Holy Spirit filled me with his presence. The same Spirit that raised Jesus from the dead abides within me. God is able to do all things through me according to the power of God that works in me.

Memory Verse: Psalms 103:1-3

"Bless the Lord, O my soul: and all that is within me, bless his holy name. Bless the Lord, O my soul, and forget not all his benefits: who forgives all your iniquities; who heals all your diseases;"

To every family member: *"I love you; you are blessed, and you are a blessing."*
Don't forget the hugs.

September 25th

Scripture: Romans 10:8-10 (HCSB)

"On the contrary, what does it say? The message is near you, in your mouth and in your heart. This is the message of faith that we proclaim: If you confess with your mouth, "Jesus is Lord," and believe in your heart that God raised Him from the dead, you will be saved. One believes with the heart, resulting in righteousness, and one confesses with the mouth, resulting in salvation."

In your prayer journal, identify in this portion of scripture a promise to receive or a command to obey.

Prayer:

Lord, my God, I believe that Jesus is Lord of all. I believe he died in my place, taking my judgment for sin. I believe you raised him from the dead. According to your Word I am saved. I am healed and delivered, set free and made whole. I receive the righteousness of God as a gift. I did not earn it but simply received it by faith. Thank you, Father, for loving me. Help me to walk in the constant revelation of your abiding presence so my prayers are bold and full of faith to call your will into my life and into the lives of those for whom I pray. I give you praise in Jesus' name, Amen.

Proclamation:

The faith I need is not way off in some distant place, but according to the Word of God, it is near me, even in my mouth and in my heart.

Memory Verse: Psalms 103:1-3

"Bless the Lord, O my soul: and all that is within me, bless his holy name. Bless the Lord, O my soul, and forget not all his benefits: who forgives all your iniquities; who heals all your diseases;"

To every family member: *"I love you; you are blessed, and you are a blessing."*
Don't forget the hugs.

September 26th

Scripture: Daniel 3:22-25 (KJV)

"Therefore because the king's commandment was urgent, and the furnace exceeding hot, the flames of the fire slew those men that took up Shadrach, Meshach, and Abednego. And these three men, Shadrach, Meshach, and Abednego, fell down bound into the midst of the burning fiery furnace. Then Nebuchadnezzar the king was astonished, and rose up in haste, and spake, and said unto his counsellors, Did not we cast three men bound into the midst of the fire? They answered and said unto the king, True, O king. He answered and said, Lo, I see four men loose, walking in the midst of the fire, and they have no hurt; and the form of the fourth is like the Son of God."

In your prayer journal, identify in this portion of scripture a promise to receive or a command to obey.

Prayer:

My Father, you said the events recorded in your Word are written for me as examples of faith to follow. You saved the three Hebrew men from the fires of the furnace because they would not bow down to a false god. You amazed the king and his counselors, causing them to know you are the only true God. Help me to live with the same confidence as these three when they boldly declared, "our God...he will deliver us". You Lord, are my shield and fortress, and you will keep me from every evil work. Thank you for your mighty power that keeps me, protects me and empowers me to be bold and glorify you. In Jesus' name I pray, Amen.

Proclamation:

My God is able to keep me from every evil work of the enemy. I am blessed beyond measure and filled with the joy of my salvation.

Memory Verse: Psalms 103:1-3

"Bless the Lord, O my soul: and all that is within me, bless his holy name. Bless the Lord, O my soul, and forget not all his benefits: who forgives all your iniquities; who heals all your diseases;"

To every family member: "I love you; you are blessed, and you are a blessing." Don't forget the hugs.

September 27th

Scripture: Romans 9:30-33 (PHILLIPS)

"Now, how far have we got? That the Gentiles who never had the Law's standard of righteousness to guide them, have attained righteousness, righteousness-by-faith. But Israel, following the Law of righteousness, failed to reach the goal of righteousness. And why? Because their minds were fixed on what they achieved instead of on what they believed. They tripped over that very stone the scripture mentions: 'Behold, I lay in Zion a stumbling stone and rock of offence, and whoever believes on him will not be put to shame'."

In your prayer journal, identify in this portion of scripture a promise to receive or a command to obey.

Prayer:

God, my Father, I thank you for your righteousness you have freely given to me. I could never earn righteousness, but you have made me righteous when I believed on Jesus as Lord of all. I pray for so many who are attempting to be good enough to get into heaven and don't know their best attempts are futile. I pray for the truth of the gospel of the Lord Jesus Christ to penetrate the heart of the people and show them their need to receive Jesus as their Lord. Reveal to them that he was the only one who was good, who was sinless and who made a way for all to come to him and receive his righteousness as a gift without any effort of their own. I pray people would not trip over the very stone God has laid as the foundation for them to build their lives upon, the only foundation that cannot be shaken. Father, I pray for those who do not yet believe. I pray for their eyes to be opened to the eternal life that is only in Jesus our Lord. Help them to know this life cannot be earned but only received by faith. I pray today in Jesus' name, Amen.

Proclamation:

Salvation is by faith alone. No works are required.

Memory Verse: Psalms 103:1-3

"Bless the Lord, O my soul: and all that is within me, bless his holy name. Bless the Lord, O my soul, and forget not all his benefits: who forgives all your iniquities; who heals all your diseases;"

To every family member: "I love you; you are blessed, and you are a blessing." Don't forget the hugs.

September 28th

Scripture: 1 Kings 3:11-13 (AMP)

"God said to him, Because you have asked this and have not asked for long life or for riches, nor for the lives of your enemies, but have asked for yourself understanding to recognize what is just and right, Behold, I have done as you asked. I have given you a wise, discerning mind, so that no one before you was your equal, nor shall any arise after you equal to you. I have also given you what you have not asked, both riches and honor, so that there shall not be any among the kings equal to you all your days."

In your prayer journal, identify in this portion of scripture a promise to receive or a command to obey.

Prayer:

My Father, you are the source of all wisdom and understanding. You know all things. You know the end from the beginning; there is nothing that escapes your knowledge. I pray to receive wisdom and understanding just as Solomon did. Help me today to make wise and godly choices and good and righteous decisions that will be a blessing to my family and me and will bring glory and praise to your great name. I know you will bless the works of my hands and the meditation of my heart, establishing my thoughts to agree with your will so my plans will be established and succeed. I thank you that I do not lack or have need or want of any good thing, for you abundantly furnish me with everything I need. You give me power and strength to accomplish your will and to fulfill every assignment you give me. I thank you for these things now in Jesus' name, Amen.

Proclamation:

My God is the supplier of all I need. He gives me wisdom and revelation in the knowledge of his will. He brings to me everything I need and blesses me in everything I do. I am greatly blessed of God today.

Memory Verse: Psalms 103:1-3

"Bless the Lord, O my soul: and all that is within me, bless his holy name. Bless the Lord, O my soul, and forget not all his benefits: who forgives all your iniquities; who heals all your diseases;"

To every family member: "I love you; you are blessed, and you are a blessing." Don't forget the hugs.

September 29th

Scripture: Proverbs 17:22 (NRSV)
"A cheerful heart is a good medicine, but a downcast spirit dries up the bones."

In your prayer journal, identify in this portion of scripture a promise to receive or a command to obey.

Prayer:

Heavenly Father, you have told me to rejoice in the Lord always. Your Word describes your kingdom as righteousness, peace and joy. In your presence is fullness of joy, and the joy of the Lord is my strength. I pray I walk in the revelation of who you are and what you have done for me so that I am filled with the joy of your salvation. Father, I am thankful that you are not sad or sorrowful, but you delight in me and want me to walk in your joy, enjoying all the good things you have prepared for me. I pray for a cheerful heart that is like medicine to me, to strengthen me and cause me to walk in health and soundness of spirit, soul and body. I refuse to be downcast and full of sorrow, for you are my help in times of trouble; you are my deliverer, my healer and my provider. Lord, I delight in you. Sorrow and sadness must flee away from me, for you give me the oil of joy for mourning and the garment of praise for the spirit of heaviness that I might walk in the blessings of the Lord and bring glory and praise to you. In the name of Jesus I thank you, Amen.

Proclamation:

I am redeemed and delivered. I am free from depression and sorrow by the Spirit of God. He is working in me and helping me to walk in the fullness of joy.

Memory Verse: Psalms 103:1-3
"Bless the Lord, O my soul: and all that is within me, bless his holy name. Bless the Lord, O my soul, and forget not all his benefits: who forgives all your iniquities; who heals all your diseases;"

To every family member: "I love you; you are blessed, and you are a blessing."
Don't forget the hugs.

September 30th

Scripture: Acts 27:22-25 (NIV)

"But now I urge you to keep up your courage, because not one of you will be lost; only the ship will be destroyed. Last night an angel of the God to whom I belong and whom I serve stood beside me and said, 'Do not be afraid, Paul. You must stand trial before Caesar; and God has graciously given you the lives of all who sail with you.' So keep up your courage, men, for I have faith in God that it will happen just as he told me."

In your prayer journal, identify in this portion of scripture a promise to receive or a command to obey.

Prayer:

God, my Father, I thank you for your Word to encourage me when I am in a difficult time. Help me to put my trust in you and listen to your Word instead of listening to the wind and the waves of the storm that has come against me. As Paul encouraged all on board a sinking ship not to fear, help me to encourage others who find themselves in difficult and dangerous circumstances. You will always make a way for those who call upon you. Your arm is not short that it cannot save, and neither do you despise the cry of your children. You are greater than our problems and able to do exceedingly more than we can even imagine. Help me today to look at the things that cannot be seen with my natural eyes to see the promises of your Word and to know that what you have spoken you will surely do. It is in Jesus' name I pray, Amen.

Proclamation:

The Lord is mighty; he will save; he will rejoice over me with singing. He will deliver me out of the mire and muck of life and set my feet on his sure foundation.

Memory Verse: Psalms 103:1-3

"Bless the Lord, O my soul: and all that is within me, bless his holy name. Bless the Lord, O my soul, and forget not all his benefits: who forgives all your iniquities; who heals all your diseases;"

To every family member: "I love you; you are blessed, and you are a blessing." Don't forget the hugs.

October 1st

Scripture: Proverbs 29:18 (KJV)
"Where there is no vision, the people perish: but he that keepeth the law, happy is he."

In your prayer journal, identify in this portion of scripture a promise to receive or a command to obey.

Prayer:

Heavenly Father, you give insight and wisdom to those who ask you. You give vision and revelations, dreams and understanding to direct my ways and bring confirmation regarding things I seek you about. I pray you help me see the things you want me to see. Open my eyes to behold the hidden treasures in your Word and to see clearly your purpose and direction for my life. Your Word declares, "Where there is no vision, the people perish." Help me to see with divine vision so I will not be distracted by unworthy or unimportant pursuits that keep me from fulfilling your will for my life. Give me eyes to see and ears to hear the things the Spirit of God shows me and speaks to me about, for the things you have prepared for me are revealed by the Holy Spirit. Father, I thank you now for spiritual sight that causes me to see things as you see them and to hear your voice so I will always know what to do. I ask you for these things in Jesus' name, Amen.

Proclamation:

I have eyes to see and ears to hear what the Spirit of God will show me. He reveals to me the wonderful things God, my Father, has prepared for me and given me that I might perform all his will and walk in the blessings of my inheritance in Christ Jesus my Lord.

Memory Verse: John 1:12-13
"But as many as received him, to them gave he power to become the sons of God, even to them that believe on his name. Which were born, not of blood, nor of the will of the flesh, nor of the will of man, but of God."

To every family member: *"I love you; you are blessed, and you are a blessing."*
Don't forget the hugs.

October 2nd

Scripture: 1 Corinthians 6:19-20 (PHILLIPS)

"Have you forgotten that your body is the temple of the Holy Spirit, who lives in you, and that you are not the owner of your own body? You have been bought, and at what a price! Therefore bring glory to God both in your body and your spirit, for they both belong to him."

In your prayer journal, identify in this portion of scripture a promise to receive or a command to obey.

Prayer:

My Father, I praise you and thank you for this day that you have made. I will rejoice and be glad in it. I belong to you, for you have redeemed me at an unimaginable price. You paid for my sin with the blood of your Son, and you washed me, cleansing me from all unrighteousness. You brought me into your family and called me by your name. Help me today to glorify you in everything I do. Strengthen me to make decisions that will honor you. Remind me that the Spirit of God lives inside me. Thank you for hearing me and helping me. In Jesus' name, Amen.

Proclamation:

My body is the temple of the Holy Spirit who lives inside of me. I do not belong to myself, for I have been purchased by the blood of the Son of God, who loved me and gave himself for me. I am greatly loved, not because of what I have done or have not done, but because the love of God moved him to intervene in my life. Jesus rescued me from the judgment my sin required and gave me his righteousness and the Spirit of God to dwell with me forever.

Memory Verse: John 1:12-13

"But as many as received him, to them gave he power to become the sons of God, even to them that believe on his name. Which were born, not of blood, nor of the will of the flesh, nor of the will of man, but of God."

To every family member: *"I love you; you are blessed, and you are a blessing."*
Don't forget the hugs.

October 3rd

Scripture: Proverbs 31:25-26 (KJV)

"Strength and honour are her clothing; and she shall rejoice in time to come. She openeth her mouth with wisdom; and in her tongue is the law of kindness."

In your prayer journal, identify in this portion of scripture a promise to receive or a command to obey.

Prayer:

Heavenly Father, you are good and your mercies endure forever. You have shown me in your Word how to live in prosperity and walk successfully in this world. The diligence of the woman described in Proverbs reveals the attributes I should have. She walks in strength and clothes herself with honor. When she speaks, wisdom is heard, and in her tongue is the law of kindness. I pray for your strength and wisdom to work in my life today so I always bring honor to you. I ask you to help me guard my mouth from speaking words that are hurtful or unkind. Help me to live in such a way that I will rejoice in the days ahead. Thank you for your grace that provides for me everything I will ever need to live in victory and walk in honor before you. In Jesus' name I pray, Amen.

Proclamation:

I choose this day to live by the law of kindness. Every word that comes out of my mouth will be tempered with the love of God. My words bring encouragement to those who hear me.

Memory Verse: John 1:12-13

"But as many as received him, to them gave he power to become the sons of God, even to them that believe on his name. Which were born, not of blood, nor of the will of the flesh, nor of the will of man, but of God."

To every family member: "I love you; you are blessed, and you are a blessing."
Don't forget the hugs.

October 4th

Scripture: Romans 3:22-26 (NCV)

"God makes people right with himself through their faith in Jesus Christ. This is true for all who believe in Christ, because all people are the same: Everyone has sinned and fallen short of God's glorious standard, and all need to be made right with God by his grace, which is a free gift. They need to be made free from sin through Jesus Christ. God sent him to die in our place to take away our sins. We receive forgiveness through faith in the blood of Jesus' death. This showed that God always does what is right and fair, as in the past when he was patient and did not punish people for their sins. And God gave Jesus to show today that he does what is right. God did this so he could judge rightly and so he could make right any person who has faith in Jesus."

In your prayer journal, identify in this portion of scripture a promise to receive or a command to obey.

Prayer:

My Father, I am so thankful for your love for me. You have made me righteous by faith in the Lord Jesus Christ. You have forgiven me and restored me to a right relationship with you. Lord, you did all the work. All you ask me to do is to believe. I know I must purposely receive your gift of righteousness by faith because without faith it is impossible to please you. I believe that you are God and you reward those who diligently seek you. I pray for all of those who attempt to please you by their good works, for they do not understand that righteousness is a gift to receive and not something that can be earned. Lord, open their eyes and give them the ability to believe and receive this gift. In Jesus' name I pray, Amen.

Proclamation:

Every good and perfect gift comes from God. He rewards me with good things because I believe in him, and I will diligently seek after him this day.

Memory Verse: John 1:12-13

"But as many as received him, to them gave he power to become the sons of God, even to them that believe on his name. Which were born, not of blood, nor of the will of the flesh, nor of the will of man, but of God."

To every family member: *"I love you; you are blessed, and you are a blessing."*
Don't forget the hugs.

October 5th

Scripture: James 3:2-5 (KJV)

"For in many things we offend all. If any man offend not in word, the same is a perfect man, and able also to bridle the whole body. Behold, we put bits in the horses' mouths, that they may obey us; and we turn about their whole body. Behold also the ships, which though they be so great, and are driven of fierce winds, yet are they turned about with a very small helm, whithersoever the governor listeth. Even so the tongue is a little member, and boasteth great things. Behold, how great a matter a little fire kindleth!"

In your prayer journal, identify in this portion of scripture a promise to receive or a command to obey.

Prayer:

God, my Father, I give you thanks for this good day. I pray for the wisdom of God to teach me and the power of the Spirit of God to help me speak words of life that will establish my ways and create good in me and in those who hear me. Help me to speak life and not death and to have the realization that my words are powerful and they set in motion the events I will experience today. I know my mouth will speak what my heart is filled with. Help me to fill my heart with the Word of God and with those things that are lovely, pure, just and will bring a good report. I pray in Jesus' name, Amen.

Proclamation:

My words are powerful, and when I speak, I set in motion the things that produce life and death. I choose this day to speak life, to speak what I want instead of how I might feel at the moment.

Memory Verse: John 1:12-13

"But as many as received him, to them gave he power to become the sons of God, even to them that believe on his name. Which were born, not of blood, nor of the will of the flesh, nor of the will of man, but of God."

To every family member: *"I love you; you are blessed, and you are a blessing."*
Don't forget the hugs.

October 6th

Scripture: Romans 13:8-10 (NIV)

"Let no debt remain outstanding, except the continuing debt to love one another, for whoever loves others has fulfilled the law. The commandments, 'You shall not commit adultery,' 'You shall not murder,' 'You shall not steal,' 'You shall not covet,' and whatever other command there may be, are summed up in this one command: 'Love your neighbor as yourself.' Love does no harm to a neighbor. Therefore love is the fulfillment of the law."

In your prayer journal, identify in this portion of scripture a promise to receive or a command to obey.

Prayer:

Heavenly Father, your love is at work in me this day. It is because of the love of God that I have been forgiven, and it is the love of God that causes faith to work in me mightily. Your Word declares that "the love of God has been shed abroad in [my heart by] the Holy Spirit." I thank you for the grace of God that fills my life and helps me to draw on your love residing within me. It is my desire to walk in love and forgiveness toward everyone. I believe your grace is sufficient for me this day to love those who may consider themselves my enemies and to respond in love to those who are less than loving towards me. Thank you for your grace to sincerely love all who are my neighbors. I receive your grace now in Jesus' name, Amen.

Proclamation:

The most powerful force in the universe is the love of God. God's love has been deposited within me so I can walk in sincere love towards everyone. God's love is why my faith works. God's love will never fail and will never end.

Memory Verse: John 1:12-13

"But as many as received him, to them gave he power to become the sons of God, even to them that believe on his name. Which were born, not of blood, nor of the will of the flesh, nor of the will of man, but of God."

To every family member: *"I love you; you are blessed, and you are a blessing."*
Don't forget the hugs.

October 7th

Scripture: Psalms 24:1-5 (AMP)

"The earth is the Lord's, and the fullness of it, the world and they who dwell in it. For He has founded it upon the seas and established it upon the currents and the rivers. Who shall go up into the mountain of the Lord? Or who shall stand in His Holy Place? He who has clean hands and a pure heart, who has not lifted himself up to falsehood or to what is false, nor sworn deceitfully. He shall receive blessing from the Lord and righteousness from the God of his salvation."

In your prayer journal, identify in this portion of scripture a promise to receive or a command to obey.

Prayer:

Blessed be the name of the Lord my God forever and ever. He is great and worthy of all praise. He has created all things, and by the Word of his power, everything is established and maintained. He invites me to come boldly to his throne to pray and declare his Word and establish his will in the earth just as it is in heaven. God has washed me and purged me by the blood of Jesus, so my hands are clean and my heart is pure. I can come into his presence with confidence and joy, knowing I will receive what my petitions require because answered prayer brings glory to God the Father. Lord, I am overwhelmed by these truths; thank you for faith to believe and the Spirit of God to teach me, anoint me and help me to fulfill your will. In Jesus' name, Amen.

Proclamation:

The Spirit of God who anoints me and helps me pray in faith and walk in love changes me day to day, from glory to glory.

Memory Verse: John 1:12-13

"But as many as received him, to them gave he power to become the sons of God, even to them that believe on his name. Which were born, not of blood, nor of the will of the flesh, nor of the will of man, but of God."

To every family member: "I love you; you are blessed, and you are a blessing."
Don't forget the hugs.

October 8th

Scripture: John 1:12-13 (HCSB)

"But to all who did receive Him, He gave them the right to be children of God, to those who believe in His name, who were born, not of blood or of the will of the flesh or of the will of man, but of God."

In your prayer journal, identify in this portion of scripture a promise to receive or a command to obey.

Prayer:

Heavenly Father, thank you for the life you have given me. I was born in the flesh in this world, but I was born-again in the spirit by the incorruptible seed of your Word. I believe in the Lord Jesus Christ, that he is Lord of all. I know my ancestry, my own will or the desires of someone else could not make me a child of God. It was the love of God that brought me your Word, gave me faith and responded to my prayer that made me a child of God. I know you love every person born into this world, but I am so grateful to you for revealing to me your love and Lordship. As you have made me, once again, in your image and likeness, help me to grow in the knowledge of your will. Help me to receive every gift you have given me and to live as you intended people to live, walking in authority and dominion and seeing your will accomplished in this world. It is in Jesus' name I pray, Amen.

Proclamation:

God has birthed me into his family, called me by his name and given me an inheritance with all those who believe so I can live in the kingdom of God all the days of my life.

Memory Verse: Philippians 4:8

"Finally, brethren, whatsoever things are true, whatsoever things are honest, whatsoever things are just, whatsoever things are pure, whatsoever things are lovely, whatsoever things are of good report; if there be any virtue, and if there be any praise, think on these things."

To every family member: *"I love you; you are blessed, and you are a blessing."*
Don't forget the hugs.

October 9th

Scripture: Psalms 46:1-3 (NKJV)

"God is our refuge and strength, a very present help in trouble. Therefore we will not fear, even though the earth be removed, and though the mountains be carried into the midst of the sea; Though its waters roar and be troubled, though the mountains shake with its swelling. Selah"

In your prayer journal, identify in this portion of scripture a promise to receive or a command to obey.

Prayer:

God, you are my refuge and strength, and you are my very present help in times of trouble. I can call upon you, and you answer me and show me things that only you know and only you can do. Because you are with me, I will not fear regardless of what is going on around me. You said, "a thousand may fall at my side and ten-thousand at my right hand, but it shall not come near to me". The mountains may shake and the seas roar, but you are my help and my refuge. I pray I will always look to you for your direction. Make my way plain today so I can walk before you with confidence, knowing my choices are right and you are there to help me in every situation. I thank you for these things now, in Jesus' name, Amen.

Proclamation:

My God is with me. He will keep me safe, even in times of trouble. He is my refuge and strength, my high tower and fortress. I will not fear, but I will be strong and filled with courage for God is with me.

Memory Verse: Philippians 4:8

"Finally, brethren, whatsoever things are true, whatsoever things are honest, whatsoever things are just, whatsoever things are pure, whatsoever things are lovely, whatsoever things are of good report; if there be any virtue and if there be any praise, think on these things."

To every family member: "I love you; you are blessed, and you are a blessing." Don't forget the hugs.

October 10th

Scripture: Matthew 21:12-14 (KJV)

"And Jesus went into the temple of God, and cast out all them that sold and bought in the temple, and overthrew the tables of the moneychangers, and the seats of them that sold doves, And said unto them, It is written, My house shall be called the house of prayer; but ye have made it a den of thieves. And the blind and the lame came to him in the temple; and he healed them."

In your prayer journal, identify in this portion of scripture a promise to receive or a command to obey.

Prayer:

Heavenly Father, I know that my body is the temple of the Holy Spirit who lives in me. Just as Jesus cleansed the physical temple in Jerusalem from the activities that distracted the people and hindered them from praying and receiving, I thank you for cleansing me from the distractions that get in my way and occupy the place of priority only you should have. It is my desire that you would have the preeminence in my life, for you are my Lord. I submit my life to your will this day. I thank you for loving me and desiring to fellowship with me, to speak to me and share with me your thoughts, your plans and your life. I am awed by your greatness and your willingness to speak to me and show me great and mighty things. Thank you Father. I pray in Jesus' name, Amen.

Proclamation:

God lives in me. He speaks to me and reveals to me his goodness. God gives me his wisdom and is willing to demonstrate his power to fulfill his promises for my life.

Memory Verse: Philippians 4:8

"Finally, brethren, whatsoever things are true, whatsoever things are honest, whatsoever things are just, whatsoever things are pure, whatsoever things are lovely, whatsoever things are of good report; if there be any virtue and if there be any praise, think on these things."

To every family member: "I love you; you are blessed, and you are a blessing."
Don't forget the hugs.

October 11th

Scripture: Romans 8:26-28 (NET)

"In the same way, the Spirit helps us in our weakness, for we do not know how we should pray, but the Spirit himself intercedes for us with inexpressible groanings. And he who searches our hearts knows the mind of the Spirit, because the Spirit intercedes on behalf of the saints according to God's will. And we know that all things work together for good for those who love God, who are called according to his purpose."

In your prayer journal, identify in this portion of scripture a promise to receive or a command to obey.

Prayer:

My Father, thank you for the promise that, when I don't know how to pray, the Spirit of God will help me pray so everything will begin to work in harmony for my good and will accomplish what you please. I yield myself to the Spirit of God now and pray in the spirit as he directs me until his purpose is established and the will of God for my good is accomplished. I do not lean to my own understanding, but I put my trust in you, for you Lord see the end from the beginning and you will always lead me in righteous paths, blessing the works of my hands and the meditations of my heart. Thank you, Father. In Jesus' name I pray, Amen.

Proclamation:

I am so thankful for the Holy Spirit. He dwells in me and will never leave me. He is my Helper, my Comforter and my Intercessor. I depend on the Spirit of God to help me pray when I do not know how to pray correctly. He takes hold together with me in the area of my weakness to help me pray and bring about the will of God my Father.

Memory Verse: Philippians 4:8

"Finally, brethren, whatsoever things are true, whatsoever things are honest, whatsoever things are just, whatsoever things are pure, whatsoever things are lovely, whatsoever things are of good report; if there be any virtue and if there be any praise, think on these things."

To every family member: *"I love you; you are blessed, and you are a blessing."*
Don't forget the hugs.

October 12th

Scripture: Ephesians 5:17-21 (NIV)

"Therefore do not be foolish, but understand what the Lord's will is. Do not get drunk on wine, which leads to debauchery. Instead, be filled with the Spirit, speaking to one another with psalms, hymns, and songs from the Spirit. Sing and make music from your heart to the Lord, always giving thanks to God the Father for everything, in the name of our Lord Jesus Christ. Submit to one another out of reverence for Christ."

In your prayer journal, identify in this portion of scripture a promise to receive or a command to obey.

Prayer:

Lord, it is your will that I would be under the influence and control of the Holy Spirit. I ask you to fill me afresh with the Spirit of God. I will speak to myself and to others with the written psalms, learned songs and songs the Spirit of God gives me to glorify you. I pray my heart is always filled with thanksgiving for everything you do for me. I will submit myself to you and to others who are led by the Spirit of God and walk in your anointing. Father, I thank you for the joy of the Lord that fills my life and strengthens me for every good work. I pray in Jesus' name, Amen.

Proclamation:

The foolish say that God's will cannot be known, but God has commanded us to understand his will, to be controlled by the Spirit and to sing songs of thanksgiving and praise to glorify his name. We are to walk in harmony with one another and to respond to every situation in life with the love of God. I choose today to do the will of God.

Memory Verse: Philippians 4:8

"Finally, brethren, whatsoever things are true, whatsoever things are honest, whatsoever things are just, whatsoever things are pure, whatsoever things are lovely, whatsoever things are of good report; if there be any virtue and if there be any praise, think on these things."

To every family member: "I love you; you are blessed, and you are a blessing." Don't forget the hugs.

October 13th

Scripture: 2 Kings 5:13-14 (AMP)

"And his servants came near and said to him, My father, if the prophet had bid you to do some great thing, would you not have done it? How much rather, then, when he says to you, Wash and be clean? Then he went down and dipped himself seven times in the Jordan, as the man of God had said, and his flesh was restored like that of a little child, and he was clean."

In your prayer journal, identify in this portion of scripture a promise to receive or a command to obey.

Prayer:

My Heavenly Father, you cleansed Naaman of his leprosy when he obeyed the word of the prophet and dipped seven times in the Jordan River. He almost missed his miracle because the word he was given seemed foolish to him. I pray I would not miss out on the miracles you want to do in my life because your Word may not make sense to my mind or seem practical for the moment. Lord, help me to recognize your instructions and obey your Word without hesitation. You said to become skillful with the Word of God so I know what is good and what is not. I know that everything you do is good and righteous and every work of God is measured by your love and compassion. Father, give me ears to hear the voice of the Spirit and wisdom to discern your will. I pray in Jesus' name, Amen.

Proclamation:

I choose to walk in the spirit and follow the directions God's Word prescribes. The natural man does not understand spiritual things because they seem foolish to him, but I am not carnal, but spiritual, for I have received the Spirit of God and he reveals to me all the things God has prepared for me.

Memory Verse: Philippians 4:8

"Finally, brethren, whatsoever things are true, whatsoever things are honest, whatsoever things are just, whatsoever things are pure, whatsoever things are lovely, whatsoever things are of good report; if there be any virtue and if there be any praise, think on these things."

To every family member: "I love you; you are blessed, and you are a blessing."
Don't forget the hugs.

October 14th

Scripture: Mark 16:19-20 (NET)

"After the Lord Jesus had spoken to them, he was taken up into heaven and sat down at the right hand of God. They went out and proclaimed everywhere, while the Lord worked with them and confirmed the word through the accompanying signs."

In your prayer journal, identify in this portion of scripture a promise to receive or a command to obey.

Prayer:

Bless the Lord, O my soul; praise his holy name, for he is worthy. He has triumphed over all mine enemies. He has redeemed my life by paying the price required for my forgiveness. Jesus died for my sin but was raised again victorious over death and has ascended into heaven to sit at the right hand of God. Lord, as you sent out your disciples to declare your Word, you confirmed the message they spoke with signs and wonders and revealed to all your power and presence. I thank you that you still watch over your Word to perform it today. As I put your Word in my mouth, I know you will confirm your Word and bring to pass whatever I ask in Jesus' name, Amen.

Proclamation:

God is faithful to confirm his Word. If he said it he will bring it to pass; if he spoke it he will surely do it, for God has exalted his Word even above his name.

Memory Verse: Philippians 4:8

"Finally, brethren, whatsoever things are true, whatsoever things are honest, whatsoever things are just, whatsoever things are pure, whatsoever things are lovely, whatsoever things are of good report; if there be any virtue and if there be any praise, think on these things."

To every family member: *"I love you; you are blessed, and you are a blessing."*
Don't forget the hugs.

October 15th

Scripture: 1 Peter 1:6-8 (WEB)

"Wherein you greatly rejoice, though now for a little while, if need be, you have been put to grief in various trials, that the proof of your faith, which is more precious than gold that perishes even though it is tested by fire, may be found to result in praise, glory, and honor at the revelation of Jesus Christ— whom not having known you love; in whom, though now you don't see him, yet believing, you rejoice greatly with joy unspeakable and full of glory."

In your prayer journal, identify in this portion of scripture a promise to receive or a command to obey.

Prayer:

My Father, I thank you for being faithful even when life seems difficult. I know the devil is out to steal your Word from me and challenge my faith through various trials. My faith is more precious than gold, and if he can't steal my faith, he can't steal my joy or rob me of my victory. I know trials and temptations do not come from you, for Jesus warned me that in this world there will be trouble, but I can rejoice, for he overcame the world for me. Lord, my God, you always make a way of escape from every temptation, and you always bring me strength to endure in every situation so that, after I have done the will of God, I will remain standing in victory. Thank you that I can rejoice in you this day with joy unspeakable and full of glory. In Jesus' name, Amen.

Proclamation:

Every promise of God is challenged by the devil, but if I submit myself to God and resist the devil, he will run from me.

Memory Verse: 1 Peter 2:9

"But you are a chosen generation, a royal priesthood, a holy nation, a peculiar people; that you should show forth the praises of him who has called you out of darkness into his marvelous light."

To every family member: *"I love you; you are blessed, and you are a blessing."*
Don't forget the hugs.

October 16th

Scripture: Psalms 9:9-10 (GW)
"The Lord is a stronghold for the oppressed, a stronghold in times of trouble. Those who know your name trust you, O Lord, because you have never deserted those who seek your help."

In your prayer journal, identify in this portion of scripture a promise to receive or a command to obey.

Prayer:
God, my Father, you are my refuge and help in times of trouble. I put my trust in you because you will never leave me without help. Your name is greater than any other name, and your names reveal your works and your ways. You are my Righteousness, my Sanctification and my Peace. You are Ever Present with me to Heal me and to Provide for me. You are my Shepherd and under the Banner of your love is where I live. Lord, without you I cannot do anything, but all things are possible in your presence. Thank you for giving me access to your throne of mercy to find grace and mercy in times of need. I give you praise for these things in Jesus' name, Amen.

Proclamation:
The name of the Lord is a high tower, and the righteous run into it, and they are safe. The name of the Lord is mighty, and at the mention of his name, every knee must bow and every tongue must confess that Jesus Christ is Lord to the glory of God the Father.

Memory Verse: 1 Peter 2:9
"But you are a chosen generation, a royal priesthood, a holy nation, a peculiar people; that you should show forth the praises of him who has called you out of darkness into his marvelous light."

To every family member: *"I love you; you are blessed, and you are a blessing."* Don't forget the hugs.

October 17th

Scripture: Isaiah 40:8 (AMP)
"The grass withers, the flower fades,
but the word of our God will stand forever."

In your prayer journal, identify in this portion of scripture
a promise to receive or a command to obey.

Prayer:

God, my Father, I know that everything was created by the power of your Word. You spoke the universe into existence. All of creation is held in place by the Word of God. The oceans do not pass their God ordained boundaries, and the heavens declare your glory and majesty. Father, I believe your Word is eternal. What you have said will surely come to pass. If you said it, you will do it, for you have exalted your Word even above your name. There was a time when your voice shook the earth. After that you promised you would shake the earth and the heavens to remove all things that can be shaken so the things that cannot be shaken would be all that remains. Your kingdom cannot be shaken but will last forever. Thank you for the power and promise of your Word. In Jesus' name I pray, Amen.

Proclamation:

The Word of the Lord endures forever; therefore I put my trust in the promises of God and rest in the certainty of his fulfilled Word. The Word of the Lord is not just written as marks on a page, but his Word is spirit and life. It is to me life and health, wisdom and strength, and brings to me his peace and causes faith to come alive inside of me so I can live in his kingdom and do those things that bring glory to his name.

Memory Verse: 1 Peter 2:9
"But you are a chosen generation, a royal priesthood, a holy nation, a peculiar people; that you should show forth the praises of him who has called you out of darkness into his marvelous light."

To every family member: "I love you; you are blessed, and you are a blessing."
Don't forget the hugs.

October 18th

Scripture: Psalms 1:1-3 (NLT)

"Oh, the joys of those who do not follow the advice of the wicked or stand around with sinners or join in with mockers. But they delight in the law of the Lord, meditating on it day and night. They are like trees planted along the riverbank, bearing fruit each season. Their leaves never wither and they prosper in all they do."

In your prayer journal, identify in this portion of scripture a promise to receive or a command to obey.

Prayer:

Heavenly Father, I thank you for blessing me with the knowledge of your will to make me fruitful and prosperous in everything I do. I ask you to protect me from the advice of the wicked, for I will delight in your Word. Keep me from the ways of the carnal man who does not follow you and from those who mock the things of God and will soon be destroyed. I pray my life is filled with the fruit of the Spirit and I demonstrate to the world the abundant life you have given to those who love you. Put your Word in my mouth and help me to boldly declare the truth of your love and forgiveness to all who believe in Jesus name, Amen.

Proclamation:

I do not follow the way of the wicked. I do not live like sinners or speak the words of those who mock. My delight is in the Word of the Lord, and his Word nourishes me, making me fruitful and fulfilled in all I do.

Memory Verse: 1 Peter 2:9

"But you are a chosen generation, a royal priesthood, a holy nation, a peculiar people; that you should show forth the praises of him who has called you out of darkness into his marvelous light."

To every family member: *"I love you; you are blessed, and you are a blessing."*
Don't forget the hugs.

October 19th

Scripture: Mark 10:27 (KJV)

"And Jesus looking upon them saith, With men it is impossible, but not with God: for with God all things are possible."

In your prayer journal, identify in this portion of scripture a promise to receive or a command to obey.

Prayer:

Lord, you can do everything. Nothing is beyond your reach. Your hand is not short that you cannot save; neither is there anything you do not see. All things are revealed to you, so you see us as we really are. I thank you today for knowing what I need even before I ask. You have shown me in your Word your will for me and your way for me to access the things you have freely given me, so I will never be without for you are my Shepherd; therefore, I shall not be in want or need of any good thing. I seek after you this day. I desire to know you and to hear your voice and to follow your instructions, for you are able to do exceeding abundantly above all I could ever think or imagine according to the power that is at work within me. I pray for your power and your anointing to rest upon me and rise up within me so I will be equipped and prepared to do your will and to believe for your will to be done in the earth even as it is done in heaven. I thank you for this good work of God working in me so I might bring praise and glory to your great name. It is in the name of my Lord Jesus I pray, Amen.

Proclamation:

Nothing is too difficult for God, and nothing is impossible for those who believe. I believe. Therefore, there is nothing impossible for me.

Memory Verse: 1 Peter 2:9

"But you are a chosen generation, a royal priesthood, a holy nation, a peculiar people; that you should show forth the praises of him who has called you out of darkness into his marvelous light."

To every family member: *"I love you; you are blessed, and you are a blessing."*
Don't forget the hugs.

October 20th

Scripture: 2 Corinthians 3:3 (NCV)
"You show that you are a letter from Christ sent through us. This letter is not written with ink but with the Spirit of the living God. It is not written on stone tablets but on human hearts."

In your prayer journal, identify in this portion of scripture a promise to receive or a command to obey.

Prayer:
My Father, I bless your wonderful name today. I thank you for this great salvation you have freely given to me. Thank you for the New Covenant that is so much better than the old. I could never keep the external laws written in stone, but because Jesus kept them for me, your Word has been written inside of me. You have made me to be a brand new person on the inside by joining my spirit with yours, forgiving me and cleansing me and bringing me into your kingdom as a member of your family. You, Lord, are helping me to transform my soul from one level of glory to the next as you empower me to walk in the spirit and not live according to my senses. I believe your Word that declares you are working in me and even causing me to will and to do your good pleasure. I thank you for this good work you have begun in me and will continue until my life brings glory and praise to you. In Jesus' name I pray, Amen.

Proclamation:
I am a living epistle. The Word of God has been written on my heart, so as I live the Word and speak the Word, my life will give demonstration of the living, eternal Word of God. I have been born-again in God's image and after his likeness, so his light fills my life and my life shines with the light of his glory.

Memory Verse: 1 Peter 2:9
"But you are a chosen generation, a royal priesthood, a holy nation, a peculiar people; that you should show forth the praises of him who has called you out of darkness into his marvelous light."

To every family member: *"I love you; you are blessed, and you are a blessing."*
Don't forget the hugs.

October 21st

Scripture: Ephesians 1:5-8 (NCV)

"Because of his love, God had already decided to make us his own children through Jesus Christ. That was what he wanted and what pleased him and it brings praise to God because of his wonderful grace. God gave that grace to us freely, in Christ, the One he loves. In Christ we are set free by the blood of his death, and so we have forgiveness of sins. How rich is God's grace, which he has given to us so fully and freely."

In your prayer journal, identify in this portion of scripture a promise to receive or a command to obey.

Prayer:

God, my Father, you are worthy of all praise. You have made me your child so I can call you Abba (Daddy) Father. Thank you for this wonderful love you have given me by your grace. Your gift of grace is granted to me, free for the taking, because I believe that Jesus Christ is the Son of God. He came to live a perfect sin-free life and then die under the judgment of my sin so his righteousness could be given to me, not by my works but by his. Father, make me always conscious of your presence in my life. Help me to put on the character of God so your love, patience, forgiveness and hope are such a natural part of my life that others look at me and see you. I pray in Jesus' name, Amen.

Proclamation:

I am a child of God. I belong to his family, and I have been given the authority of his name to call into being his will. God's grace is mine. It was freely given to me because it is God's will and pleasure to love me, forgive me and bless me.

Memory Verse: 1 Peter 2:9

"But you are a chosen generation, a royal priesthood, a holy nation, a peculiar people; that you should show forth the praises of him who has called you out of darkness into his marvelous light."

To every family member: *"I love you; you are blessed, and you are a blessing."*
Don't forget the hugs.

October 22nd

Scripture: 2 Timothy 1:6-7 (NKJV)

"Therefore I remind you to stir up the gift of God which is in you through the laying on of my hands. For God has not given us a spirit of fear, but of power and of love and of a sound mind."

In your prayer journal, identify in this portion of scripture a promise to receive or a command to obey.

Prayer:

My Father, I thank you today for the Holy Spirit of God who lives in me, speaks to me and supplies me with your wisdom, your knowledge and your power. I did not receive the spirit of fear when the Holy Spirit came into my life, but I received power, love and a sound mind. I ask you to help me realize who is with me when I feel afraid or uncertain. The love of God has filled my life, and I know your perfect love casts out all fear. Help me to stir up the gift of God that is within me so I will not live as if you are nowhere around. You have given me the choice to walk in the spirit or follow after the flesh. I choose to follow after the Spirit of God so I will recognize the things you have freely given me, and I will hear your voice and not the accusing voice of the enemy. I thank you for this now in Jesus' name, Amen.

Proclamation:

The Spirit of God lives in me. He gives me power. He reveals to me the love of God, so the peace of God will keep me free of fear and full of courage to follow after the Lord with all my heart.

Memory Verse: 2 Timothy 1:7

"For God has not given us the spirit of fear; but of power and of love and of a sound mind."

To every family member: *"I love you; you are blessed, and you are a blessing."*
Don't forget the hugs.

October 23rd

Scripture: 1 Chronicles 4:10 (NIV)

"Jabez cried out to the God of Israel, "Oh, that you would bless me and enlarge my territory! Let your hand be with me, and keep me from harm so that I will be free from pain." And God granted his request."

In your prayer journal, identify in this portion of scripture a promise to receive or a command to obey.

Prayer:

Father, I know that you do not respect one person over another, but what you did for one, you will do for all who ask you. Jabez asked you to "bless him and increase his territory and to know that [you] are with him and will keep [him] from harm and free of pain," and you gave him what he asked. I also ask you to bless me today and cause me to: increase in my realm of influence as well as my personal possessions, empower me with your strong right hand and protect me from harm and keep me from pain. I believe you grant me this request, for you have declared, "All things whatsoever [I] ask in prayer believing, [I] will receive". I believe I receive now in Jesus' name, Amen.

Proclamation:

The Lord desires to give me the desires of my heart. I ask and receive because that is the will of God my Father. He has ordained answered prayer to be an important part of my life, for that will bring glory to his great name and demonstrate to the world his willingness to show himself to be mighty and strong on my behalf.

Memory Verse: 2 Timothy 1:7

"For God has not given us the spirit of fear; but of power and of love and of a sound mind."

To every family member: "I love you; you are blessed, and you are a blessing."
Don't forget the hugs.

October 24th

Scripture: 2 Chronicles 5:13-14 (AMP)

"And when the trumpeters and singers were joined in unison, making one sound to be heard in praising and thanking the Lord, and when they lifted up their voice with the trumpets and cymbals and other instruments for song and praised the Lord, saying, For He is good, for His mercy and loving-kindness endure forever, then the house of the Lord was filled with a cloud, So that the priests could not stand to minister because of the cloud, for the glory of the Lord filled the house of God."

In your prayer journal, identify in this portion of scripture a promise to receive or a command to obey.

Prayer:

Father, I desire to see the glory of the Lord filling the church every time we meet together. I know it is in the place of agreement and unity that you have commanded the blessings of God. I pray this day that the people of God would be in perfect agreement in worshiping and praising your name. Remove from us the division and strife that impede the manifested glory of your presence. Help us to truly dwell together in unity. Fill us afresh with your Spirit and bring us into that place of unity where we are with one voice declaring your mercy and loving-kindness that endures forever. I thank you for bringing this to pass in your church, in Jesus' name, Amen.

Proclamation:

The Spirit of the Lord is at work to bring the body of Christ together in a place of harmony and agreement. We will speak the same things and do everything with sincere hearts and pure motives to glorify God. We will see his glory filling his church and the people of the world seeing his love and goodness.

Memory Verse: 2 Timothy 1:7

"For God has not given us the spirit of fear; but of power and of love and of a sound mind."

To every family member: "I love you; you are blessed, and you are a blessing."
Don't forget the hugs.

October 25th

Scripture: 2 Timothy 2:1-2 (NLT)

"Timothy, my dear son, be strong through the grace that God gives you in Christ Jesus. You have heard me teach things that have been confirmed by many reliable witnesses. Now teach these truths to other trustworthy people who will be able to pass them on to others."

In your prayer journal, identify in this portion of scripture a promise to receive or a command to obey.

Prayer:

Heavenly Father, I praise you and thank you for teaching me about the things of God. You have blessed me with the knowledge of your salvation, and you continue to reveal to me wonderful truths from your Word. I ask you to equip me and enable me not to just obey your Word and walk in the ways of God, but to also teach others who will learn and grow and bring to the next generation the words and works of your kingdom. As you have commanded us to make disciples of all nations, I pray for your Word to cover the earth. I ask you to raise up many who will go into all the world and reap the harvest of people, prepared to hear and embrace the gospel. Send forth your Word and the power of the Spirit of God to confirm what is preached and demonstrate your love to all nations. I pray in Jesus' name, Amen.

Proclamation:

The Word of the Lord is mighty to save. It will transform nations and the hungry hearts of those who hear.

Memory Verse: 2 Timothy 1:7

"For God has not given us the spirit of fear; but of power and of love and of a sound mind."

To every family member: *"I love you; you are blessed, and you are a blessing."*
Don't forget the hugs.

October 26th

Scripture: Matthew 5:43-48 (NLT)

"'You have heard the law that says, "Love your neighbor" and hate your enemy. But I say, love your enemies! Pray for those who persecute you! In that way, you will be acting as true children of your Father in heaven. For he gives his sunlight to both the evil and the good, and he sends rain on the just and the unjust alike. If you love only those who love you, what reward is there for that? Even corrupt tax collectors do that much. If you are kind only to your friends, how are you different from anyone else? Even pagans do that. But you are to be perfect, even as your Father in heaven is perfect.'"

In your prayer journal, identify in this portion of scripture a promise to receive or a command to obey.

Prayer:

God and Father of my Lord Jesus Christ, I bless your holy name. It is my desire to hear and obey your every Word. Help me to walk in love to those who love me and also to those who do not. Lord, you are kind to everyone and send your blessings to all. You loved me so much that, even when I was an enemy, Jesus died to redeem me. I pray I walk in the same love as Jesus did. You Lord, have deposited in my heart the love of God. You have given me your Spirit. I call upon you today to strengthen me with sincere faith and love that reveals your heart, and your desire for all to be saved and come to a knowledge of the truth. I ask these things in Jesus' name, Amen.

Proclamation:

I choose to walk in love this day toward everyone. It is not my love but God's. He empowers me to love those who are not lovely or kind because his love always wins and it will never end.

Memory Verse: 2 Timothy 1:7

"For God has not given us the spirit of fear;
but of power and of love and of a sound mind."

To every family member: "*I love you; you are blessed, and you are a blessing.*"
Don't forget the hugs.

October 27th

Scripture: Luke 22:39-46 (NKJV)

"Coming out, He went to the Mount of Olives, as He was accustomed, and His disciples also followed Him. When He came to the place, He said to them, 'Pray that you may not enter into temptation.' And He was withdrawn from them about a stone's throw, and He knelt down and prayed, saying, 'Father, if it is Your will, take this cup away from Me; nevertheless not My will, but Yours, be done.' Then an angel appeared to Him from heaven, strengthening Him. And being in agony, He prayed more earnestly. Then His sweat became like great drops of blood falling down to the ground. When He rose up from prayer, and had come to His disciples, He found them sleeping from sorrow. Then He said to them, 'Why do you sleep? Rise and pray, lest you enter into temptation.'"

In your prayer journal, identify in this portion of scripture a promise to receive or a command to obey.

Prayer:

Lord, my God, I know it is through prayer that you strengthen me to do your will and to keep me from entering into temptation. As Jesus prayed and was strengthened by an angel, I pray for your strength now. I desire my will to conform to your will so I always do those things that please you. I know that you are not the source of temptation, but you are the one who gives me power to overcome temptation when it comes to distract me or destroy me. If only the disciples had prayed, they would not have suffered the shame of denying you when their lives were threatened. Help me today to recognize temptation when it comes and to have the certainty that you will give me strength to overcome all temptation. Because I pray, you will deliver me from temptation and keep me from evil. In Jesus' name, Amen.

Proclamation:

In this world, I will have trouble and temptation will come my way, but as I pray, I will not enter into temptation, for the Lord keeps me in all my ways.

Memory Verse: 2 Timothy 1:7
"For God has not given us the spirit of fear; but of power and of love and of a sound mind."

To every family member: "I love you; you are blessed, and you are a blessing."
Don't forget the hugs.

October 28th

Scripture: Isaiah 61:10-11 (KJV)

"I will greatly rejoice in the Lord, my soul shall be joyful in my God; for he hath clothed me with the garments of salvation, he hath covered me with the robe of righteousness, as a bridegroom decketh himself with ornaments, and as a bride adorneth herself with her jewels. For as the earth bringeth forth her bud, and as the garden causeth the things that are sown in it to spring forth; so the Lord God will cause righteousness and praise to spring forth before all the nations."

In your prayer journal, identify in this portion of scripture a promise to receive or a command to obey.

Prayer:

God, my Father, I praise you. You have covered my sin with the robe of righteousness. You have adorned me with the fruit of the Spirit and given me great and precious promises. You load me down with blessings and have freely given me heavenly gifts. As the earth produces what is sown in it I thank you for the things you have sown into me so my life buds and bring forth as a garden the fragrance of your presence and the fruit of your Spirit. I will be joyful in you this day, for you have clothed me with garments of salvation and prepared me as for a wedding day with all the finest things. Thank you, my Father, in Jesus' name, Amen.

Proclamation:

I will rejoice in the Lord my God. He has raised me up from the dead and given me life. He has covered me with his presence and filled me with joy. I am greatly blessed by the Lord this day.

Memory Verse: 2 Timothy 1:7

"For God has not given us the spirit of fear; but of power and of love and of a sound mind."

To every family member: "I love you; you are blessed, and you are a blessing." Don't forget the hugs.

October 29th

Scripture: Luke 18:1 (AMP)
"Also [Jesus] told them a parable to the effect that they ought always to pray and not to turn coward (faint, lose heart, and give up)."

In your prayer journal, identify in this portion of scripture a promise to receive or a command to obey.

Prayer:
Father, you have declared in your Word that all believers are to "pray without ceasing". You said to pray so we would not faint, lose heart, grow weary or give up. I ask you to teach me to pray. Help me to be in a continuous conversation with you wherever I am and in whatever I am doing. I desire to include you in every decision I make so I have a God consciousness instead of only being aware of the things I see around me. I acknowledge your presence and ask your advice and listen to hear your voice so I do not lean to my own understanding about things, but I am led of the Spirit of God. Bring these things to pass in my life today. I pray, Father, in Jesus' name, Amen.

Proclamation:
I am led by the Holy Spirit of God. He teaches me and speaks to me and gives me wisdom and direction because I pray and ask God to help me in every decision I make. Because I pray, I do not faint, lose heart, grow weary or give up. I do not become a coward when opposition stands against me because I am made strong by praying and hearing God's voice and following his directions.

Memory Verse: Luke 6:38
"Give and it will be given to you. A good measure, pressed down, shaken together and running over, will be poured into your lap. For with the measure you use, it will be measured to you."

To every family member: *"I love you; you are blessed, and you are a blessing."*
Don't forget the hugs.

October 30th

Scripture: 2 Timothy 2:15 (NASB)

"Be diligent to present yourself approved to God as a workman who does not need to be ashamed, accurately handling the word of truth."

In your prayer journal, identify in this portion of scripture
a promise to receive or a command to obey.

Prayer:

My Heavenly Father, I thank you for the abundant promises in your Word. I pray I am diligent to study your Word and to meditate on it day and night and give it the highest priority in my life so the promises of your Word work for me and I am able to teach and encourage others with your Word of truth. I know you expect all believers to become skillful in the Word of God. I pray I do not just read your Word, but I am skillful to apply your Word and experience it, not just believe it is true. I desire to be approved by you as a workman who is accomplishing the things that please you and producing the things that honor you. Father, help me today to skillfully apply your Word so your will is accomplished in me and in the lives of those for whom I pray and to whom I minister. I receive your help now in Jesus' name, Amen.

Proclamation:

The Word of God is mighty and more powerful than any two-edged sword. It will accomplish everything the Lord has spoken. I do not just randomly speak the scriptures as religious clichés, but I accurately declare his Word as a skilled swordsman, defeating the enemy and living in victory.

Memory Verse: Luke 6:38

"Give and it will be given to you. A good measure, pressed down, shaken together and running over, will be poured into your lap. For with the measure you use, it will be measured to you."

To every family member: *"I love you; you are blessed, and you are a blessing."*
Don't forget the hugs.

October 31st

Scripture: Mark 11:25-26 (WEB)

"Whenever you stand praying, forgive, if you have anything against anyone; so that your Father, who is in heaven, may also forgive you your transgressions. But if you do not forgive, neither will your Father in heaven forgive your transgressions."

In your prayer journal, identify in this portion of scripture a promise to receive or a command to obey.

Prayer:

My Heavenly Father, I stand before you this day to pray and to obey your Word. I choose today to forgive anyone who has hurt me or offended me in any way. I know Jesus has paid the price for my sin as well as the sin of the entire world. Because you have forgiven all who have sinned against you, I have no right to hold on to any wrong that was done to me. The price Jesus paid to forgive my sin was the same price paid to forgive all sin. I forgive any and all who have sinned against me, and because I do, my Heavenly Father forgives me and releases me from the judgments I have held against others. I give forgiveness, and I receive forgiveness now in Jesus' name, Amen.

Proclamation:

The blood of Jesus was the price that was paid to forgive me of all sin. The blood of Jesus satisfied the righteous and legal requirements of God to release me from all sin. I will not hold against anyone a wrong done to me. I will not exalt my sin or the sin of another above the paid price of the blood of Jesus.

Memory Verse: Luke 6:38

"Give and it will be given to you. A good measure, pressed down, shaken together and running over, will be poured into your lap. For with the measure you use, it will be measured to you."

To every family member: "I love you; you are blessed, and you are a blessing."
Don't forget the hugs.

November 1st

Scripture: 1 Thessalonians 3:12-13 (NKJV)

"And may the Lord make you increase and abound in love to one another and to all, just as we do to you, so that He may establish your hearts blameless in holiness before our God and Father at the coming of our Lord Jesus Christ with all His saints."

In your prayer journal, identify in this portion of scripture a promise to receive or a command to obey.

Prayer:

Father, I thank you for your love that you have given to me. I pray that your love increases and abounds in my life more and more so I walk in love towards other believers and to all people whether they believe or not. I pray that my ways and my words, those things I purpose in my heart and the reason I do the things I do are motivated by the love of God and not by my own desires that are sometimes selfish. Lord, I ask you today to establish my heart (my thoughts and desires) in holiness (sincere and complete devotion to God). I desire to be without blame before you in every area of my life so, when Jesus returns, my life has glorified him and others have experienced the love of God. I thank you for this good work of God you are working in me today in Jesus' name, Amen.

Proclamation:

The Holy Spirit has put in me the love of God. This love is increasing more and more every day. I choose to walk in love. I love those who love me and those who do not. My love for God is greater today than yesterday, and my desire is to please him every day and in every way.

Memory Verse: Luke 6:38

"Give and it will be given to you. A good measure, pressed down, shaken together and running over, will be poured into your lap. For with the measure you use, it will be measured to you."

To every family member: *"I love you; you are blessed, and you are a blessing."*
Don't forget the hugs.

November 2nd

Scripture: Mark 6:56 (KJV)

"And whithersoever he entered, into villages, or cities, or country, they laid the sick in the streets, and besought him that they might touch if it were but the border of his garment: and as many as touched him were made whole."

In your prayer journal, identify in this portion of scripture a promise to receive or a command to obey.

Prayer:

Lord, you are great and greatly to be praised. You are mighty and limitless in power. You call things into existence that are not, and they come into being. Lord, as the multitudes touched the hem of your clothes by faith and were healed, I by faith touch you and receive healing for my body. What you did for the multitudes you will do for me. You do not prefer one above another, but you said, "whosoever will" can receive. Thank you for the promises in your Word and the faith it produces in me to receive. If you said it, you will do it, and if you have spoken it, you will bring it to pass. I now receive the power of God to drive sickness and disease out of my body and to make me perfectly whole. I receive these things now in Jesus' name, Amen.

Proclamation:

Jesus bore my sickness and carried my disease. He paid the price for my healing. He sent his Word to heal me and to deliver me from all my distresses. I am whole and complete in him who loves me and has given himself for me so I can live free of the curse of sickness and disease and rest in the love of his divine power.

Memory Verse: Luke 6:38

"Give and it will be given to you. A good measure, pressed down, shaken together and running over, will be poured into your lap. For with the measure you use, it will be measured to you."

To every family member: *"I love you; you are blessed, and you are a blessing."*
Don't forget the hugs.

November 3rd

Scripture: Luke 19:10 (KJV)
"For the Son of man is come to seek and to save that which was lost."

In your prayer journal, identify in this portion of scripture a promise to receive or a command to obey.

Prayer:

My Heavenly Father, I am amazed at your goodness and your love for me. Your Word declares that Jesus came to seek and to save everything we had lost, including ourselves. I was lost and could not find my way back to you or to the life you purposed for me to live. I thank you, Lord, for seeking me and saving me from the darkness that blinded my eyes and the destruction for which I was headed. You brought me into your kingdom and delivered me from guilt and shame and from all the results of sin that caused me to lose my way. I will forever praise you for loving me and restoring me to a right relationship with you and to the peace and joy I so greatly desire. Thank you for seeking me and restoring me. In Jesus' name, Amen.

Proclamation:

The Son of God came to earth to fulfill the will of God his Father. He searched for me as a shepherd for a lost sheep. He found me and brought me back to the safety of his kingdom and to the exceeding rich blessings of his love. I am whole and complete in him who loved me and gave himself for me. I have been made whole by his brokenness, blessed by his taking my curse, and because he was judged for my sin, I walk in his righteousness.

Memory Verse: Luke 6:38

"Give and it will be given to you. A good measure, pressed down, shaken together and running over, will be poured into your lap. For with the measure you use, it will be measured to you."

To every family member: *"I love you; you are blessed, and you are a blessing."*
Don't forget the hugs.

November 4th

Scripture: Matthew 1:23 (NKJV)

"Behold, the virgin shall be with child, and bear a Son, and they shall call His name Immanuel, which is translated, God with us."

In your prayer journal, identify in this portion of scripture a promise to receive or a command to obey.

Prayer:

Heavenly Father, thank you for your Son Jesus, born of a virgin and uncontaminated by the nature of man. As your Son, he is perfect, righteous and holy. As a man, born of a woman, he is qualified to function as a man according to your original design with authority and power because you were with him. Father, it was Moses who cried to you and asked to see your glorious presence. He refused to go to the land you promised Israel if you did not go with them. It is your presence that makes the people of God different than any other people. In your presence is great joy, and you invite us to come boldly into your presence to worship and praise and pray. I pray that you make me always aware of your presence with me. Because Jesus is God with us, we can see your mercy and kindness to forgive and your compassion to heal and set free those in bondage. I rejoice in your presence with me and your promise to never leave or forsake me. Because if you are with me, none can ever stand against me. I praise you for your presence. In Jesus' name, Amen.

Proclamation:

I rejoice in the presence of the Lord. He is not far away from me. He does not ignore me, and neither is he ignorant of my current circumstances or needs. My prayers do not have to travel to the far ends of the universe because God hears me and he abides in me.

Memory Verse: Luke 6:38

"Give and it will be given to you. A good measure, pressed down, shaken together and running over, will be poured into your lap. For with the measure you use, it will be measured to you."

To every family member: "I love you; you are blessed, and you are a blessing." Don't forget the hugs.

November 5th

Scripture: Psalms 106:1-3 (NKJV)

"Praise the Lord! Oh, give thanks to the Lord, for He is good! For His mercy endures forever. Who can utter the mighty acts of the Lord? Who can declare all His praise? Blessed are those who keep justice, And he who does righteousness at all times!"

In your prayer journal, identify in this portion of scripture a promise to receive or a command to obey.

Prayer:

Lord my God, I praise you today. You are good, and your mercy endures forever. Your mercies are new every day. Every day will I bless you and praise your great name. You, Lord, are Almighty and All Powerful, yet you treat me with tender mercies, and your great goodness is poured out upon me today. You give me your righteousness so that your blessings can come upon me and surround me. I pray for your grace and wisdom to rest upon me so I bring praise to your name by doing what is right and good in your eyes. I desire to walk in all the blessings of God so freely given to me. Thank you for these things this day in Jesus' name, Amen.

Proclamation:

The Lord is good. He has defeated all my enemies. Even if they gather against me, they will not succeed. No weapon that is formed against me shall prosper, for the Lord is my help. Sickness and disease, fear and torment, lack and need have no place in my life, for the Lord has defeated these enemies and given me victory over them by his great love and mighty power.

Memory Verse: John 10:10

"A thief comes only to steal and to kill and to destroy. I have come so that they may have life and have it in abundance."

To every family member: "I love you; you are blessed, and you are a blessing." Don't forget the hugs.

Faith Family Minute | 311

November 6th

Scripture: John 8:12 (HCSB)

"Then Jesus spoke to them again: 'I am the light of the world. Anyone who follows Me will never walk in the darkness but will have the light of life.'"

In your prayer journal, identify in this portion of scripture a promise to receive or a command to obey.

Prayer:

O Lord my God, you, are great and worthy of all praise. As you spoke and light exploded into the darkness at creation, so Jesus brought us the light, the revelation of your love and your will for our lives. Thank you for your promise to me that I will never walk in darkness if I follow the light Jesus shines on the path of life. Help me today to walk in the true light that comes only from you. Keep me from the confusion darkness brings and make my way plain so I will see clearly and recognize what is of you and what is not. I pray the light of God in me will shine brighter and brighter day by day so others will see your light and follow after you. I pray in Jesus' name, Amen.

Proclamation:

Jesus is the light of the world. His light shined in my darkness and revealed to me abundant life. I do not stumble in the darkness because my way is made plain. Today I will follow the Lord to walk in his light and to behold the wonderful things he has prepared for me. Those who walk in darkness cannot see the goodness of God, but I will follow Jesus and walk in the light of life.

Memory Verse: John 10:10

"A thief comes only to steal and to kill and to destroy. I have come so that they may have life and have it in abundance."

To every family member: "I love you; you are blessed, and you are a blessing." Don't forget the hugs.

November 7th

Scripture: Psalms 9:1-2 (GNT)

"I will praise you, Lord, with all my heart; I will tell of all the wonderful things you have done. I will sing with joy because of you. I will sing praise to you, Almighty God."

In your prayer journal, identify in this portion of scripture a promise to receive or a command to obey.

Prayer:

Lord, my God, there is no other God but you. You are the Creator of all things, and with you is all might and power. Father, you have redeemed me from destruction and given me life. You said I may call you Abba (Daddy) Father because I am your child, created in your image and for your purpose. Father, I know that your desire for me is always good because there is nothing dark or evil in you. Everything you do is good and righteous and holy. It is your good pleasure to give me your kingdom. It is your delight when I pray and purpose to enter your presence to worship and to praise you for all the glorious things you have done for me. I thank you today for your great love for me. I thank you for your abiding presence in my life and your promise to never leave me nor forsake me. You are with me, and you cause your goodness and mercy to chase me down and overtake me because you delight in me. Father, I know these blessings are not mine because I deserve them but because you choose to bless me because you are good and you love me. I thank you for these things in Jesus' name, Amen.

Proclamation:

I walk in the revelation of God's love for me today. He is always with me everywhere I go, and in every situation of life, he is there. I do not fear, for if God is for me, who can be against me?

Memory Verse: John 10:10

"A thief comes only to steal and to kill and to destroy. I have come so that they may have life and have it in abundance."

To every family member: "I love you; you are blessed, and you are a blessing." Don't forget the hugs.

November 8th

Scripture: 1 Corinthians 13:13 (WEB)
"But now faith, hope, and love remain—these three. The greatest of these is love."

In your prayer journal, identify in this portion of scripture a promise to receive or a command to obey.

Prayer:

Heavenly Father, I treasure your love above everything else. The promises of your Word are mine because of your love. Faith only works by love, and the hope of those things that cannot be seen is maintained because I am certain of your love. I pray you protect me from the things that distract me from your love. Your commandments to me are to love you with all my heart and to love others. Thank you, Lord, for your love that you have placed in me. It is only by your love that I can fulfill your will. Anything I do that is not motivated by love is empty and of no real or lasting value. It is faith in your love for me that keeps me from fear and makes me complete. I pray you will constantly remind me of your love for me and your love will move me to do your will. In Jesus' name, Amen.

Proclamation:

Love never fails. Everything else will come to an end, but love endures forever. I will walk in God's love today. I will not allow anything else to take the place of God's love, for nothing else will last forever, but God's love never ends.

Memory Verse: John 10:10
"A thief comes only to steal and to kill and to destroy. I have come so that they may have life and have it in abundance."

To every family member: *"I love you; you are blessed, and you are a blessing."* Don't forget the hugs.

November 9th

Scripture: Galatians 5:1 (NCV)

"We have freedom now, because Christ made us free. So stand strong. Do not change and go back into the slavery of the law."

In your prayer journal, identify in this portion of scripture a promise to receive or a command to obey.

Prayer:

God, my Father, I am free, for you have made me free. Jesus freed me from the law of sin and death. He bore my sin and took upon himself my death so I am free from the judgment of sin, and death has no more power over me. Keep me from the temptation of returning to the law of works to be accepted by you. Lord, keep me from judging others by their works instead of by your grace. I know there is nothing I can do to earn your favor or forgiveness. It is not by right works I can do, but only by your mercy I am saved. Father, give me a clear vision of your grace and the work Jesus accomplished for me. Keep me from becoming entangled by the idea that you only accept me or reject me by how I perform instead of believing that Jesus performed in my place the things I could never do for myself. I declare this day that I have been made righteous before God and forgiven of all sin by faith alone in what Jesus did for me. I praise you for this great salvation. In Jesus' name, Amen.

Proclamation:

Jesus took all the commandments of God requiring my obedience or my death and satisfied each one of them by receiving my judgment for disobedience and giving me a spiritual receipt that says, "paid in full."

Memory Verse: John 10:10

"A thief comes only to steal and to kill and to destroy. I have come so that they may have life and have it in abundance."

To every family member: *"I love you; you are blessed, and you are a blessing."*
Don't forget the hugs.

November 10th

Scripture: 1 John 2:27 (NASB)

"As for you, the anointing which you received from Him abides in you, and you have no need for anyone to teach you; but as His anointing teaches you about all things, and is true and is not a lie, and just as it has taught you, you abide in Him."

In your prayer journal, identify in this portion of scripture a promise to receive or a command to obey.

Prayer:

Father, I thank you for the anointing of God that rests upon me today. You have anointed me with the Holy Spirit of God who abides in me. You said he would teach me all things and remind me of the things Jesus said. He would take the things of God and reveal them to me and show me the things I need to know. I believe the Spirit of God who raised Jesus from the dead lives in me. He helps me pray when I don't know how to pray, and he intercedes in my behalf, so even when trouble comes against me I can see his goodness working to bring me victory. Father, I pray for this anointing you have given me to flow through me as a river that brings life to everything it touches. Thank you for teaching me to know and having the power to do all of your good pleasure by the anointing of the Spirit of God. In Jesus' name, Amen.

Proclamation:

The Spirit of God enables me to do the will of my heavenly Father. It is not by my might or by my own power that I will get things done. But, it is by the Spirit of God who reveals to me the things of God and anoints me to do his will.

Memory Verse: John 10:10

"A thief comes only to steal and to kill and to destroy.
I have come so that they may have life and have it in abundance."

To every family member: "I love you; you are blessed, and you are a blessing."
Don't forget the hugs.

November 11th

Scripture: Hebrews 1:1-3 (TLB)

"Long ago God spoke in many different ways to our fathers through the prophets, in visions, dreams, and even face to face, telling them little by little about his plans. But now in these days he has spoken to us through his Son to whom he has given everything and through whom he made the world and everything there is. God's Son shines out with God's glory, and all that God's Son is and does marks him as God. He regulates the universe by the mighty power of his command. He is the one who died to cleanse us and clear our record of all sin, and then sat down in highest honor beside the great God of heaven."

In your prayer journal, identify in this portion of scripture a promise to receive or a command to obey.

Prayer:

My Father, you are glorious and worthy of all praise. You created everything by our Lord Jesus Christ, and by him the entire universe is sustained at his command. He revealed to us your love and your plan for our redemption. He was the only one who qualified to cleanse us from sin, and having finished the work, he sat down at your right hand. I thank you today for the free gift of righteousness and for qualifying me to receive this gift because of what Jesus accomplished on my behalf. I see in the life of Jesus who you are and what you are like. Thank you, Father, for your unearned love and your desire for me to walk in every blessing and to be successful in accomplishing your will for my life through your power and grace. I pray in Jesus' name, Amen.

Proclamation:

When I see the love and compassion of Jesus, I see the heart of God, the Father. Everything Jesus did, he did at the direction of the Father because it is the will of God to heal and deliver, to comfort and encourage.

Memory Verse: John 10:10

"A thief comes only to steal and to kill and to destroy. I have come so that they may have life and have it in abundance."

To every family member: *"I love you; you are blessed, and you are a blessing."* Don't forget the hugs.

November 12th

Scripture: 1 Timothy 6:17-19 (NCV)

"Command those who are rich with things of this world not to be proud. Tell them to hope in God, not in their uncertain riches. God richly gives us everything to enjoy. Tell the rich people to do good, to be rich in doing good deeds, to be generous and ready to share. By doing that, they will be saving a treasure for themselves as a strong foundation for the future. Then they will be able to have the life that is true life."

In your prayer journal, identify in this portion of scripture a promise to receive or a command to obey.

Prayer:

Heavenly Father, you have richly blessed me with provision and abundance. You have promised me that I will not lack or be in need or want of any good thing for you are my provider. I pray for a heart of compassion and a willingness to reach out and meet the needs of others. I know the rich blessings of God are not dependent on the current economy. I can prosper in times of famine, and I can receive from your hand enough to meet all my need and also give to every good work. As I give, I am laying up in a heavenly account treasures available for my future. My trust is in you and not in the abundance of things I possess. Because you are my source, I cannot fail. This world will pass away, but you abide forever. It is in Jesus' name I give you praise, Amen.

Proclamation:

My bank account balance or the amount of food in my pantry does not determine my security. I give to advance the kingdom of God, and I give to people who are in need. I am not diminished by giving, but increased. When I give to others, I am storing up in my heavenly account for my future needs ,and what I give is given again to me in good measure, pressed down and running over.

Memory Verse: Ephesians 4:29

"Let no corrupt communication proceed out of your mouth, but that which is good to the use of edifying, that it may minister grace unto the hearers."

To every family member: *"I love you; you are blessed, and you are a blessing."*
Don't forget the hugs.

November 13th

Scripture: Philippians 1:27 (AMP)

"Only be sure as citizens so to conduct yourselves [that] your manner of life [will be] worthy of the good news (the Gospel) of Christ, so that whether I [do] come and see you or am absent, I may hear this of you: that you are standing firm in united spirit *and* purpose, striving side by side *and* contending with a single mind for the faith of the glad tidings (the Gospel)."

In your prayer journal, identify in this portion of scripture a promise to receive or a command to obey.

Prayer:

Heavenly Father, thank you for making me a citizen of heaven, a member of your family, an ambassador of your kingdom and one who has the privilege of carrying your name. I ask you for wisdom to know and the discipline to do your will and to live in such a way as to honor you and glorify your name. Help me to walk in love, standing in the place of agreement with all those who declare the good news of the Gospel of Jesus. I pray for the love of God to be seen in me and heard as I speak your words of life. I thank you for hearing me and helping me in Jesus' name, Amen.

Proclamation:

I will live my life in such a way that all who see me or hear my voice will know God loves them. I will strive to stay in unity and live in peace with everyone who calls on the name of the Lord Jesus Christ.

Memory Verse: Ephesians 4:29

"Let no corrupt communication proceed out of your mouth, but that which is good to the use of edifying, that it may minister grace unto the hearers."

To every family member: "*I love you; you are blessed, and you are a blessing.*" Don't forget the hugs.

November 14th

Scripture: Ephesians 1:17-23 (HCSB)

"I pray that the God of our Lord Jesus Christ, the glorious Father, would give you a spirit of wisdom and revelation in the knowledge of Him. I pray that the perception of your mind may be enlightened so you may know what is the hope of His calling, what are the glorious riches of His inheritance among the saints, and what is the immeasurable greatness of His power to us who believe, according to the working of His vast strength. He demonstrated this power in the Messiah by raising Him from the dead and seating Him at His right hand in the heavens far above every ruler and authority, power and dominion, and every title given, not only in this age but also in the one to come. And He put everything under His feet and appointed Him as head over everything for the church, which is His body, the fullness of the One who fills all things in every way."

In your prayer journal, identify in this portion of scripture a promise to receive or a command to obey.

Prayer:

Father, I pray to know you and the glory of your kingdom. Only by the revelation you give, could I possibly know your greatness and realize the hope of your calling. You have called me to a glorious inheritance. Help me to understand the mighty power of God that raised Jesus from the dead and seated him at your right hand where he rules with all authority and power. You have given him dominion over all things and made him to be the head of the church. I pray all members of this glorious church know their relationship to Christ and receive the authority, power and dominion that flows from him through us to accomplish the will of God, for there is no obstacle or adversary who can stand against him. Thank you for these things in Jesus' name, Amen.

Proclamation:

Jesus is the head of the church. I am a member of his glorious body, and everything he received, I have also received. God has made me one with Christ.

Memory Verse: Ephesians 4:29

"Let no corrupt communication proceed out of your mouth, but that which is good to the use of edifying, that it may minister grace unto the hearers."

To every family member: *"I love you; you are blessed, and you are a blessing."*
Don't forget the hugs.

November 15th

Scripture: Galatians 1:3-5 (KJV)

"Grace be to you and peace from God the Father, and from our Lord Jesus Christ, Who gave himself for our sins, that he might deliver us from this present evil world, according to the will of God and our Father: To whom be glory for ever and ever. Amen."

In your prayer journal, identify in this portion of scripture a promise to receive or a command to obey.

Prayer:

Lord my God, I bless your holy name. I exalt and praise you for you are worthy. You have given me grace and peace. You have delivered me from the evil of this world through my Lord Jesus Christ. Jesus took my judgment and carried away my sin so I can live in peace and walk in your grace that gives me everything I will ever need. Your grace is always sufficient to put me over and give me victory in every situation of life. I receive your blessings, your favor and every good and perfect gift that comes from you. You love me more than I can comprehend, and because I know you love me, I know you will always help me, comfort me, protect me and empower me to choose what pleases you. Thank you, Father, in Jesus name, Amen.

Proclamation:

God loves me. He causes his grace and peace to fill my life, so I will never be afraid.

Memory Verse: Ephesians 4:29

"Let no corrupt communication proceed out of your mouth, but that which is good to the use of edifying, that it may minister grace unto the hearers."

To every family member: *"I love you; you are blessed, and you are a blessing."*
Don't forget the hugs.

November 16th

Scripture: Isaiah 30:18 (KJV)

"And therefore will the Lord wait, that he may be gracious unto you, and therefore will he be exalted, that he may have mercy upon you: for the Lord is a God of judgment: blessed are all they that wait for him."

In your prayer journal, identify in this portion of scripture a promise to receive or a command to obey.

Prayer:

Lord my God, you are faithful in all your ways. You desire to be gracious and merciful to us. In your great wisdom, you search for ways to bless us and keep us from every evil work. You said all who wait upon you will be blessed. I pray that I would not become impatient or presumptuous to do things prematurely or to step out in my own strength or wisdom to try and make something happen before the time. Your timing is always right to accomplish your purpose. Give me wisdom to know when it is time to move and when it is time to wait. Give me ears to hear your voice clearly and to recognize the seasons of my life. I pray in Jesus' name, Amen.

Proclamation:

I will not be moved by my own desires or by the opinion of others; I will only be moved by the Spirit of the Lord. As I wait upon the Lord, he is putting in order the people, the provision and the plan of action that will accomplish his purpose, glorify his name and bring me into the perfect place at the perfect time.

Memory Verse: Ephesians 4:29

"Let no corrupt communication proceed out of your mouth, but that which is good to the use of edifying, that it may minister grace unto the hearers."

To every family member: *"I love you; you are blessed, and you are a blessing."*
Don't forget the hugs.

November 17th

Scripture: Psalms 107:19-21 (NASB)

"Then they cried out to the Lord in their trouble; He saved them out of their distresses. He sent His word and healed them, and delivered them from their destructions. Let them give thanks to the Lord for His lovingkindness, and for His wonders to the sons of men!"

In your prayer journal, identify in this portion of scripture a promise to receive or a command to obey.

Prayer:

Lord my Father, I want to give thanks to you today for the wondrous things you have done for me. You have rescued me from trouble when I called upon you. You sent your Word and healed me and delivered me from my distress. You have not ignored me in times of trouble, but you have moved on my behalf because of your loving kindness and tender mercies. You have kept me from troubles I didn't even know about. You have protected me and hidden me from the purposes of the adversary. I thank you for your abiding presence and your compassion for me. I bless you in the glorious name of Jesus Christ my Lord, Amen.

Proclamation:

I walk in God's favor and with his blessings. He watches over me to keep me in all my ways. He delivers me from trouble, and in times of distress, he comes to my rescue. He sends his Word to heal me when I'm sick, and he showers me with his loving kindnesses and tender mercies. I will praise and exalt his name forever.

Memory Verse: Ephesians 4:29

"Let no corrupt communication proceed out of your mouth, but that which is good to the use of edifying, that it may minister grace unto the hearers."

To every family member: *"I love you; you are blessed, and you are a blessing."*
Don't forget the hugs.

November 18th

Scripture: Matthew 6:6 (NKJV)

"But you, when you pray, go into your room, and when you have shut your door, pray to your Father who is in the secret place; and your Father who sees in secret will reward you openly."

In your prayer journal, identify in this portion of scripture a promise to receive or a command to obey.

Prayer:

Lord, I thank you for the promise of your Word to hear me when I pray. I want to always pray with a pure and sincere heart. It is not my desire for others to hear me so they might help me. I do not want to try and gain some kind of praise from people. I do not want to try to please people or have them think of me as spiritual or holy because they hear me pray. I desire to follow your Word and to enter into that secret place of your presence and to pray so only you will hear the cries of my heart. Lord, you have promised to hear me and to answer me. You have also promised to reward me publicly when I pray privately for the purpose of your kingdom and the accomplishment of your will. In Jesus' name, Amen.

Proclamation:

Jesus said to pray for God's kingdom to come and for his will to be done on earth just as it is always done in heaven. I know he would not tell me to pray for something I could not have. I will enter into that secret place of God's presence and pray so only he can hear me. I will declare to him his Word, and I will receive from him those things I have asked for in faith. As I pray in private, God answers me publicly, and the kingdom of God will come, and the will of God will be done here as it is there.

Memory Verse: Ephesians 4:29

"Let no corrupt communication proceed out of your mouth, but that which is good to the use of edifying, that it may minister grace unto the hearers."

To every family member: *"I love you; you are blessed, and you are a blessing."*
Don't forget the hugs.

November 19th

Scripture: 2 Timothy 1:13-14 (NIV)

"What you heard from me, keep as the pattern of sound teaching, with faith and love in Christ Jesus. Guard the good deposit that was entrusted to you—guard it with the help of the Holy Spirit who lives in us."

In your prayer journal, identify in this portion of scripture a promise to receive or a command to obey.

Prayer:

Heavenly Father, I know you have deposited within me the very life of God. You have given me your righteousness and the person of the Holy Spirit who has made me to be a brand new created being made in your image and after your likeness. Help me to hold on to the truth you have taught me by the Word and Spirit of God. Help me to guard my heart through the power of the Spirit of God within me so I will not allow the things you have deposited in me to be stolen away. I will treasure your Word and the things you have done for me above all else. I will rejoice in you all the days of my life. Thank you for this abundant life that is mine. In Jesus' name, Amen.

Proclamation:

I will acknowledge every good thing that God has given me. I do not focus on failures of my past, but I look upon the promises God has given me. I will treasure the Word of God, for it is life to me and health to all my flesh. I will keep my eyes upon him, for he will fulfill the desires of my heart and bring rest to my soul.

Memory Verse: Hebrews 11:1

"Now faith is the substance of things hoped for, the evidence of things not seen."

To every family member: *"I love you; you are blessed, and you are a blessing."*
Don't forget the hugs.

November 20th

Scripture: Romans 4:16-17 (NLT)

"So the promise is received by faith. It is given as a free gift. And we are all certain to receive it, whether or not we live according to the law of Moses, if we have faith like Abraham's. For Abraham is the father of all who believe. That is what the Scriptures mean when God told him, 'I have made you the father of many nations.' This happened because Abraham believed in the God who brings the dead back to life and who creates new things out of nothing."

In your prayer journal, identify in this portion of scripture a promise to receive or a command to obey.

Prayer:

My Heavenly Father, you called Abraham the father of faith because he chose to believe your promise when it looked impossible. You fulfilled your promise to Abraham and Sarah by giving them a child in their old age because they decided to believe in your ability to fulfill your promise more than the facts of their circumstances. I ask you to help me walk by faith in your Word instead of living by the facts I can feel. You call those things that do not yet exist into being because you promised them to those who would believe. Help me believe for your protection in the face of adversity. Help me to receive healing for my body when the facts are saying it can't be done. Help me to receive your provision when the circumstances seem hopeless, for you are able to do all things. Thank you for faith that will take hold of your promises and boldly declare your will in the midst of all opposition. I pray in Jesus' name, Amen.

Proclamation:

Faith is the reality of things that cannot be seen with the natural eye. Faith sees by the Word of God those things God has promised and is pleased to do.

Memory Verse: Hebrews 11:1

"Now faith is the substance of things hoped for, the evidence of things not seen."

To every family member: "*I love you; you are blessed, and you are a blessing.*" Don't forget the hugs.

November 21st

Scripture: Luke 7:6-10 (PHILLIPS)

"So Jesus went with them, but as he approached the house, the centurion sent some of his personal friends with the message, "Don't trouble yourself, sir! I'm not important enough for you to come into my house—I didn't think I was fit to come to you in person. Just give the order, please, and my servant will recover. I am used to working under orders, and I have soldiers under me. I can say to one, 'Go', and he goes, or I can say to another, 'Come here', and he comes; or I can say to my slave, 'Do this job', and he does it." These words amazed Jesus and he turned to the crowd who were following behind him, and said, "I have never found faith like this anywhere, even in Israel!" Then those who had been sent by the centurion returned to the house and found the slave perfectly well."

In your prayer journal, identify in this portion of scripture a promise to receive or a command to obey.

Prayer:

Heavenly Father, you said there is nothing impossible to those who believe. As the centurion believed in the authority of your Word and saw the power of God released to heal his servant, I pray for the revelation of your authority and power in my life. What you have spoken, you will bring to pass. Help me put your Word in my mouth and declare it with boldness. Help me to see, not the things that are, but those things that can only be seen by the vision your Word creates. As I speak your Word in the authority of the name of Jesus, things will change to line up with your Word because your Word is able to change the things that are and to create the things that are not yet. I thank you for this awesome privilege in Jesus' name, Amen.

Proclamation:

God spoke the universe into existence. God upholds all creation by the power of his Word. I will do what he has instructed me. I will seek God's Word and speak God's Word and see the power of God's Word change what is wrong and make it right.

Memory Verse: Hebrews 11:1

"Now faith is the substance of things hoped for, the evidence of things not seen."

To every family member: "I love you; you are blessed, and you are a blessing." Don't forget the hugs.

November 22nd

Scripture: John 4:23-24 (AMP)

"A time will come, however, indeed it is already here, when the true (genuine) worshipers will worship the Father in spirit and in truth (reality); for the Father is seeking just such people as these as His worshipers. God is a Spirit (a spiritual Being) and those who worship *Him* must worship Him in spirit and in truth (reality)."

In your prayer journal, identify in this portion of scripture a promise to receive or a command to obey.

Prayer:

My Father, I worship and praise you for who you are and for what you have done for me. I seek after you. I desire to worship you in spirit and reality. I am not just going through the motions of prayer and praise as a duty to perform, but I sincerely desire to honor you by seeking after you with all my heart. I make pray and worship the priority of my day, for there is nothing as important as my time with you. You are worthy of my time and my attention. My greatest need is to hear your voice and to obey your Word. My greatest delight is to know your presence. I ask you to fill me afresh with the Spirit of God and help me guard my heart from every distraction that would attempt to rob me of this time with you. I pray in Jesus' name, Amen.

Proclamation:

God is seeking those who will worship him above everything else. I will worship the Lord in spirit and truth. I will seek him first when my day begins because there is nothing as important as hearing his voice. Everything I will need this day is contained in God's wisdom and his instructions for me.

Memory Verse: Hebrews 11:1

"Now faith is the substance of things hoped for, the evidence of things not seen."

To every family member: "*I love you; you are blessed, and you are a blessing.*"
Don't forget the hugs.

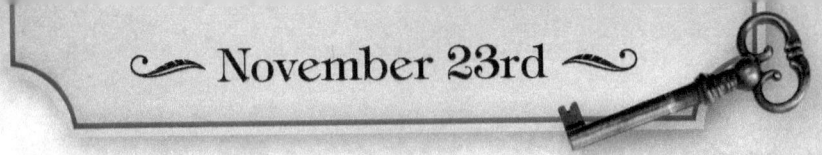

November 23rd

Scripture: 2 Corinthians 6:1-2 (TLB)

"As God's partners, we beg you not to toss aside this marvelous message of God's great kindness. For God says, "Your cry came to me at a favorable time, when the doors of welcome were wide open. I helped you on a day when salvation was being offered." Right now God is ready to welcome you. Today he is ready to save you."

In your prayer journal, identify in this portion of scripture a promise to receive or a command to obey.

Prayer:

Heavenly Father, I thank you for this great salvation that you have given me. You have opened the door of salvation for us to enter in so we might experience abundant life free from condemnation, guilt and shame. As a partner with us, you give us this message of forgiveness and an open invitation for all who will come and enter into your kingdom through the Lord Jesus Christ. I pray for your favor to rest upon me today and for the anointing to speak the Word of your salvation to everyone who wants to receive. I ask you to create opportunities for me today to declare your Word and share your love. In Jesus' name I pray, Amen.

Proclamation:

I am a partner with God to declare the message of his kindness that the day of salvation has come. The door to the kingdom of God is open, and today is the day of God's salvation for everyone who will believe.

Memory Verse: Hebrews 11:1

"Now faith is the substance of things hoped for, the evidence of things not seen."

To every family member: "I love you; you are blessed, and you are a blessing." Don't forget the hugs.

November 24th

Scripture: 2 Kings 6:16-17 (KJV)

"And he answered, Fear not: for they that be with us are more than they that be with them. And Elisha prayed, and said, Lord, I pray thee, open his eyes, that he may see. And the Lord opened the eyes of the young man; and he saw: and, behold, the mountain was full of horses and chariots of fire round about Elisha."

In your prayer journal, identify in this portion of scripture a promise to receive or a command to obey.

Prayer:

My Father, I know you are always with me and I am never out of your sight. Even when I can't see what is really around me, you are there to protect me. Elisha saw the angelic host protecting him when the young man who was with him could not see until you opened his eyes. I ask you, Lord, to open my eyes to see the things you want me to see. Those things that are not seen with natural sight but can only be seen by the revelation you give. You have told me to look at the things that are not seen. I pray to see those invisible things your words declare and to look with spiritual eyes seeing what the Holy Spirit reveals, so I will not be moved by the things my eyes see but only by the things you reveal to me. I thank you for this great work of God in me today in Jesus' name, Amen.

Proclamation:

I allow the Word of God to create for me the vision that I see. I will not live according to my senses but according to what God reveals to me by his Spirit and his Word.

Memory Verse: Hebrews 11:1

"Now faith is the substance of things hoped for, the evidence of things not seen."

To every family member: *"I love you; you are blessed, and you are a blessing."*
Don't forget the hugs.

November 25th

Scripture: Hebrews 1:13-14 (AMP)

"Besides, to which of the angels has He ever said, Sit at My right hand [associated with Me in My royal dignity] till I make your enemies a stool for your feet? Are not the angels all ministering spirits (servants) sent out in the service [of God for the assistance] of those who are to inherit salvation?"

In your prayer journal, identify in this portion of scripture a promise to receive or a command to obey.

Prayer:

My Heavenly Father, you have exalted the Lord Jesus to sit on the throne of your glory. You have put all his enemies under his feet and given him all authority and power. You sent the angels of heaven to minister to me and to all who are heirs of salvation. I thank you that I have the authority of the name of Jesus and the indwelling presence of God, as well as, the angels of God who are assigned to me. I cannot fail or be defeated, for if you are for me, who can be against me? You are my help in time of need. You are my fortress and strength. I bless your wonderful name for the things you have done. Help me walk in the reality of your victory. I pray in Jesus' name, Amen.

Proclamation:

Jesus defeated death and is victorious over all the power of the enemy. He is the Lord of Lords and the King of kings, and his kingdom will never end. He is Lord of all.

Memory Verse: Hebrews 11:1

"Now faith is the substance of things hoped for, the evidence of things not seen."

To every family member: *"I love you; you are blessed, and you are a blessing."*
Don't forget the hugs.

November 26th

Scripture: Haggai 2:18-19 (AMP)

"Consider, I pray you, from this day onward, from the twenty-fourth day of the ninth month, even from the day that the foundation of the Lord's temple was [re]laid, consider this: Is the harvested grain any longer in the barn? As to the grapevine, the fig tree, the pomegranate, and the olive tree—they have not yet borne. From this day on I will bless you."

In your prayer journal, identify in this portion of scripture a promise to receive or a command to obey.

Prayer:

God, my Father, your desire is to bless us and cause us to prosper and walk in the joy of your salvation. When the people of Judea obeyed your Word and made the building of your house their priority, you turned their lack and scarcity to a season of great blessing and plenty. Your blessings are upon me this day to give me the wisdom, the way and the resources to build into my life and into those you have placed in my life the things that are most important to you. Father, it is my desire to give to you the best part of my time, my energy and my possessions. I worship you and put you first above everything else. I ask you to bless the work of my hands, and I pray that the very thoughts of my heart bless and glorify you. I pray these things now in Jesus' name, Amen.

Proclamation:

I purpose this day to honor the Lord by giving to him the first fruits of my increase. I begin my day by seeking his face and hearing his voice so I can accomplish his will and rejoice in his blessings.

Memory Verse: Luke 18:1

"And he spoke a parable unto them to this end, that men ought always to pray and not to faint."

To every family member: *"I love you; you are blessed, and you are a blessing."*
Don't forget the hugs.

November 27th

Scripture: Galatians 5:13-15 (NKJV)

"For you, brethren, have been called to liberty; only do not use liberty as an opportunity for the flesh, but through love serve one another. For all the law is fulfilled in one word, even in this: "You shall love your neighbor as yourself." But if you bite and devour one another, beware lest you be consumed by one another!"

In your prayer journal, identify in this portion of scripture a promise to receive or a command to obey.

Prayer:

Lord, my God, I stand before you today to worship and praise you. I come boldly before your throne, for you have invited me to pray and to declare your Word and do your will. You have commanded us to love one another and serve each other instead of only pleasing ourselves. Help me to walk in your love today. I pray for your grace to rest upon me and remind me that in every situation of life I can choose to walk in love. Your love never fails. You will always bring me through every difficult place to the place of your blessing. You will lift me up above the troubles I face and cause me to stand in your joy. Thank you for your victory in Jesus' name, Amen.

Proclamation:

Love will always cause me to choose what is pleasing to God. God has called me to walk in liberty. He has freed me from the bondage that judgment and criticism of others brings. I will walk in love, and because I do, many will be encouraged, and they will encourage others.

Memory Verse: Luke 18:1

"And he spoke a parable unto them to this end, that men ought always to pray and not to faint."

To every family member: *"I love you; you are blessed, and you are a blessing."*
Don't forget the hugs.

November 28th

Scripture: Genesis 2:15-17 (NCV)

"The Lord God put the man in the garden of Eden to care for it and work it. The Lord God commanded him, 'You may eat the fruit from any tree in the garden, but you must not eat the fruit from the tree which gives the knowledge of good and evil. If you ever eat fruit from that tree, you will die!'"

In your prayer journal, identify in this portion of scripture a promise to receive or a command to obey.

Prayer:

Lord, you gave man everything and instructed him because you loved him. I pray you will keep me from the temptation to think I know better than you. You see the end from the beginning. You know all things. You desire for me to walk in dominion and authority and overcome every evil work of the enemy. I know I can only fulfill these things when I trust you and obey you. You know what is good and what is evil. I know you desire to bless me because you love me. Help me today not to be deceived as Adam was by the subtlety of the devil. I will walk in obedience to your Word as you lead me today by your Spirit and fill me with your grace. In Jesus' name, Amen.

Proclamation:

The devil is a liar. His intentions are to steal, to kill and to destroy everything that is good. God is good. His desire is for me to enjoy every good thing he has created for me.

Memory Verse: Luke 18:1

"And he spoke a parable unto them to this end, that men ought always to pray and not to faint."

To every family member: "I love you; you are blessed, and you are a blessing."
Don't forget the hugs.

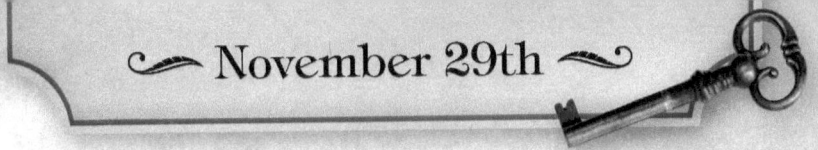

November 29th

Scripture: 1 John 3:1-2 (GW)

"Consider this: The Father has given us his love. He loves us so much that we are actually called God's dear children. And that's what we are. For this reason the world doesn't recognize us, and it didn't recognize him either. Dear friends, now we are God's children. What we will be isn't completely clear yet. We do know that when Christ appears we will be like him because we will see him as he is."

In your prayer journal, identify in this portion of scripture a promise to receive or a command to obey.

Prayer:

Heavenly Father, you love me and made a way for me to become a child of God. Although I do not know all I will become, I know that when Christ appears I will be made like him. I will see him as he is and I will see what you have done for me. How awesome it is to think you have made me to be your child, a member of your family. You gave me a place in your kingdom. I know others will not understand if they have not experienced your love. I pray to be constantly reminded of what you have done for me. Help me today to live in the realization that you, the Almighty God and Creator of all things are my Father. You have brought me into your family and given me your name. Thank you for what you have done for me. In Jesus' name I pray, Amen.

Proclamation:

Who could imagine that God, infinite in wisdom and power, the Creator of all things and the one who created me, would love me and redeem me, creating me in his image and birthing me by his Spirit into his family as a royal member of his kingdom.

Memory Verse: Luke 18:1

"And he spoke a parable unto them to this end, that men ought always to pray and not to faint."

To every family member: *"I love you; you are blessed, and you are a blessing."*
Don't forget the hugs.

Faith Family Minute

November 30th

Scripture: Acts 4:12 (KJV)

"Neither is there salvation in any other: for there is none other name under heaven given among men, whereby we must be saved."

In your prayer journal, identify in this portion of scripture a promise to receive or a command to obey.

Prayer:

God, my Father, you have saved me from destruction by delivering me from the judgment of sin. Jesus took my curse so I could receive his righteousness. He took my judgment so I could live in his blessings. Lord, I know there is not any forgiveness or blessing, there is no victory or life except by my Lord Jesus Christ. No one else could have or would have paid the price for my forgiveness. No one loves me and was willing to do for me what you have done. There is no other name under heaven that gives me this great salvation. I praise you and thank you in the name of my Lord and Savior, Jesus Christ, Amen.

Proclamation:

There was nothing I could do to erase my sin and make myself acceptable to God. There was no amount of good I could do or payment I could make that would remove my sin and give me life. But Jesus came by the plan of God to take my place in righteousness and in judgment. I am righteous and no longer under judgment because Jesus purchased my righteousness and received my judgment. In the name of Jesus, I am right with God and free of sin. There is salvation in no other name but in the name of Jesus Christ the Lord.

Memory Verse: Luke 18:1

"And he spoke a parable unto them to this end, that men ought always to pray and not to faint."

To every family member: *"I love you; you are blessed, and you are a blessing."*
Don't forget the hugs.

December 1st

Scripture: Jude 1:20-21 (MSG)
"But you, dear friends, carefully build yourselves up in this most holy faith by praying in the Holy Spirit, staying right at the center of God's love, keeping your arms open and outstretched, ready for the mercy of our Master, Jesus Christ. This is the unending life, the *real* life!"

In your prayer journal, identify in this portion of scripture a promise to receive or a command to obey.

Prayer:
Heavenly Father, your love and mercy are overwhelming. Thank you for the immeasurable love you have shown me. Holy Spirit, help me pray so I can be strong in the Lord and have the power of his might working in me. Build me up and make me strong so I will keep myself in the center of your love. I pray for the compassion of God to fill me so I will show others God's love. You said when I pray in the spirit, I am speaking mysteries with God and as I pray in the spirit I am to pray for the understanding. Help me to release the will of God into every situation of my life as the Spirit of God gives me words to pray. I thank you for this good work of God in my life now in Jesus' name, Amen.

Proclamation:
I will build myself up on my most holy faith by praying in the spirit. I call forth the will of God to be done. As I pray, I am strengthened to stay in the love of God regardless of what else is going on around me. The Spirit of God reveals to me the things of God, and I am made strong to walk in his ways and to accomplish his will.

Memory Verse: Luke 18:1
"And he spoke a parable unto them to this end, that men ought always to pray and not to faint."

To every family member: "I love you; you are blessed, and you are a blessing."
Don't forget the hugs.

December 2nd

Scripture: James 2:8 (KJV)

"If ye fulfil the royal law according to the scripture, Thou shalt love thy neighbour as thyself, ye do well"

In your prayer journal, identify in this portion of scripture a promise to receive or a command to obey.

Prayer:

Father, it is my desire to follow the commandment you have given. You said if I love you to keep your commandments of walking in faith and loving one another. I know love is not a feeling but a decision and commitment to do towards someone else the same as I would want done to me. I see in your Word this is the royal commandment. The commandment of the King is above everything else. Thank you for helping me fulfill this commandment because I love you and because I want to please you more than myself. I know your promise for me to do well will come to pass as I obey your Word. I believe you will give me wisdom and strength to walk in love this day in Jesus' name, Amen.

Proclamation:

I will walk today in the royal law of love. Jesus said if I obey this commandment I have already fulfilled every commandment. Laying down my life, my comfort and convenience, for someone else's benefit is truly the demonstration of God's love.

Memory Verse: Luke 18:1

"And he spoke a parable unto them to this end, that men ought always to pray and not to faint."

To every family member: "I love you; you are blessed, and you are a blessing." Don't forget the hugs.

December 3rd

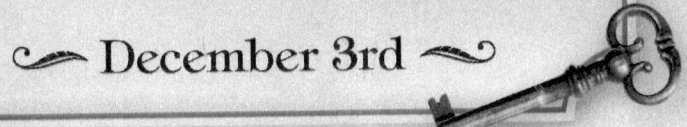

Scripture: Proverbs 25:28 (AMP)

"He who has no rule over his own spirit is like a city that is broken down and without walls."

In your prayer journal, identify in this portion of scripture a promise to receive or a command to obey.

Prayer:

My Heavenly Father, I bless you and praise your great and glorious name. There is no one like you. You are above all, and you have exalted your Word even above your name. You have warned me to guard my heart, my thoughts, from the lies of the wicked one. I do not want to be as a city with no defenses, but as a walled city that carefully determines what is allowed in and what goes out. I ask you to help me protect my heart from fears and doubts that would rob me of your peace. I thank you for the power to stand against every crafty device of the devil. Help me recognize what is of God and what is not so my life, my city, will be well protected and secure. I receive this good work of God now in Jesus' name, Amen.

Proclamation:

God is my refuge and strength. He will be to me as a wall of fire that surrounds me and keeps me. He is my high tower lifting me above the chaos and confusion of this world. I will not be moved from my position of peace and safety that is in his presence.

Memory Verse: Joshua 1:8

"This book of the law shall not depart out of your mouth, but you shall meditate therein day and night that you may observe to do according to all that is written therein, for then you shall make your way prosperous and then you shall have good success."

To every family member: *"I love you; you are blessed, and you are a blessing."*
Don't forget the hugs.

December 4th

Scripture: 1 John 3:23-24 (RSV)

"And this is his commandment, that we should believe in the name of his Son Jesus Christ and love one another, just as he has commanded us. All who keep his commandments abide in him, and he in them. And by this we know that he abides in us, by the Spirit which he has given us."

In your prayer journal, identify in this portion of scripture a promise to receive or a command to obey.

Prayer:

Heavenly Father, your kingdom is different than all the kingdoms of this world. Your kingdom is described as everything that is right, and it brings peace and produces joy. Your kingdom is ruled by the royal law of love. I desire to abide in your love, and when I do, I know I am abiding in you and your kingdom is continuing in me. I ask you for your grace that gives me both the desire and the ability to walk in your love and keep your commandment to love one another. I receive your grace and faith to access everything your grace can give me now in Jesus' name, Amen.

Proclamation:

All the kingdoms of this world function by fear and greed. Strife and confusion reign in the chaos of these kingdoms. I live in this world, but I do not live according to the kingdoms of this world. I have been delivered from the kingdom of darkness into the kingdom of God. I live by his love and keep his commandment to love one another, and I know the Spirit of God abides in me to teach me, lead me and help me to please God and enjoy life to its fullest.

Memory Verse: Joshua 1:8

"This book of the law shall not depart out of your mouth, but you shall meditate therein day and night that you may observe to do according to all that is written therein, for then you shall make your way prosperous and then you shall have good success."

To every family member: "I love you; you are blessed, and you are a blessing." Don't forget the hugs.

December 5th

Scripture: Psalms 42:11 (NIV)
"Why, my soul, are you downcast? Why so disturbed within me? Put your hope in God, for I will yet praise him, my Savior and my God."

In your prayer journal, identify in this portion of scripture a promise to receive or a command to obey.

Prayer:
God, my Father, you have freely given me all things that have to do with life and living the abundant life. When I get discouraged, I know that discouragement did not come from you. You have commanded me to be of good courage and to be strong in faith, trusting you in everything. I will declare your promises and reject sorrow and sadness, for you have not given me a spirit of fear, but a spirit of love and a sound and healthy mind. I receive from you now the joy of your salvation. I am greatly blessed for you are always with me. I praise you for this good and prosperous day. In Jesus' name I pray, Amen.

Proclamation:
I will not be discouraged or defeated, for God is with me. Sorrow and depression are enemies of my soul, so I speak to them in the name of Jesus and command them to flee away. I will stand in faith and declare the Word of the living God who loves me and gave himself for me so I could have life and life more abundantly. I am greatly blessed by the Lord, and everything I do brings me prosperity and good success. My faith pleases God, and he rewards those who seek after him. I seek the Lord this day. Therefore, I am blessed beyond measure.

Memory Verse: Joshua 1:8
"This book of the law shall not depart out of your mouth, but you shall meditate therein day and night that you may observe to do according to all that is written therein, for then you shall make your way prosperous and then you shall have good success."

To every family member: *"I love you; you are blessed, and you are a blessing."*
Don't forget the hugs.

December 6th

Scripture: Exodus 17:10-12 (KJV)

"So Joshua did as Moses had said to him, and fought with Amalek: and Moses, Aaron, and Hur went up to the top of the hill. And it came to pass, when Moses held up his hand, that Israel prevailed: and when he let down his hand, Amalek prevailed. But Moses' hands were heavy; and they took a stone, and put it under him, and he sat thereon; and Aaron and Hur stayed up his hands, the one on the one side, and the other on the other side; and his hands were steady until the going down of the sun."

In your prayer journal, identify in this portion of scripture a promise to receive or a command to obey.

Prayer:

My Father, you brought Israel victory over their enemies when Moses' hands were raised. When Moses became weary you sent Aaron and Hur to help him and to hold up his hands until the victory was won. I pray for those you would send to me to help hold up my hands in times of trouble until the victory comes. Lord, I also pray you would show me those who need my help. Help me to recognize those I can come along side to help through difficult times. You have commanded us to love one another with more than just our words. I pray for those who will help me and for those who need my help so we can strengthen each other in Jesus' name, Amen.

Proclamation:

One can put a thousand to flight, and two can chase ten thousand. Our strength is greatly multiplied when we work together and watch out for one another. The Lord is on our side, and he will bless us and prosper us and cause us to war in victory and walk in prosperity. I will not lack any good thing. I will have all I need to be a blessing to me and my family and much more to give to every good work and be a blessing to help those in need.

Memory Verse: Joshua 1:8

"This book of the law shall not depart out of your mouth, but you shall meditate therein day and night that you may observe to do according to all that is written therein, for then you shall make your way prosperous and then you shall have good success."

To every family member: "I love you; you are blessed, and you are a blessing."
Don't forget the hugs.

December 7th

Scripture: Numbers 6:23-27 (TLB)

"'Tell Aaron and his sons that they are to give this special blessing to the people of Israel: "May the Lord bless and protect you; may the Lord's face radiate with joy because of you; may he be gracious to you, show you his favor, and give you his peace." This is how Aaron and his sons shall call down my blessings upon the people of Israel; and I myself will personally bless them.'"

In your prayer journal, identify in this portion of scripture a promise to receive or a command to obey.

Prayer:

My Heavenly Father, I thank you for your great love for me. You have blessed me in every way. Even as you instructed Aaron and the priests to bless the people by pronouncing words over them, I also declare your words of blessing. I ask you Lord to protect me and cause your face to radiate with joy because of me. Lord, be gracious to me and show me your favor and give me your peace. I receive this blessing of the Lord now by faith in Jesus' name, Amen.

Proclamation:

I am blessed of the Lord. When I wake up and when I walk through the day until I lie down and rest and even through the night, the blessings of the Lord are upon me. As Aaron and the priests spoke blessing over the people and the Lord blessed them, I speak the blessings of the Lord over my life and receive his blessings. I will bring pleasure to the Lord this day, and I will be a blessing to many.

Memory Verse: Joshua 1:8

"This book of the law shall not depart out of your mouth, but you shall meditate therein day and night that you may observe to do according to all that is written therein, for then you shall make your way prosperous and then you shall have good success."

To every family member: *"I love you; you are blessed, and you are a blessing."*
Don't forget the hugs.

December 8th

Scripture: Genesis 12:1-3 (NKJV)

"Now the Lord had said to Abram: 'Get out of your country, from your family and from your father's house, to a land that I will show you. I will make you a great nation; I will bless you and make your name great; and you shall be a blessing. I will bless those who bless you, and I will curse him who curses you; and in you all the families of the earth shall be blessed.'"

In your prayer journal, identify in this portion of scripture a promise to receive or a command to obey.

Prayer:

God, my Father, you are faithful. You will perform your Word. What you have promised you will certainly bring to pass. You blessed Abraham when he believed your Word. You blessed him in all his ways, and you kept him from the enemies that purposed to deceive him and destroy him. You miraculously provided for him, protected him and fulfilled your promise to give him a son when he and his wife were too old for nothing is impossible with you. Your Word declares that you are no respecter of persons, and whoever believes and obeys you, you will bless and fulfill your Word to them. Help me to be like Abraham who believed in your power to even create what did not exist to bring to pass your promise. You said all things are possible for those who believe. I choose to believe you this day. In Jesus' name, Amen.

Proclamation:

My God is able to do more than I could ever think or imagine. He will bless me because I am in Christ, and if I am in Christ, then I am Abraham's seed and an heir according to his promise to Abraham. I am in Christ; therefore Abraham's blessings are mine.

Memory Verse: Joshua 1:8

"This book of the law shall not depart out of your mouth, but you shall meditate therein day and night that you may observe to do according to all that is written therein, for then you shall make your way prosperous and then you shall have good success."

To every family member: "I love you; you are blessed, and you are a blessing." Don't forget the hugs.

December 9th

Scripture: Job 23:11-12 (KJV)

"My foot hath held his steps, his way have I kept, and not declined. Neither have I gone back from the commandment of his lips; I have esteemed the words of his mouth more than my necessary food."

In your prayer journal, identify in this portion of scripture a promise to receive or a command to obey.

Prayer:

Father, I bless you and praise you and honor your great and glorious name this day. You are worthy of all praise. You have created all things, and you created them to be perfect and good. I know that every word you have spoken is for my good and blessing. I ask you to help me recognize your ways so I walk in your steps and follow your commandments. You said the one who delights greatly in your Word is blessed by the Lord. I choose to delight in your Word, to prize your words more highly than even my daily food. Father, open my ears to hear and understand your Word and help me to remember and apply your Word to every decision I make every day of my life. I pray in Jesus' name, Amen.

Proclamation:

The Word of the Lord is to be prized above everything else. God spoke the universe into being by the words of his mouth. He has declared that his Word is exalted even above his name and it is to be valued more than fine gold or treasures of this world. I will value God's Word above anything and everything else, for it is my life and health this day.

Memory Verse: Joshua 1:8

"This book of the law shall not depart out of your mouth, but you shall meditate therein day and night that you may observe to do according to all that is written therein, for then you shall make your way prosperous and then you shall have good success."

To every family member: *"I love you; you are blessed, and you are a blessing."*
Don't forget the hugs.

December 10th

Scripture: 1 John 2:15-17 (WEB)

"Don't love the world or the things that are in the world. If anyone loves the world, the Father's love isn't in him. For all that is in the world, the lust of the flesh, the lust of the eyes, and the pride of life, isn't the Father's, but is the world's. The world is passing away with its lusts, but he who does God's will remains forever."

In your prayer journal, identify in this portion of scripture a promise to receive or a command to obey.

Prayer:

Lord, I bless your glorious name this day. I thank you for delivering me out from this world's system of lust and greed and for bringing me into your kingdom. I know that I am not of this world even while I live in this world. Father, keep me by your power and grace not to live according to this world, but to live according to the things of your kingdom. Your kingdom is not of this world, but your kingdom lives in me even while I am in this world. Help me to do your will today. Help me to walk in love and faithfully perform your Word so the kingdom of God will be clearly seen in me today. In Jesus' name I pray, Amen.

Proclamation:

I do not love the system of this world that controls people through lust and pride. I will walk in love towards every one I meet, and I will humble myself to follow the Lord. My purpose is to please God above all else.

Memory Verse: 1 John 2:15-17

"Love not the world, neither the things that are in the world. If any man love the world, the love of the Father is not in him. For all that is in the world, the lust of the flesh and the lust of the eyes and the pride of life, is not of the Father, but is of the world. And the world passes away and the lust thereof: but he that does the will of God abides for ever."

To every family member: *"I love you; you are blessed, and you are a blessing."*
Don't forget the hugs.

December 11th

Scripture: Romans 10:11-13 (HCSB)

"Now the Scripture says, Everyone who believes on Him will not be put to shame, for there is no distinction between Jew and Greek, since the same Lord of all is rich to all who call on Him. For everyone who calls on the name of the Lord will be saved."

In your prayer journal, identify in this portion of scripture a promise to receive or a command to obey.

Prayer:

My Heavenly Father, I thank you for your Word and your promise of salvation to all who call upon you. You save and deliver, rescue and make me well and whole when I call upon you, for you are my salvation. You will keep me from shame and I will never be disappointed because you are my help. Jew or Gentile, male or female, people of all nations and tongues are welcomed into your kingdom when they call upon the name of the Lord Jesus Christ. I will call upon you in my time of need, for you are faithful to rescue and deliver me. Thank you for this great salvation that is mine now in Jesus' name, Amen.

Proclamation:

I will not be put to shame because I have called upon the name of the Lord Jesus Christ who saves me. He is Lord of all, and he is rich unto all who call upon him.

Memory Verse: 1 John 2:15-17

"Love not the world, neither the things that are in the world. If any man love the world, the love of the Father is not in him. For all that is in the world, the lust of the flesh and the lust of the eyes and the pride of life, is not of the Father, but is of the world. And the world passes away and the lust thereof: but he that does the will of God abides for ever."

To every family member: "*I love you; you are blessed, and you are a blessing.*"
Don't forget the hugs.

December 12th

Scripture: John 14:27 (NLT)

"Peace I leave with you. My peace I give to you. I do not give peace to you as the world gives. Do not let your hearts be troubled or afraid."

In your prayer journal, identify in this portion of scripture a promise to receive or a command to obey.

Prayer:

Father, you have given me your peace. I will not be afraid. My peace does not depend on my circumstances, but depends only on you. The peace I have is not my own but your peace which you have freely given me. Your grace empowers me to receive and walk in your peace. Help me to experience this peace that passes all understanding. I will guard my heart from fearful thoughts that would try to rob me of your peace. You said not to let my heart be troubled, so I will keep my heart from fear because my trust in you. You are faithful, so I can walk in peace and live in peace, and peace will rule over me all the days of my life, for I will not be afraid. Thank you for this peace that is at work in me now in Jesus' name, Amen.

Proclamation:

The peace of God rules in my heart. I will not be afraid. The peace of God is what Jesus gave me; therefore, the world cannot take it from me. I do not fear. I will not be afraid, for the perfect love of God casts out all fear.

Memory Verse: 1 John 2:15-17

"Love not the world, neither the things that are in the world. If any man love the world, the love of the Father is not in him. For all that is in the world, the lust of the flesh and the lust of the eyes and the pride of life, is not of the Father, but is of the world. And the world passes away and the lust thereof: but he that does the will of God abides for ever."

To every family member: "I love you; you are blessed, and you are a blessing."
Don't forget the hugs.

December 13th

Scripture: Isaiah 48:17 (AMP)

"Thus says the Lord, your Redeemer, the Holy One of Israel: I am the Lord your God, Who teaches you to profit, Who leads you in the way that you should go."

In your prayer journal, identify in this portion of scripture a promise to receive or a command to obey.

Prayer:

Heavenly Father, you are above all. Your might and strength and power are greater than can be measured. You alone are God. You are worthy of all praise, for everything you do is righteous and good. I thank you for teaching me to profit in all I do. You lead me in righteous paths. You go before me and prepare my way, and you stand behind me to keep me safe. I ask you to make my path plain and teach me to be fruitful, increasing me and prospering me in all I do. Grant me wisdom to make wise choices and decisions that will honor you and bring me your blessings. I pray in Jesus' name, Amen.

Proclamation:

I will walk with the Lord and follow his leading every day of my life. His Spirit will give me wisdom, and the Word of God will make my way plain. I will not go to the left or the right. I will not walk in darkness, but I will walk in the light of life. I did not receive the spirit of this world, but I received the Spirit of God, so I can know the things God has freely given to me.

Memory Verse: 1 John 2:15-17

"Love not the world, neither the things that are in the world. If any man love the world, the love of the Father is not in him. For all that is in the world, the lust of the flesh and the lust of the eyes and the pride of life, is not of the Father, but is of the world. And the world passes away and the lust thereof: but he that does the will of God abides for ever."

To every family member: *"I love you; you are blessed, and you are a blessing."*
Don't forget the hugs.

Faith Family Minute | 349

December 14th

Scripture: Matthew 12:35-37 (NKJV)

"A good man out of the good treasure of his heart brings forth good things, and an evil man out of the evil treasure brings forth evil things. But I say to you that for every idle word men may speak, they will give account of it in the day of judgment. For by your words you will be justified, and by your words you will be condemned."

In your prayer journal, identify in this portion of scripture a promise to receive or a command to obey.

Prayer:

God, my Father, I want to honor you in everything I do and say. Help me to treasure the good things of God in my heart so my mouth will speak good words. I don't want my words to be empty, barren or unemployed so they would judge and condemn me. I pray my words produce good fruit in all who hear them. Let the words of my mouth and the meditation of my heart be pleasing and acceptable to you. Father, fill me anew with the Spirit of God and let your Word dwell in me richly so the good treasure of my heart overflows with praise to you. I ask you for this good work of God to continue working mightily in me today. I pray in Jesus' name, Amen.

Proclamation:

The Word of God fills my thoughts, and the love of God fills my heart. Out of the abundance of my heart flow words of praise and thanksgiving to the Lord my God.

Memory Verse: 1 John 2:15-17

"Love not the world, neither the things that are in the world. If any man love the world, the love of the Father is not in him. For all that is in the world, the lust of the flesh and the lust of the eyes and the pride of life, is not of the Father, but is of the world. And the world passes away and the lust thereof: but he that does the will of God abides for ever."

To every family member: "I love you; you are blessed, and you are a blessing."
Don't forget the hugs.

December 15th

Scripture: Luke 21:1-4 (ESV)

"Jesus looked up and saw the rich putting their gifts into the offering box, and he saw a poor widow put in two small copper coins. And he said, 'Truly, I tell you, this poor widow has put in more than all of them. For they all contributed out of their abundance, but she out of her poverty put in all she had to live on.'"

In your prayer journal, identify in this portion of scripture a promise to receive or a command to obey.

Prayer:

My Heavenly Father, you see the things that no one else sees. You saw this widow's heart, and you saw her gift, and you knew this tiny amount was all she had. No one else could measure the value of her gift for only you could see her heart. I pray for a pure heart that is willing to give all I have to you. I desire to treasure you above all else. I know that everything I have has come from you and anything I give is simply returning what I have received. I know you are not interested in my gifts, but in my heart. When my heart is right, my giving is generous, and whatever I am prompted to give, you return to me and more. I thank you for seeing my heart and working in me to make me useful to you and the kingdom of God. I pray in Jesus' name, Amen.

Proclamation:

I know the Lord sees my heart. He sees the reasons I do what I do. I will honor the Lord with my heart, and with my possessions I will bring praise to his name.

Memory Verse: 1 John 2:15-17

"Love not the world, neither the things that are in the world. If any man love the world, the love of the Father is not in him. For all that is in the world, the lust of the flesh and the lust of the eyes and the pride of life, is not of the Father, but is of the world. And the world passes away and the lust thereof: but he that does the will of God abides for ever."

To every family member: "I love you; you are blessed, and you are a blessing."
Don't forget the hugs.

December 16th

Scripture: 1 Corinthians 15:57 (AMP)

"But thanks be to God, Who gives us the victory [making us conquerors] through our Lord Jesus Christ."

In your prayer journal, identify in this portion of scripture a promise to receive or a command to obey.

Prayer:

Heavenly Father, I bless your wonderful name this day. Thank you for the victory that is mine because of the work of the Lord Jesus Christ. You did not create me and then leave me to just do the best I can. You have never asked me to do what I cannot do, but you have created me and given me faith to believe your Word and receive the victory Jesus gained for me. I receive your victory over every enemy (sin, sickness, depression, hopelessness and fear) that rise up against me. I know what Jesus did he did for me on my behalf because I was incapable of obtaining forgiveness or righteousness on my own. I declare today I am more than a conqueror because my Lord Jesus Christ has freely given me abundant life and victory over all the works of the enemy. It is in Jesus' name I give you thanks, Amen.

Proclamation:

I am more than a conqueror today. Jesus took my place. He lived righteously so he could give me his righteousness. He died for me so he would receive my judgment for my sin. He arose from the dead to defeat death and give me eternal life. It is God's will for me to walk in his victory this day and forever.

Memory Verse: 1 John 2:15-17

"Love not the world, neither the things that are in the world. If any man love the world, the love of the Father is not in him. For all that is in the world, the lust of the flesh and the lust of the eyes and the pride of life, is not of the Father, but is of the world. And the world passes away and the lust thereof: but he that does the will of God abides for ever."

To every family member: *"I love you; you are blessed, and you are a blessing."*
Don't forget the hugs.

December 17th

Scripture: Galatians 5:22-23 (KJV)

"But the fruit of the Spirit is love, joy, peace, longsuffering, gentleness, goodness, faith, meekness, temperance: against such there is no law."

In your prayer journal, identify in this portion of scripture a promise to receive or a command to obey.

Prayer:

God, my Father, everything you do is good. Every good and perfect gift comes from you. The Spirit of God has come to live with me and in me, to produce love, joy, peace, long-suffering, gentleness, goodness, faith, meekness and self-control. If I live my life by the Spirit of God within me, I will enjoy the fruit of the Spirit. Lord, you said if I lay down my life I can live in your life. I choose to lay down my life this day so your life will be seen and the fruit of your Spirit will be enjoyed by all. I thank you for this grace now in the name of Jesus, Amen.

Proclamation:

I do not walk after the flesh, but I live according to the Spirit of God who lives within me. The fruit of the Spirit hangs on the branches of my life, so everyone around me can eat of this fruit and I can say, "O, taste and see that the Lord is good: blessed is the one who trusts in him."

Memory Verse: Philemon 1:6

"That the sharing of your faith may become effective by the acknowledgment of every good thing which is in you in Christ Jesus."

To every family member: *"I love you; you are blessed, and you are a blessing."*
Don't forget the hugs.

Faith Family Minute | 353

December 18th

Scripture: Ephesians 2:11-13 (NLV)

"Do not forget that at one time you did not know God. The Jews, who had gone through the religious act of becoming a Jew by man's hands, said you were people who do not know God. You were living without Christ then. The Jewish people who belonged to God had nothing to do with you. The promises He gave to them were not for you. You had nothing in this world to hope for. You were without God. But now you belong to Christ Jesus. At one time you were far away from God. Now you have been brought close to Him. Christ did this for you when He gave His blood on the cross."

In your prayer journal, identify in this portion of scripture a promise to receive or a command to obey.

Prayer:

Heavenly Father, you have brought all mankind together through the Lord Jesus Christ. There is now no difference between Jews or Gentiles, men or women, but people of all nations and tribes and tongues have an equal inheritance in the Kingdom of God. As you made man in your image and after your likeness in the beginning, all who come to Jesus are made brand new, again in the image of God. I thank you that I am a son of God and an heir of God and a joint-heir with Christ Jesus my Lord. I have been given access to the very throne of God so I can come in faith and receive by grace anything I will ever need. Thank you for this great salvation. In Jesus' name I pray, Amen.

Proclamation:

The goodness of God has been poured out on all people of all ages, and in every nation, those who call on God by Christ Jesus are saved from darkness and brought into the glorious kingdom of God's Son.

Memory Verse: Philemon 1:6

"That the sharing of your faith may become effective by the acknowledgment of every good thing which is in you in Christ Jesus."

To every family member: *"I love you; you are blessed, and you are a blessing."*
Don't forget the hugs.

December 19th

Scripture: Colossians 3:12-13 (GW)

"As holy people whom God has chosen and loved, be sympathetic, kind, humble, gentle, and patient. Put up with each other, and forgive each other if anyone has a complaint. Forgive as the Lord forgave you."

In your prayer journal, identify in this portion of scripture a promise to receive or a command to obey.

Prayer:

My Heavenly Father, I thank you for loving me and forgiving me and giving me this great salvation. You chose me and loved me; you are kind and gentle and patient with me. You are careful to do for me everything you ask me to do for others. I pray for your great grace to work in me today to help me put up with those who are unkind and rude. Help me to forgive as you have forgiven me. Help me to also walk in sincere love that will never fail but will always bring me into a place of victory. I thank you for these things now in Jesus' name, Amen.

Proclamation:

Love never fails. I will walk in love today with everyone. If they are kind and helpful to me or if they are rude and hateful to me, it will make no difference because I decide right now to forgive anyone who hurts or offends me. If they criticize and condemn me and purpose to dishonor or disrespect me, I forgive them. If they choose to hurt me purposefully or unintentionally, it will make no difference because I choose to forgive and walk in love with everyone, and God gives me the grace to do it. I am more than a conqueror by the grace of God.

Memory Verse: Philemon 1:6

"That the sharing of your faith may become effective by the acknowledgment of every good thing which is in you in Christ Jesus."

To every family member: *"I love you; you are blessed, and you are a blessing."*
Don't forget the hugs.

December 20th

Scripture: 2 Corinthians 3:18 (CEB)

"All of us are looking with unveiled faces at the glory of the Lord as if we were looking in a mirror. We are being transformed into that same image from one degree of glory to the next degree of glory. This comes from the Lord, who is the Spirit."

In your prayer journal, identify in this portion of scripture a promise to receive or a command to obey.

Prayer:

Heavenly Father, you are great and greatly to be praised. You have delivered me out from the authority of darkness into the kingdom of your dear Son. You have birthed me into your family and called me by your name. You have given me your Word to transform my thinking and to show me your glory. As I look into your Word, I pray to see the glory of God. I ask you to change me into the same image I see, as I see you, in your Word. Father, show me your glory in the mirror of your Word. Thank you for hearing me and continuing to accomplish this good work in me. In Jesus' name I pray, Amen.

Proclamation:

As I look into the Word of God today, I see the glory of God in the face of Jesus Christ, and I am changed into the same image from glory to glory by the power of the Holy Spirit.

Memory Verse: Philemon 1:6

"That the sharing of your faith may become effective by the acknowledgment of every good thing which is in you in Christ Jesus."

To every family member: *"I love you; you are blessed, and you are a blessing."*
Don't forget the hugs.

December 21st

Scripture: Matthew 16:19 (NKJV)

"And I will give you the keys of the kingdom of heaven, and whatever you bind on earth will be bound in heaven, and whatever you loose on earth will be loosed in heaven."

In your prayer journal, identify in this portion of scripture a promise to receive or a command to obey.

Prayer:

God, my Father, you have greatly blessed me in many ways. I am very thankful for the wonderful things you have done for me and given to me. You have given me authority to pray in the name of Jesus and to call forth your will on the earth as it is done in heaven. You have given to me the keys of the kingdom of God to bind and loose, to lock and unlock and to allow and forbid on earth what corresponds to your will in heaven. I ask you to remind me of all the things you have freely given to me. The Word of God declares, "eye has not seen nor ear heard neither has it entered into the heart of man the things the Lord has prepared for those that love him, but these things are revealed to us by the Spirit of God". Lord, help me to stand in the place of authority you have given me and to declare your Word with all boldness instead of always asking you to do what you have given me the authority to accomplish. I pray in Jesus' name, Amen.

Proclamation:

Jesus gave me the keys to the kingdom of God. I am to speak his Word with all boldness and to command that which is contrary to the will of God to be bound and forbidden to function. I am also to release the will of God by speaking forth his Word and commanding his will to be done on earth as it is in heaven.

Memory Verse: Philemon 1:6

"That the sharing of your faith may become effective by the acknowledgment of every good thing which is in you in Christ Jesus."

To every family member: *"I love you; you are blessed, and you are a blessing."*
Don't forget the hugs.

December 22nd

Scripture: 1 Peter 2:2 (NKJV)

"As newborn babes, desire the pure milk of the word, that you may grow thereby."

In your prayer journal, identify in this portion of scripture a promise to receive or a command to obey.

Prayer:

My Heavenly Father, thank you for the Word of God that you have given me. You, who created the universe and everything in it can certainly write and preserve a pure Word for us to follow. You said your Word is eternal and exalted, even above your great name. You are not a man that you should lie or repent, and if you said it, you will certainly bring it to pass. You will supply all my needs and will create what does not exist if that is what is necessary to fulfill your Word and promise. Thank you for the power of your Word. I will desire your Word as a treasure, precious and valuable, that I might grow spiritually and become strong in faith and in the power of your might. For I know you can do exceeding abundantly above all I could ever ask or think according to the powerful working of your Word in me. In Jesus' name, I pray, Amen.

Proclamation:

The Word of the Lord is forever. It is forever settled in heaven, and both heaven and earth bear witness to the Word's commands. All things were created by the Word of God, and all things are maintained by that same Word. It never needs to be updated or modified; it never grows weak or obsolete. The Word of the Lord is eternal.

Memory Verse: Philemon 1:6

"That the sharing of your faith may become effective by the acknowledgment of every good thing which is in you in Christ Jesus."

To every family member: "I love you; you are blessed, and you are a blessing." Don't forget the hugs.

December 23rd

Scripture: Isaiah 1:19 (KJV)
"If ye be willing and obedient, ye shall eat the good of the land"

In your prayer journal, identify in this portion of scripture
a promise to receive or a command to obey.

Prayer:

Father, I worship you. I bless your holy name. Thank you for your great grace that rests upon me today. Your mercies are new everyday, and I know that every good and perfect gift comes from you. I am blessed this day. I have divine favor, and your goodness and mercies chase me down and overtake me. You said that I would eat the good of the land when I am willing and obedient. I know you desire to bless me, so help me to stay in that place of your blessings. Help me to quickly recognize your voice and not hesitate to obey you. Help me to remain willing to choose your will over mine and obey you with a joyful heart. I receive this day your grace to make your will plain to me and my will totally submitted to yours. I declare these things this day in Jesus' name, Amen.

Proclamation:

I will follow after the Lord with all my heart. I seek first the kingdom of God and his righteousness, and all the things others seek after will be freely given to me. I will eat the good of the land because I am quick to obey the voice of the Lord, and I follow his leading with a willing and joyful heart. I know that it is my Heavenly Father's will for me to walk in his blessings and abundance. I know the way to walk in these things is to follow the leading of the Spirit of God with a right heart and a willing mind, and as I follow him, he will lead me in paths of righteousness and will satisfy the desires of my heart.

Memory Verse: Philemon 1:6
"That the sharing of your faith may become effective by the acknowledgment of every good thing which is in you in Christ Jesus."

To every family member: "I love you; you are blessed, and you are a blessing."
Don't forget the hugs.

December 24th

Scripture: 2 John 1:6 (CEB)

"This is love: that we live according to his commands. This is the command that you heard from the beginning: live in love."

In your prayer journal, identify in this portion of scripture a promise to receive or a command to obey.

Prayer:

My Father, it is my desire to honor you and to keep your commandments. I know I am no longer under the law of the ten commandments, but if I love you, I am instructed to demonstrate my love by keeping your New Covenant commandments of believing on the Lord Jesus Christ and loving others. Without faith, it is impossible to please you, but your Word brings me faith to believe, and the Spirit of God empowers me to love others with the genuine God-kind of love that is unconditional and unlimited. I pray for your grace to cover me this day so I will draw on your perfect love and obey your Word and the leading of the Holy Spirit who also strengthens me to walk in love, not only to those who love me, but also to those who don't. I will love my friends and my enemies alike because I love you and desire to please you in everything I do. Thank you for this grace that is at work in me now. In Jesus' name I pray, Amen.

Proclamation:

The Spirit of the Lord lives in me and has anointed me to live by the faith of the Son of God and to love God and man with God's unconditional, unlimited and never failing love.

Memory Verse: Proverbs 18:20

"A man's belly shall be satisfied with the fruit of his mouth; and with the increase of his lips shall he be filled."

To every family member: *"I love you; you are blessed, and you are a blessing."* Don't forget the hugs.

December 25th

Scripture: Hebrews 2:1 (KJV)

"Therefore we ought to give the more earnest heed to the things which we have heard, lest at any time we should let them slip."

In your prayer journal, identify in this portion of scripture a promise to receive or a command to obey.

Prayer:

Heavenly Father, you have spoken wonderful things for us to hear. The shepherds heard the angel's announcement of the birth of Christ in the fields around Bethlehem. The wise men heard of the promised arrival of a king when they saw a new star arise. You have spoken by the prophets of old, and all creation declares your glory. I ask you to help me guard my heart so the Word of God is not stolen from me or obscured by the busyness of life. I pray your Word remains planted in my heart and will grow and bring forth fruit that will honor you and bring to pass the things you have promised in my life. In Jesus' name, Amen.

Proclamation:

I will fill my heart with the Word of God. The Spirit of God will remind me of God's Word so I will live everyday according to the will of God. As I meditate on the Word day and night and observe it and do it, I will be blessed and prosper in everything I do. The Word will be a light that brings light to my darkness and reveals the path of life the Lord sets before me today. As the star shined a light that guided the wise men to the manger and as the instructions to the shepherds directed them to Jesus, the Word of God brings me light and direction.

Memory Verse: Proverbs 18:20

"A man's belly shall be satisfied with the fruit of his mouth; and with the increase of his lips shall he be filled."

To every family member: "*I love you; you are blessed, and you are a blessing.*"
Don't forget the hugs.

December 26th

Scripture: Psalms 33:1 (HCSB)

"Rejoice in the Lord, you righteous ones; praise from the upright is beautiful."

In your prayer journal, identify in this portion of scripture a promise to receive or a command to obey.

Prayer:

God, my Father, I praise your great and glorious name. I rejoice in you this day, for you are faithful in all your ways, and your promises are certain to those who will take hold of them. You desire praise from a sincere and humble heart. You even inhabit the praises of those who will lift up their voices to offer to you the sacrifice of praise. When kings of old believed your Word, they marched into battle with the singers and musicians in front of their armies knowing you would fight their battles and bring them victory. Victory came not by the strength or skill of their military, but by the hand of their God. You defeated kings and rulers of wickedness by praise that flowed from the lips of children. I desire to praise you and rejoice in you at all times. Father, receive my praise and the thanks flowing from my heart, for I am truly grateful to you. You have loved me when I was unlovable. You forgave me when forgiveness was undeserved. You protect me from evil and bless all I do. I give you thanks in Jesus' name, Amen.

Proclamation:

I will praise the Lord at all times. His praise will continually be in my mouth. For the Lord is worthy. He is great and greatly to be praised. The wicked will flee at the presence of the Lord, but the righteous will be glad and put their trust in him.

Memory Verse: Proverbs 18:20

"A man's belly shall be satisfied with the fruit of his mouth; and with the increase of his lips shall he be filled."

To every family member: *"I love you; you are blessed, and you are a blessing."* Don't forget the hugs.

December 27th

Scripture: Hebrews 10:15-17 (KJV)

"Whereof the Holy Ghost also is a witness to us: for after that he had said before, This is the covenant that I will make with them after those days, saith the Lord, I will put my laws into their hearts, and in their minds will I write them; And their sins and iniquities will I remember no more."

In your prayer journal, identify in this portion of scripture a promise to receive or a command to obey.

Prayer:

God, my Father, thank you for forgiving me, and not remembering my sins or iniquities. You said, you would write your law on my mind and in my heart so my life would not be governed by external rules, but by the leading of the Holy Spirit. You did not give me the spirit that is of this world and is controlled by lust and greed, but you have given me the Holy Spirit who lives with me and abides in me to give me wisdom and instruction for every event in life. Father, lead me by the Spirit of God into your truth and righteousness. You will lead me in good places. As green pastures and still waters supply all the needs of the sheep in the field, so the Spirit of God will guide me into places where there is no lack and where my soul is refreshed and comforted in the presence of the Lord. Help me to recognize quickly what the Spirit of God is saying to me and to see clearly where he is leading me so I will not waste time or talent in unfruitful places. Make my way plain, I pray in Jesus' name, Amen.

Proclamation:

The Spirit of God within me will lead me where I should go and will reveal to me the things God wants me to know so I will always be at the right place at the right time doing the right thing that will please the Lord.

Memory Verse: Proverbs 18:20

"A man's belly shall be satisfied with the fruit of his mouth; and with the increase of his lips shall he be filled."

To every family member: "I love you; you are blessed, and you are a blessing." Don't forget the hugs.

December 28th

Scripture: John 15:5 (ESV)

"I am the vine; you are the branches. Whoever abides in me and I in him, he it is that bears much fruit, for apart from me you can do nothing."

In your prayer journal, identify in this portion of scripture a promise to receive or a command to obey.

Prayer:

Heavenly Father, I thank you for life and life more abundantly. You desire for me to bear much fruit, good fruit, to show the world the goodness of God. I know fruit only comes on the branch when the branch remains attached to the vine. I know without you I cannot do anything. Father, I pray to remain attached to you. Keep me from trying to produce good fruit on my own in my own strength and by my own efforts. Help me to draw upon your life within me so the fruit I display will be the good fruit that only you can produce. I thank you for these things now in Jesus' name, Amen.

Proclamation:

The fruit on the branches comes from the life of the vine. I will abide in the Lord, and his Word will continue in me so I can ask whatever I will and it shall be done for me. The fruit I display is answered prayer—prayer that brings forth the will of God that is seen and heard and felt. I will do the will of God and pray the will of God and call forth the will of God to be done on earth even as it is always done in heaven.

Memory Verse: Proverbs 18:20

"A man's belly shall be satisfied with the fruit of his mouth; and with the increase of his lips shall he be filled."

To every family member: *"I love you; you are blessed, and you are a blessing."*
Don't forget the hugs.

December 29th

Scripture: Hebrews 11:3 (KJV)

"Through faith we understand that the worlds were framed by the word of God, so that things which are seen were not made of things which do appear."

In your prayer journal, identify in this portion of scripture a promise to receive or a command to obey.

Prayer:

Heavenly Father, I know that your words created everything. You spoke what did not exist into being. I believe your Word is powerful to create. I believe your Word is able to accomplish everything you sent it forth to do. I ask for the understanding and revelation your Word can bring me so I am not concerning myself with things that have no real value. You have warned me about being preoccupied with foolish questions, fables, lengthy genealogies and vain traditions that strip the Word of its power to fulfill your will. Help me ,Father, to keep what is most important at the center of my life. Help me to pray your Word and to speak your Word in order to see your Word bring life and hope to everyone who hears it. I pray in Jesus' name, Amen.

Proclamation:

The Word of God is living. It is not a historical record written by the hands of men, but it is the very breath of God sent forth with power to accomplish what God desires.

Memory Verse: Proverbs 18:20

"A man's belly shall be satisfied with the fruit of his mouth; and with the increase of his lips shall he be filled."

To every family member: "*I love you; you are blessed, and you are a blessing.*" Don't forget the hugs.

December 30th

Scripture: Psalms 35:27 (AMP)

"Let those who favor my righteous cause and have pleasure in my uprightness shout for joy and be glad and say continually, Let the Lord be magnified, Who takes pleasure in the prosperity of His servant."

In your prayer journal, identify in this portion of scripture a promise to receive or a command to obey.

Prayer:

Heavenly Father, you have made all things for your pleasure and your purpose. You made man in your image and likeness and desired for him to prosper, being fruitful and increasing, growing strong in wealth and wisdom to do your will. Over and over again, you reveal your heart, your desire for us to walk in your blessings, and you are displeased when we fail and are defeated. I pray for your will to be fulfilled in my life. I ask you to prosper me and make me to increase and abound in every good work that will glorify you and will be a blessing to me and to many others. Father, bless the work of my hands. Grant me favor today with all those you have put in my path to help me accomplish your will. It is in the name of Jesus I pray, Amen.

Proclamation:

The Lord takes pleasure in me, when I live according to his Word and do his will, prospering in every good work. I am blessed beyond measure. The exceedingly abundant blessings of God are available for me to receive today.

Memory Verse: Proverbs 18:20

"A man's belly shall be satisfied with the fruit of his mouth; and with the increase of his lips shall he be filled."

To every family member: "I love you; you are blessed, and you are a blessing." Don't forget the hugs.

December 31st

Scripture: Psalms 136:1-6 (KJV)

"O give thanks unto the Lord; for he is good: for his mercy endureth for ever. O give thanks unto the God of gods: for his mercy endureth for ever. O give thanks to the Lord of lords: for his mercy endureth for ever. To him who alone doeth great wonders: for his mercy endureth for ever. To him that by wisdom made the heavens: for his mercy endureth for ever. To him that stretched out the earth above the waters: for his mercy endureth for ever."

In your prayer journal, identify in this portion of scripture a promise to receive or a command to obey.

Prayer:

Heavenly Father, I give you thanks for your great goodness and mercy which you have shown me. You have done great and mighty things. You have demonstrated both your great power and unfathomable love. I know you can do all things, and yet I see in your Word that you have given to man authority to choose and to do whatever he pleases. I pray for your wisdom so I will always choose what is right and good to you. I ask you to bless the meditations of my heart and the works of my hands so I accomplish your purpose and glorify your name. My greatest desire is to hear you say to me, "Well done, good and faithful servant." In Jesus' wonderful name I pray, Amen.

Proclamation:

I am a child of the King of kings and Lord of lords. I am blessed in all my ways, for God is with me, and if God is with me, who can stand against me? Over all challenges and adversaries, I am more than a conqueror because Jesus loved me and gave his life for me so I can live with him.

Memory Verse: 1 Corinthians 13:8

"Love never fails...."

To every family member: *"I love you; you are blessed, and you are a blessing."*
Don't forget the hugs.

www.ingramcontent.com/pod-product-compliance
Lightning Source LLC
Chambersburg PA
CBHW021115300426
44113CB00006B/164